Complete Guide to Testosterone

James Francis

Medical Disclaimer.

Medical Disclaimer.

The information in this book, whether provided as an e-book or in printed form is for informational purposes and nothing contained in it is intended to be construed as anything other than general information and advise.

It does not take into account your individual health, physical or emotional situation or your needs. It assumes that you are a normal healthy functioning man, not suffering with any serious medical conditions.

The information provided in this book is not an absolute substitute for medical attention, treatment or medical advice. It is a proposed alternative to testosterone replacement therapy. It is not intended to provide a clinical diagnosis nor to take the place of proper medical advice from a fully qualified medical practitioner.

You should, before you act on or use any of this information consider the appropriateness of this information having regard to your own personal situation and needs.

You are responsible for consulting a suitable medical professional before using any of the information or materials contained herein before trying any treatments or taking any course of action that may directly or indirectly affect your health or well being.

Contents

1

Preface.

Welcome to my complete guide to testosterone. Inside you will find absolutely everything that you can possibly be doing to optimise your T levels. You will also find everything that you can possibly be doing to maintain those T levels as you get older.

From between the ages of 30 and 40 your testosterone levels in most men will begin to decline with age. At least this is what is widely thought. What is not so widely known is that it is entirely possible to slow down this age related decline.

Is it possible to completely stop this decline? Fortunately yes it is. And slowing that decline and the effects of that decline for most men is entirely possible.

Testosterone levels in general have been following a declining trend in the last 50 years. The average T levels nowadays of 400ng/DL, was considered to be typically normal for a 60 year old in the 1970s. Now that is quite some decline. I address this problem inside this guide and offer explanations as to why this is happening. It is not one thing that is causing this it is many. I will show you how to fix this.

The object of this guide is to stop and reverse that decline. I want all the 50 year old guys of the future to have T levels like mine. I offer myself up as an example of what is possible with the right knowledge and lifestyle choices.

I am also completely natural. I use a few key natural supplements. Everything that I do to maintain my T levels is well within your reach. I do not need to go onto Testosterone Replacement Therapy, and it is my intention to never have to. I already know that this will never be necessary for me. I have that much confidence in what I am doing. I will reveal everything that I am doing now, and have been doing, for the last two decades.

The main aim of this whole guide is to put forward a realistically viable solution that is an effective alternative to Testosterone Replacement Therapy, or TRT. To empower men to take control of their testosterone by completely natural means.

Often when men experience symptoms of low testosterone they take a blood test and often discover that they have a low total testosterone level. Then they believe that they need TRT, or will be needing it at some point in the near future.

Did you know that among many guys out there the popular consensus is that late 30s is a normal age for guys to be considering TRT? You should be still in your prime at this age! Follow this guide and you *will* be still in your prime at that age!

If you already have low T levels? Then here you will discover everything you can possibly do to naturally boost your T levels within this guide.

So what if you have lower testosterone levels? Is this OK? Does this make you any less of a man? Unfortunately it can and does have an effect on manhood. There is no escaping this truth.

This fact makes many men decide to use TRT as a means of preserving their masculinity.

But by following what is laid out within this guide there is no reason why you cannot raise your T levels naturally. In some cases to double, or even triple your baseline level is going to be possible. But remember there are no miracles, this is going to take some dedication and efforts from you. If you are prepared to put in the work then you will inevitably see results. You are a man and with grit, determination and some effort and hard work you will see results.

This is a completely natural solution. And it works. I am living breathing proof of this. This little book will demonstrate everything you can do naturally to boost your testosterone levels and to maintain those levels as you age.

This is also a guide aimed at teaching everything you can possibly do to optimise and maintain your T levels and to keep your testosterone levels to optimum levels as you get older.

You *can* and you *will*. Of that I am already sure. Because I have already done it.

Come on inside and lets get started.

Introduction.

The studies of the last few decades shows an alarming trend in the declining testosterone levels of men.

It has been demonstrated that the current generation of 20 some-things have similar testosterone levels to the 60 some-things of 50 years ago.

This has quite naturally risen to much cause for concern as testosterone is seen as a big part of what a man is. It is largely responsible for energy levels, grit, discipline determination, libido, mental clarity and focus, passion and drive, and so much more.

It is also a major contributory factor in building muscles and recovery time, your body's ability to store and burn fat, and in your stamina and endurance levels. It will help you prevent many age related diseases later in life. It will also affect your mood, your brain function and even your outlook on life. It is fundamental to both your physical and mental wellbeing.

And with testosterone levels beginning a natural decline as most men age, on average 1-2% per year, as well as the alarming downward trend for lower peak T levels in men this has led to a lot of concern.

This has also led to an increase in the use of TRT, Testosterone Replacement Therapy, in men of much younger ages, as they feel the need to have higher T levels.

The problem with using synthetic testosterone solutions of any kind is that they can inhibit and shut off natural testosterone production, leading to a dependence on these supplements to maintain the increased levels of testosterone they provide.

I am 50 years old and recently had my blood work done and that revealed that I have a total testosterone level range between 771-1004 ng/DL, and a free testosterone level of 169-194 pg/ml. I will show you the regime I have followed over the last 20 years to maintain my testosterone levels. I will show you what works, and what doesn't work. The truth is that it has been recently demonstrated in studies that in healthy older men, there is no significant or drastic decline in testosterone. This guide explains all the things you need to consider to make this happen.

There seems to be a trend of content which promises to reveal secrets to doubling or even tripling your T levels. A hard fact is that this is going to involve a lot of hard work on your part. There are no natural easy or fast results. You must consider your entire human organism here, there is no secret one great thing that will provide you with instant natural results. This is the most important thing to consider when optimising your testosterone levels.

The reality is that this consists of many smaller things you can do which when **combined together**, and adopted into your lifestyle, will improve and then maintain your T levels. *The main principle to all this is balance.* Everything in nature is balanced and it is this balance that sustains your bodily functions.

Any health issue can negatively affect your testosterone levels. This is why it is particularly important to focus on your entire bodily organism when optimising your hormone production. Anything from high blood pressure, high blood sugar, low blood oxygen and many other bodily ailments can affect testosterone. A healthy balanced body tends to have healthy balanced hormones.

For this reason buying home devices that monitor blood sugar, blood pressure, heart rate, and blood oxygen levels can be a good idea. Regular observation of these outputs can bring your attention to many problems and potential health conditions before they manifest into something serious. So pay attention to your entire organism if you want optimised T levels.

When it comes to the reality of whether it is possible to double or even triple your testosterone levels, if you are a guy that has previously led a sedentary lifestyle, and have not observed a healthy balanced diet, then it is entirely possible that you could double, or even triple your baseline testosterone levels. If you are already active and have already been observing a good diet, then there are are still things you can do to up your T levels and keep them maintained, but just bear in mind that massive gains, like levels 3 times higher, are going to be highly unlikely.

According to medical science the normal functioning T levels for most men start to decline between the ages of 30 and 40. This can take place before or after this age depending on the individual and their lifestyle. Following the advice in this guide will give you every chance that you will never be affected by any significant decline.

Lets now consider what are generally considered to be normal ranges when it come to T levels.

Medical science says that at around age 18 - 20 men have between 300-1,200ng/DL of testosterone. This is the age at which men enjoy their peak testosterone levels. In men in their 20s, the normal levels are between 280-950ng/DL.

For men between the ages of 40 and 49, the normal levels are somewhere between 252-916ng/DL, and between the ages of 50 and 59 this becomes between 215-878ng/DL. So from this you can see that my levels are within normal ranges for my age. And my levels are healthy for my age.

Testosterone levels in most men decline at a rate of 1-2% per year as they get older, but should we be so concerned with the number of ng/DL? So many guys see increasing this magic number to be their primary target. We are obsessed with keeping score and competing against each other.

A thing to consider here is that we are all different. We all have our own optimum levels and personal requirements. T levels can also naturally fluctuate by as much as 40%. It does not stay the same, all of the time. Your T levels on waking in the morning will be higher than your T levels at the end of the day. This is completely natural.

With many promising quick results and instant fixes it is important to consider the male hormonal and reproductive cycle. As we know a woman's hormonal cycle is on a monthly basis. A man's hormonal cycle is on a daily basis.

A man's T levels will be at their highest at around 8am. Testosterone production tends to occur during sleep. From the moment we awaken those levels will begin to decline. Studies have shown that by late afternoon your T levels can decrease by as much as 40%. Don't worry this is completely normal. It is for this reason you are advised to have your blood sample taken early in the day when you are having your levels checked.

When it comes to boosting and optimising your natural T levels you must also consider this not only in the long term but also on a daily basis.

By doing as much as you can to optimise your T levels each day, then on a daily basis you will be helping to keep the natural daily decline to a minimum. Attention to this will significantly contribute towards the maintenance of your total testosterone levels.

Also the numbers are not as important as you might think. This obsession with numbers is probably the root cause of many guys resorting to TRT, when often attention to diet, lifestyle, and many other things would prove to be so much more effective in the long term.

Your size and weight will also come into this. Our body types and metabolic rates will also have an influence. Some guys can function fine and build muscle, enjoy good energy levels and a good sex drive with say 400 ng/DL and some cannot. I will explain why shortly.

The magic ng/DL number is *not* so important. What is important though is how you feel within yourself, your health and vitality, your energy levels and physical performance. If these areas are good then you're probably good.

3

Important Initial Considerations.

The male hormone cycle happens on a daily basis. Testosterone levels fluctuate each day. Your T levels never stay the same and they will not be at the same level every day. The production of testosterone mostly occurs overnight while you are asleep. Levels tend to peak at around 8am, upon waking, and are steadily decreased throughout the day. Every day.

This is because testosterone is utilised to fuel many of the critical bodily systems. And this is taking place all day every day. Think of your testosterone like your energy levels. The more you use the less you have. And then you must rest and recover to replenish. Energy levels and testosterone are very closely related.

Because testosterone levels at at their highest early in the morning blood exams concerned with measuring T levels are taken when levels will be at their highest. Testing centres also advise to get tested before eating. Because every and any use of energy or any action performed by the body utilises testosterone, and thus decreases levels of testosterone. This includes eating and digesting food.

A meal taken before the blood draw will reduce testosterone. A large meal can cause a drop of up to 47% in total testosterone levels. This is because during the 1 or 2 hours after ingesting food, the body is utilising a lot of energy to break down and absorb nutrients from the food. This use of energy utilises testosterone. Energy and testosterone are closely related and influence each other.

But of course we need to consume food to survive and maintain bodily energy levels. The human body is a finely balanced organism and eating either too little or too much will affect testosterone. This is why it is important to approach any bulking or weight loss program with a view to gradual weight gain or weight loss. Balancing the entire body is therefore very important especially in the longer term maintenance of testosterone levels, also on a daily basis.

Another thing to consider is that the production of testosterone is just one of many hormones produced in the male body. The production of testosterone is just one of the many functions of the endocrine system.

The endocrine system is made up of a system of interconnected glands that each secrete different hormones when these hormones are required by the body. Any disruptions to any part of this system can negatively affect your testosterone production.

Hormones are the body's chemical messengers. They convey information and instructions from one set of human cells to many other human cells. The endocrine system has some kind of influence over almost every cell, organ and bodily function.

The endocrine system glands release hormones into the bloodstream and this allows the hormones to circulate around the body in order for them to carry out their various functions. Things like or moods, growth and the regeneration of cells, and the functioning of our various organs, our metabolism and sexual reproduction. Testosterone is the hormone in males that performs the male reproductive capability.

The endocrine system regulates the quantities of each hormone. There are many factors that can affect this process. It can depend on how much of each hormone is present within the blood. In the case of testosterone the secretion of most of this hormone occurs when our levels have dropped and the levels require topping up. This occurs on a daily basis.

It can also depend on the levels of other hormones present in the blood. For example insulin and cortisol, which can both negatively influence testosterone production if they are not sufficiently balanced out.

Too much or too little of any hormone within the body can harm the body and throw it out of sync. *Everything must be balanced.*

For example, the hypothalamus in effect is the controller and regulator of the endocrine system. It links the endocrine system to the nervous system. The cellular information it receives from the body and its environment influence the hormones that the pituitary gland makes and releases into the bloodstream.

The hormones produced by the pituitary gland control and influence the function of the other endocrine glands. The pituitary secretes growth hormone, which makes the body regenerate cells and also has an influence over how the body absorbs nutrients.

The pituitary is also responsible for the production of prolactin, which produces breast milk in women. This is one that men should avoid allowing to get too high. It also produces thyrotropin which stimulates thyroid hormones. It also secretes hormones which produce testosterone in the testicles and regulates body water balance and influences the secretion of adrenal hormones such as DHEA and cortisol.

When it comes to the endocrine system all of these hormones have an influence over each other. This is why it is so important to optimise your entire physical body when seeking to increase testosterone production. *Any imbalances within the body will produce imbalances in hormonal output.*

Some of these imbalances include: Adrenal fatigue, resulting from long periods of stress. This produces prolonged secretion of cortisol resulting in depleted cortisol. This results in low energy and decreases to testosterone levels. Also conditions such as hypothyroidism, hyperthyroidism, either low or excessive production of thyroid hormones, will both affect testosterone production.

When the endocrine system is out of sync and not functioning properly, this results in a hormonal imbalance. A hormonal imbalance inevitably leads to diseases within the body. And many things can cause hormonal imbalance in men. Chronic prolonged stress, poor sleep, over-training, high insulin, poor nutrition, poor digestion and micro nutrient deficiencies for example.

This is why the most important thing to consider for the optimisation and maintenance of testosterone is not focusing on how to increase testosterone with quick fixes or wonder supplements, but by focusing on the entire bodily organism. Get all your health markers in check.

4

What is Testosterone and Why is it Important?

Testosterone is the primary sex hormone and androgen in males. Androgen basically means it is a steroid hormone. A naturally occurring steroid hormone. There are many different hormones in the human body. Hormones are effectively chemical messengers that regulate and balance many different processes within the human body.

Testosterone is therefore essential to the development of male characteristics. Testosterone is responsible for:

Development of the penis and testicles and their normal functions, including sex drive.

Deepening of the voice.

Facial and body hair. It is also partially responsible for hair loss and men going bald.

It is crucial to development of muscles.

It plays a role in determining your strength.

It improves fat metabolism.

It contributes towards bone strength and density.

It is vital to sperm production and the reproductive system.

It helps to regulate mood and mental quality of life.

It helps to maintain our energy levels.

It aids cognitive function, memory and thinking ability.

It plays a part in the prevention of age related diseases. It contributes towards healthy heart and blood.

It can influence a man's confidence.

So its pretty important. It is a man's masculinity, but so much more than that, it is absolutely vital to his health and mental well being.

Lets now consider how testosterone is made, The different types of testosterone and the testosterone functions and the various elements that are involved.

5

Testosterone Sub-Types

Testosterone is a steroid hormone made from cholesterol. An average man produces around 7mg of testosterone per day. When considering our T levels it is important to consider is that you may have 1000ng/DL of total testosterone, but not all that testosterone in the blood can be used by your body, right now, in this moment.

We effectively have three different types, or sub-types of testosterone.

The most important sub-type is free testosterone. This is an amount of our overall testosterone that is in our blood than can be used in this moment. It is called "free" testosterone because it is not bound to any proteins. And because it is not bound to any other molecules in the body, this free testosterone is free to activate receptors in the body to have its effect upon things like building muscle, your sex drive, your current mood and your energy levels.

So it will probably come as a surprise that this free testosterone consists of only up to 5% of our total testosterone. So does this effectively mean that we can only utilise no more than 5% of our testosterone at any one time? Well not exactly. But in a way, yes!

We have testosterone that is "bioavailable." This means that it is biologically active and can effectively be utilised. We also have an amount of testosterone that is not biologically active, it is bound testosterone, so this means that our body cannot use this testosterone right now for things like building muscle, our sex drive or affect our energy levels or mental wellness.

This is why that magic ng/DL number should not be your primary concern. Yes its pretty complicated so I will try to keep this as simple as I possibly can.

Now around 45% of our total testosterone consists of a sub-type known as albumin bound testosterone. While not free and immediately available to use, it is bound to a protein called albumin and is technically not biologically active, but it can be utilised to make free testosterone when required. Provided of course that your hormonal balance and body is all functioning well.

This process of optimising T levels and maintaining them as we age is pretty much down to optimising the efficient conversion into free testosterone. With a lack of free T you will most likely experience symptoms of low testosterone. It is your available testosterone that is the most important. Your total T level just helps to maintain your free T in a way.

Around half of our total testosterone consists of what is called SHBG bound testosterone. SHBG, or Sex Hormone Binding Globulin, is a protein that is produced in the liver. The role of SHBG is to is to regulate the amount of free testosterone available in our bodies. This regulation correlates to the balance in our hormonal production. Not too little and not too much.

Too little and we experience symptoms of low T. Too much and the body will produce more estrogen to compensate as it tries to maintain balance.

This SHBG bound testosterone is biologically inactive. So our bodies cannot use this testosterone directly to build muscle, nor to boost our energy levels, sex drive or mental state. Now this is no bad thing. What is a bad thing is when we have too much of this SHGB.

Too much SHBG is when SHBG binds itself to too much testosterone and then this affects the amount of albumin bound testosterone that can be converted into free testosterone, and also the amount of bioavailable free testosterone, which is produced and made available for your body to use.

This creates the possibility that you could have a high total T magic number in ng/DL, and yet *still* suffer with symptoms related to low testosterone. Not something you want to hear, but its true.

Therefore it is fundamental that we create within ourselves a well balanced hormonal production system that effectively converts albumin bound T into free available T. When testosterone is produced some free T is also made. We want all this to keep happening.

So this is why that magic number is not so important? For context lets say we have one guy with a total T level of 1000ng/DL, and another with only 700. Based upon the magic numbers we would naturally assume that the guy packing 1000ng/DL is going to be more efficient at building muscle mass, and more likely to have higher energy levels than the guy with only 700?

But now lets say that the guy packing 1000ng/DL is not as efficient in making free T. Sure he has high T levels but for some reason, usually an imbalance of some kind, his free T levels are low. Our guy with only 700ng/DL just happens to be super efficient in making free testosterone. And with us all being different, this is scenario is quite possible.

Now if we pose the same question and ask which of these guys is more likely to have a higher sex drive and energy levels and to be more efficient at building muscle it would be the guy who only has 700ng/DL who would have the edge. Why?

Simply because he is more efficient in converting his bound testosterone into free testosterone. He is more efficient in producing free T. This is because he is more androgen sensitive. Androgen sensitivity determines how efficient you will be at making free T. This would give him a higher level of testosterone that is available to use, right now, giving him better muscle building capability and increasing the likelihood of him having a higher sex drive and more energy. It is the free testosterone available right now, that determines how we feel and how we perform, right now.

Your androgen sensitivity was genetically hard-wired into you when you were in your mother's uterus. This cannot be changed. But you *can* optimise what God gave you to a degree.

6

The Creation of Testosterone Explained.

Now for the process of how testosterone is created. This is just a simplified description. Its very complicated but you need to understand the basics of this process. This description describes the process in a normal healthy functioning male with no imbalances present, or T production issues. An understanding of how testosterone is made can give you a lot of insight into preventing decline and maintaining T levels.

The production of testosterone is controlled by a specific feedback loop that is called the hypothalamic-pituitary-gonadal axis. And here is how it works.

It all begins in the brain with the hypothalamus. The hypothalamus, acts as a kind of biological control centre. This is in the most simple terms.

In truth it is a highly complex part of the human brain and would need an entire essay to explain fully what tasks it performs and how it works. But for our purposes here its main function is to maintain a state of balance, or a stable state (ie functioning normally) which is known as homeostasis.

It functions by directly instructing your autonomic nervous system and by managing all the different hormones in the human body. It receives messages from your nerves in the brain and from the nerves in your body.

So effectively your hypothalamus reads these messages and then re-acts to these messages in order to keep your body in a state of balanced harmony, by making the adjustments necessary to keep the state of internal balance.

The hypothalamus detects (receives a message) that the body needs more testosterone. This means the testosterone present in your blood stream needs topping up. Testosterone production is an ongoing and continuous process. Your levels of all three types of testosterone are constantly adjusting and changing determined by these messages that are being sent and received. By doing everything you can to help this process, you can exercise a degree of control over these messages by making sure that everything you need is being made available to the body.

The hypothalamus then releases a hormone called gonadotropin releasing hormone to the pituitary gland. In simple terms, gonadotropins are hormones, which stimulate the testicles, or sex glands, into performing their endocrine, hormone producing, or reproductive functions. They make both sperm and testosterone.

Then when the pituitary gland detects that it has received gonadotropins, it then begins to secrete two types of hormone. Follicle Stimulating Hormone, FSH, and Lutenizing Hormone, LH. FSH is a gonadotropic hormone that is secreted to produce sperm in men. LH causes the testicles to make testosterone, which is important for sperm production. An imbalance, or low levels of either of these gonadotropic hormones, or FSH and LH, can cause low T levels.

These two hormones are then carried by the blood to the testicles. FSH focuses on sperm production and LH stimulates the Leydig cells and Sertoli cells to produce more testosterone. En route to the testes these hormones bind to cholesterol, which is the building block of testosterone.

Leydig cells and Sertoli cells function together to control the production and secretion of testosterone in the testicles. Leydig cells produce and secrete the testosterone, some of which will bind to androgen binding proteins secreted by Sertoli cells.

The Leydig cells in the testes then convert cholesterol into testosterone. Yes cholesterol, which for the last 50 years or so the medical community advises us to avoid. *Cholesterol is the building block of testosterone.* This is very important. Ingrain it into your mind. More on cholesterol and the T boosting diet later in the book.

Basically the FSH and the LH travel through the bloodstream en route to the testicles and they collect, or absorb, the cholesterol that happens to be present in the blood from all the food we ingested.

If there is not enough cholesterol in the blood then the testes can produce the cholesterol, which the Leydig cells then convert into testosterone. So I can still eat "healthy" as doctors advise, keeping my cholesterol low, AND make testosterone?

Well no. Yes. Sometimes maybe. But this is not a good thing because having our testicles doing all the work to produce all the required cholesterol all of the time, can actually inhibit the Leydig cells from producing testosterone. And that could play a big role in low T levels later on. In fact, there are loads of things that can adversely affect this process.

You have to EAT cholesterol to optimise T levels. Understand this and make it a part of your daily lifestyle and you will have already taken a massive step towards optimising your testosterone production.

So, now when the testosterone is produced in the testicles, it goes back into the blood. The majority of it will be bound to proteins and become either albumin bound T or SHBG bound T. The rest will become free testosterone which we can use right away.

When there is enough testosterone present in the blood, and the testicles have produced the required amount, the hypothalamus then instructs the pituitary gland to stop secreting FSH and LH, and the testicles then shut down production until the next time a top up is needed.

Being aware of this process will help you to understand how this all works, and to help you to prevent low T levels.

When do lower testosterone levels start to be a real problem? Why are T levels falling lower with each new generation of men? Lets consider this.

7

The Generational Decline in T Levels.

According to recent research and various studies male testosterone levels have reportedly dropped by 20% in the last 20 years. And since the 1970s levels have been claimed to have dropped by as much as 50%.

And all of this research and the clinical tests carried out all do agree on one thing. That testosterone levels are falling and it is becoming more common in more men of much younger ages.

It was discovered that men in their 70s in 1987 had average testosterone levels of 100 points higher than men in their 50s in 2002. The tests also ascertained that the decreasing levels were not restricted to age. From the results that were seen, it is claimed that a 22 year old man in 2002 had an average testosterone level which was roughly equal to that of a 67 year old in 1987.

This negative trend seems to be getting worse and occurring in men at much younger ages. Adolescent boys are also experiencing delayed puberty.

The researchers of these studies concluded that, "the decline in testosterone does not appear to be attributable to observed changes in explanatory factors, including health and lifestyle changes such as smoking and obesity." Pretty lame conclusion?

It does however seem that the tests did not comprise entirely of normally functioning and healthy subjects so the results could be a little misleading.

There have been many possible causes put forward but in conclusion, the tests, and more notably the researchers themselves, have been unable to categorically state the underlying cause/s.

Another grey area are the actual test subjects. The subjects were selected at random and little is known about their exact lifestyle and habits. All that is said is that there seemed to be increases in obesity and medication use along with a decrease in smoking. Strange considering that they concluded by denying, or failing to conclude that these factors were responsible in any way.

In the study by Travison et al, for example, the test that most people refer to on this subject, it was reported that 52% of the test subjects reported at least one chronic illness and 22% reported using at least three different prescription medications. Not at all representative of healthy subjects. These factors can all adversely affect T levels of course.

I have some theories of my own about this, which although not backed by any research at all, and not confirmed independently by anyone, do have a basis in truth.

The first proposal is medical advice. It was around 50 years ago that the medical establishment started a trend of advising people to lower their cholesterol. Cholesterol was hailed as being bad for our health and it caused clogged arteries and increased the risk of heart attacks. Which of course in the case of bad cholesterol is true to an extent. However this advise was taken literally to mean all cholesterol.

This led to the nutrition industry adopting a trend of plugging low fat diets and advising people to avoid saturated fats especially. It has now been found that eating saturated fats from good sources, not processed foods or trans fats, but from sources such as meat and eggs, has no harmful effects and does not increase the risk of a heart attack.

A point to note here is that the website for the British Heart Foundation is still advising people to eat low fat diets, and to keep cholesterol intake to a minimum.

The problem regarding testosterone is that saturated fats and essential fats provide cholesterol, which of course is the building block of testosterone. So men who have heeded this advice for the last 50 years could have caused their testosterone levels to decline.

A flaw in that theory is that the test subjects for the T level decline based research selected men at random for their studies, and that means that not all of them were guaranteed to be observing low fat diets. In fact they stated that obesity did not affect the results. A flaw in the studies and the theories of the researchers is that they did not consider this. Or if they did they decided not to declare this to be a contributory factor.

But one thing that cannot be denied cholesterol is the building block of testosterone. A deficiency in cholesterol *will* affect T levels.

Another unconfirmed theory of mine, and indeed also of many others, are the side effects of technological advances. Everything is convenient and entertainment is now available at the flick of a screen, or the push of a button. Fast forward through the last 50 years and the further forward in time you look throughout this period, the younger the users of this tech have become.

Another related factor to consider is that people are less active in the modern world. The numbers of men pursuing careers in the field of physical labour are falling and advances in technology and machinery are reducing their workload. Physical activity is fundamental to testosterone levels and staying active is very important.

Also we have our modern society based upon instant gratification and convenience. We have a plethora of tech devices that are capable of delivering entertainment and mental stimuli on demand. All day every day. Whatever your interests, they have you covered.

For children growing up in the 1970s, there were no children's channels providing 24/7 entertainment. Game consoles and computers had not yet arrived and their use was not widespread. For many children in the modern world, they are introduced to these devices at an early age, as a means of keeping them occupied, and often this becomes their staple form of amusement and entertainment and has taken the place of any physical activity for many.

Many children spend many hours in front of a screen. More children have been preferring to stay indoors and play video games, use social media or watch a never ending stream of children s TV that is now available.

This has become more widespread since the 1980s. These children have not been getting much sunlight so are lacking in vitamin D, which is known to have a profound affect on T levels and puberty development. Parents who allow children to enjoy a lot of screen time also tend to be sedentary families with sedentary lifestyles. They are more likely to observe bad diets and eat a lot of convenient processed foods and takeaways.

This would result in nutritional deficiencies in many micro nutrients, which are also known to affect T levels. A zinc deficiency in teenagers has been linked with potential delays in them reaching sexual maturity. It would also assume that their, the children's, intake of trans fats might be higher and this too can affect T levels.

I grew up in the UK in the late 1970s and 80s and we occupied ourselves by playing outdoors and partaking in physical activities every day. When our parents wanted some downtime they didn't give us a screen to keep us quiet, there weren't any. Apart from the TV which had an hour of kids programmes per day at the most. They told us to go outside and play.

This is important because an active childhood lays the foundations for an active adult life. An active childhood furthers physical development, and this must be affecting T level development too. The decline in physical activity among the young has certainly played a part in the decline in testosterone levels. That cannot be denied.

If you are someone who was not physically active as a child then you cannot go back in time or do anything about the past. You can only look ahead and you have to work and develop whatever you have got. Accept this and move on. All is not lost as you will see.

It is also certainly true that more people are on more prescription medications now. 20 years ago people in their 60s and 70s were likely to be taking up to 5 or 6 different medications. Now people in their 30s and younger, including children, are being prescribed more medications and many in their 30s and 40s are now using up to 5 or 6 prescription medications. This has become the new normal. Just like falling T levels.

Many medications for many different conditions are known to play a part in hormonal imbalances and the reduction of testosterone levels in men. And delayed puberty in boys. So this is highly likely to influence the results of these tests and be helping to contribute towards declining T levels.

Another idea that has been put forward is the rise in the use of plastics in the last 50 years. The use of plastics is more widespread in food packaging and the manufacture of many goods, including children's toys. Plastics are now known to contain endocrine disruptors, which are thought to have an affect on T levels. There is also an increase in the use of endocrine disruptors in many personal hygiene products such as toothpastes and shower gels.

Another consideration is the use of parabens and other hormone disruptors in many skin care products, which more and more men took to using more frequently the further you look throughout this same 50 year period. Men in the 1970s did not moisturise. At all. It was frowned upon. They shaved, took baths or showers, brushed their teeth and splashed some cold water on their face. They had higher T levels too.

I am not judging here, these are just testosterone related facts. I do care for my skin but I use a little known recipe that is 100% natural, very effective, non toxic and contains no hormone disruptors whatsoever. I shall reveal this later.

Now plastics have become more widespread since the 1970s so there could be truth in this. But as for men using skin care products this only really took off in the 1990s and has only become more mainstream in the last 10 years or so. This provides a little flaw to that theory. But a certain truth is that these products are full of toxins and hormonally disruptive chemicals.

These chemicals are effectively disrupting male hormones and causing men to develop hormonal imbalances, and it is thought that in some cases an elevation in estrogen levels.

This has given rise to a new social media trend known as estrogenics and the promotion of avoiding these chemicals and the products they are found in. We will look at this a little further on.

Another aspect that is not often considered are the changes in modern manufacturing processes of many goods. The main aim of these developments in manufacturing are largely down to the newer methods being more cost efficient and resulting in more profits for the manufacturers.

This trend towards cost cutting and the increasing number of toxins, hormone disruptors and other chemicals will no doubt have had an effect on declining T levels in the last 50 years. In my opinion it is not so much that one thing has caused this decline, but more a combination of all the things we have considered here.

So how do you know if you have low T levels?

8

Gyno and Hormone Imbalance.

R ecover Hormonal Balance.

Gynecomastia is becoming more common among many men now so in this section I am going to into gyno, and to put forward some ways you can adopt to help you reverse this condition naturally, without pharmaceutical drugs or surgery.

Many online sources now claim that it is normal for young guys to suffer with hormonal imbalances during puberty. This has often been cited as a principle cause of the condition and in the majority of cases this is true. In this section we will focus on methods aimed at restoring hormonal balance.

As the principle cause of gynecomastia is a hormonal imbalance, this section will offer some insight to anyone suffering with this condition. The two subjects are closely related and the principles of treating gyno and restoring hormonal balance require a very similar approach. Although I will be constantly referring to gyno in this chapter the same strategies also apply to attempting to restore hormonal balance.

When I was in puberty during the mid to late 1980s, and of course at this time surrounded by many other guys also going through puberty, I do not recall ever seeing any other guy with gyno during that period. In fact, the most common problem us guys had during puberty back then was with acne, this being due to our testosterone levels rising and becoming higher as we approached adulthood.

Of course children in the 1970s did not have so many plastic toys. There were also less endocrine disrupting chemicals added to products. Foods did not contain so many additives as they do today. Also children were a lot more active and we did not have much screen time. It is certainly a completely different environment for the children and adolescents of today.

The underlying root cause of gyno is, more often than not, a hormonal imbalance of the hormones estrogen and testosterone. Other factors that are known to be involved in triggering gyno are diet and lifestyle choices, and even some medical conditions.

Also if your body is out of sync in any way then this will increase the chances of your hormones being unbalanced.

If your estrogen is a little too high and your testosterone happens to drop at the same time this can trigger gyno. There are many things that can cause this imbalance to happen. The most important thing when you are looking to resolve this problem is to try to identify the root cause. It is this root cause that you should be principally aiming to fix. This could be a hormonal imbalance, but you must try to determine what exactly is was that caused this imbalance. This could be down to poor diet, or poor lifestyle choices. It could even be something that you would think of as being completely unrelated to testosterone such as high insulin levels.

Gyno can also be caused by some medical problems with the liver, with hypothyroidism, obesity, malnutrition, various problems with the adrenal glands or the pituitary glands and even levels of urea in the blood.

With liver problems, this can affect the way that the adrenal glands influence hormones and this can affect the way that testosterone and estrogen interact. This can result in a reduction in the body's ability to clear adrenal hormones from the liver. This can cause increased levels of SHBG, which can cause levels of free testosterone to drop and this can also possibly cause estrogen to rise.

To optimise adrenal functioning you need to be ideally following a low or no sugar diet, and cutting out caffeine intake. Nutritional supplements including vitamins B5, B6, B12 and vitamin C can be beneficial. Also ensuring adequate sleep and good stress management strategies. One of the most important hormones to balance for good adrenal function is insulin. High insulin plays havoc with adrenal function.

COMPLETE GUIDE TO TESTOSTERONE 39

Another hormone that can negatively affect adrenal function is cortisol. In a different section we looked at ways to balance out cortisol. This will also correlate to the subject of gyno.

A good idea in the case of insulin would be to test your blood glucose with a glucometer or a flash glucose monitor. Checking your blood sugar levels is always a good idea. If you have gyno it is highly recommended. High blood sugar can negatively affect hormones. Balancing out your blood sugar levels can be beneficial to improving adrenal functioning, which in turn can help to balance out your hormones and could possibly reverse your gyno if this were to be the root cause.

Should you discover that your blood sugar levels are higher than they should be, eating low GI carbs will help with regulating insulin levels. Reduce intake of high starch carbs like pasta and potatoes and instead aim to get your carbs and fibre from low starch foods such as cruciferous vegetables or leafy greens. Starchy foods spike insulin. Going low carb or keto for a month or two could be helpful in reducing insulin levels.

In the case of high insulin it can also be a good idea to moderate fruit intake too. Eating a lot of fruits can lead to increased blood glucose levels.

If you have hypothyroidism, this will apply more to older guys, then eating low iodine foods such as eggs, fruits, nuts, oats, potatoes and honey can be helpful. Eating cruciferous vegetables is also very beneficial. Also make sure that you are getting plenty of iron in your diet. Low iron levels are linked to hypothyroidism. Also supplement with selenium, zinc, and vitamin D. Ensure that you are getting plenty of healthy fats in your diet, this helps to protect thyroid health. Also using turmeric, green chillies, ginger and black pepper can be helpful.

High levels of urea in the blood have been linked to high protein diets, and in particular high meat consumption. By high protein diet, it is meant consuming more than 3g of protein per pound of body-weight. This is something that could occur if you are following the carnivore diet. Blood urea levels can be lowered by consuming less protein. Reducing protein intake to 1g per pound of bodyweight is certainly a good idea. Also consuming lots of potatoes and carrots can help alkalise the urine and lessen the effects of urea. Bear in mind that potatoes are starchy and can raise insulin. Eating healthy foods and plenty of fruits and vegetables and also in particular, cinnamon, lemon, red peppers and turmeric can also help to lower the blood urea levels.

This is why it is important to be eating a varied and balanced diet. Eating meats is beneficial for testosterone, but the possible negative side effects must be balanced out by including other types of foods in your diet.

Malnutrition is commonly associated with being starved or going without food for prolonged lengths of time. However, what is often not considered is that nutrient deficiencies caused by poor diet or restrictive diets can also cause similar effects to malnutrition. Any nutrient deficiencies are a form of malnutrition. And any form of mal-nutrition can throw the body out of sync and in turn create hormonal imbalances.

Some pharmaceutical medications can also trigger gyno. Any medications that have any effects on androgens or normal hormone production, such as steroids and synthetic androgens can cause gyno. This is also possible with hormone precursor supplements such as pregnenolone and DHEA. Also medications for ADHD, anti-anxiety, anti-depressants, antibiotics, and some heart medications can all be possible causes of gyno.

Whatever the root cause that is causing your gyno, whether that is a medical condition, poor lifestyle choices or poor diet, resolving that root cause is going to prevent the condition from ever coming back. This is why it is so important to try to identify and tackle that root cause.

Easier said than done of course. With an underlying medical condition it may not be possible to reverse the condition completely. If this is the case then effective condition management is going to be beneficial.

And there is one key point to make in trying to resolve or reverse gyno. This is not going to be easy. This is going to involve putting in some detailed thinking, careful planning, some effort, and a little bit of experimentation to discover what works for you. There are no quick fixes and this is going to take time. I am sorry but this is the truth. I cannot lie to you.

Having surgery or going onto TRT is definitely much easier and certainly less complicated but even if you have surgery to remove the excess tissue, the root cause has not been fixed and the gyno can come back.

Medications such as TRT or SERMS, which are Selective Estrogen Receptor Modulators, also do not address the root cause of gyno. All they do is to try to regulate the increased estrogen in other words treating the symptom of increased estrogen without addressing the root cause. SERMS treat the symptom of increased estrogen, and TRT increases testosterone to counter the increased estrogen. With either you will remain with a hormonal imbalance, which is the root cause of your gyno. And, as with most pharmaceutical medications, they can cause further hormonal imbalances, making the original root cause worse, and often come with many other unwanted side effects.

An important thing to consider is that there is also a condition with a similar visible effect to gyno called "pseudogynecomastia," which causes an increase in fat but not an increase of gland tissue in the chest. The main difference between the two is that gyno causes an increase in the breast gland tissue. Gyno is a hormonal reaction resulting in the accumulation of glandular tissue, and pseudogynecomastia is just normal fat accumulation.

The visible effects of both conditions are very similar in appearance and often it is very difficult to tell the difference between the two.

If you have been leading a low activity lifestyle then there is a high probability that you will have built up excess fat tissue in your chest. But this is not necessarily true gyno.

In the case of pseudogynecomastia, in the majority of cases all it will take to fix the problem is taking care of your diet and starting to work out on a regular basis. For most guys with pseudogynecomastia this is going to be enough, and the issue will likely resolve itself over time.

With true gynecomastia however, you are going to need to take care of the hormonal imbalance that caused the condition to occur in the first place. If you leave this imbalance unattended, the condition can keep reoccurring.

There is a quick test you can perform on yourself to help you determine whether you have gyno, or just excess fat tissue in the chest, without going to a doctor.

If you gently pinch the breast tissue around the nipple and the tissue is firm or has the consistency of rubber, this indicates the presence of glandular tissue, indicating a high probability of true gynecomastia. If this is the case then a visit to a doctor for confirmation is advised.

If it feels soft and fatty and pliable, this indicates pseudogynecomastia caused by a build up of excess fat. This simple test can give you an idea of where you should begin.

So is the condition reversible in a natural way without resorting to TRT, other pharma medications or surgery?

Yes it is, but as I have already said this is not going to be a quick or easy process. And you are going to have to come at this with a bit of detailed thinking as there a quite a few things to consider. And combining as many of these things together as you can is going to give you the best results. The more things you do, the better and more permanent the effects will be. This is the same method and approach that will also produce better results when it comes to your testosterone.

First thing to do is to take a photo of yourself. This is your reference point to gauge your progress. It can be difficult to notice changes so much because you see yourself in the mirror on a daily basis. Every month take another photo and then compare the two. This gives you an effective way to check your progress over time. It can also help you determine what is working for you and what is not working so well.

The first thing to consider in trying to determine the root cause of your gyno is to consider your daily habits and lifestyle choices.

For example if you have been leading a sedentary lifestyle, consuming an unhealthy diet consisting of lots of processed foods, drinking alcohol, sugary sodas, being exposed to hormone disrupting chemicals, or using recreational drugs, then first and foremost you must address these more obvious things first. Chances are if you are guilty of any of these things they will have contributed towards the condition in some way.

If you have gyno then I recommend zero alcohol and zero recreational drugs. Cut out these things immediately if this applies to you. Just one beer is not OK. People will try to say just one will do no harm. Don't listen to them. We've all been there. That one beer often leads to two or three and before you know it you're drunk and getting into this state and consuming that many drinks will crash your testosterone levels and it could take your endocrine system up to 3 to 5 days to recover. Not a good idea if you are trying to cure your gyno.

You are also going to need to pay attention to your diet. And this will need to be a detailed approach. Diet often plays a significant role in causing gyno. Diet is going to play a part in helping you to reverse the gyno.

Of course the problem with diet is that in truth, there is no such thing as a one size fits all diet that will suit absolutely everyone. So lets just consider some basic rules and guidelines.

Most important thing to consider. Especially in the long term sphere of things. You need a varied and balanced diet containing all macros and micros. A deficiency in any macro or micro-nutrient can cause health issues, throw the body out of sync, and many deficiencies can disrupt hormone production.

Your diet also preferably needs to be balanced to your own personal needs. Find your dietary sweet spot. Not too much and not too little of anything.

One thing that you should do is to avoid seed oils and vegetable oils, these are known to have a negative effect on hormones. They are also effectively processed foods and chemicals have often been added during the processing. If you must fry anything use olive oil, coconut oil, or even better use animal fats. Or even better still, don't fry. Use other cooking methods like grilling, boiling or oven baking.

Also consider consuming more raw foods. I would recommend that anything that can be consumed raw without cooking it then do so. Especially when consuming vegetables, because any cooking methods reduce their nutrient value.

Here is a valuable rule for all diets. This has to be the best piece of dietary advice that I have ever received. If it does not occur naturally in nature it is best avoided. If it has been manufactured, in any way, be wary and be very attentive to it. This would apply to things like olive oil for example. There are some very high quality oils out there in the marketplace. There are some that are not so good, and there are others that should be completely avoided, because they are very low quality and often have been bulked out with other cheaper seed oils.

You should also cut *all* processed foods and fast food from your diet. These foods are full of empty calories and are usually stuffed with added salt, sugars and chemical preservatives. All of these things make gyno harder to reverse. These things can also contribute towards gyno.

Also many of these foods come in cans or plastic containers and these usually contain hormone disrupting chemicals such as polycarbonate or bisphenol A, or BPA. Again whenever someone says to you that just once won't do any harm, ignore that advice and say no. That once is one time too many.

Many take outs contain trans fats. Yes in some countries trans fats have been banned but fast food outlets get round this by including trans fats in what they call "fat blends." The reality is that fast food has no significant or beneficial nutrient value, its also processed food, and it is bad for your testosterone and your general health anyway so just cut it out from your life.

When it comes to processed foods, consider that things like pasta, bread, and pasteurised milk are manufactured using a list of ingredients, and this effectively means they are processed and many of these products contain chemical preservatives.

Also it is a good idea to moderate your intake of dairy products if you have gyno. Many of these products contain hormones from the animals that produced them and consuming too much could mean that you are feeding yourself female hormones. Milk in particular consumed in large amounts has been linked with causing gyno. Milk is also considered to be rich in estrogen. You do not need to cut dairy out completely as it can be beneficial to health and dairy products are good sources of protein but just be aware that they contain female hormones.

Bear in mind that most animal products have been fed growth hormones, they too contain female hormones but meat is still beneficial to male hormone production. If you are concerned about this then most veal calves are male animals and do not contain any female hormones. Eggs also contain female hormones but are great for testosterone. Dairy can be beneficial too but if you have gyno, not *too* much dairy.

Also be aware that whey protein, often consumed by many guys post workout is a milk protein isolate. Often guys drink one or two of these a day and many also make desserts and puddings using whey. A good alternative post workout drink to using protein powder is to just consume 4 to 6 raw eggs either drink them on their own from a glass, or you can add a little filtered water to help it go down a little easier. Don't forget, protein powders are also effectively processed foods. Even plant based protein powders are processed.

Alternatively, make your own natural post workout drink using a blender. Take a banana, a little water, 4 raw eggs, and you could even add some ginger or a bit of raw honey and throw that all into a blender, blitz it, and you have a natural highly nutritious post workout drink that is completely unprocessed and natural and provides at least 28g protein. Use six eggs and that becomes 42g of protein. This will cost more than using protein powders but it is natural and certainly more nutritious.

Another golden dietary rule is to consume a diet based on complete whole foods. A whole food is one that consists of only one ingredient. Try to avoid food items that contain a list of ingredients. Don't forget even wholemeal bread and pasta which are seen as healthy, contain a list of ingredients and are processed foods. If it doesn't occur naturally in nature its not a whole food. Be aware that canned beans, chickpeas and other ready made legumes, often viewed as whole foods, have added salt and sugar and are processed. Better to use natural legumes.

Cut out sugary foods and drinks. *If you can cut out sugar completely then do so.* When stating this I mean to cut out all refined, processed, sugar. Remember that sugar can spike insulin and this can be bad for hormonal balance. But natural sugars from fruits and raw honey are highly beneficial. But beware that many honeys found in supermarkets can contain as much as 70 to 80g of sugar per 100g of honey. That's just as bad as consuming sugar.

You should be looking to include plenty of meats, fish, fruits, legumes, unprocessed of course, vegetables and natural whole grains in your diet. Eggs are particularly good for testosterone they are jam packed with nutrients and they also provide good amounts of cholesterol and also have a low saturated fat content. Organ meats such as liver and kidneys are excellent sources of low saturated fat cholesterol too.

When it comes to cholesterol always remember that too much cholesterol can be just as harmful as not enough. Just consuming cholesterol does not guarantee the body will use it to produce testosterone if the body is out of sync. It is important to balance out cholesterol levels. It is important to balance the whole body.

Cholesterol only ever becomes unhealthy when we allow an excess to build up within the body. This occurs when our body is not using it all up efficiently.

With gyno the objective is to reduce excess tissue so it is best to avoid any bulking diet for now at least until your hormones are balanced out.

For helping to blast off excess build up of fat tissue a keto or a low carb animal based diet could be useful to help you to kick start this process. But remember that carbs, from fruit and vegetables, are also essential for body optimisation so best to avoid staying on any restrictive diets for too long.

If you prefer to go plant based, I am not an advocate of the vegan diet although I do consume a lot of plant foods. After all, plant foods are natural whole foods that occur naturally in nature. Many of these plant foods I consume raw.

If you are going to opt for plant based I would strongly recommend including lots of eggs, 4 to 6 per day, with that and plenty of extra virgin olive oil. You need to consume adequate cholesterol in your diet to optimise your testosterone production. An unavoidable fact, hormones are made with cholesterol. Vegan diets tend to be cholesterol deficient. And no, despite what many vegans believe, your body will not make all the cholesterol it needs.

Both keto and carnivore in particular are excellent diets for losing weight and getting rid of excess fatty tissues in the body. These diets can also increase testosterone in the first few months. This is usually due to the increased fat and cholesterol intake.

However, a varied and balanced diet is best for testosterone in the long term. Including all macros and micros. Any nutrient deficiencies can have a negative effect especially when these deficiencies occur for longer duration. At some point your body is going to require some carbohydrate and dietary fibre input. Just bear this in mind.

There is no one size fits all dietary solution that is going to work for everyone. We are all different. We all have different calorific and nutritional requirements. But by applying a few ground rules and then seeking to tweak and modify your diet to suit your own needs is the best strategy you can employ.

Experiment with your diet and observe the results and then go from there. And you are going to need to combine this diet with some physical training for best results.

If I were asked to say whether carnivore, keto, or animal or plant based is best for this purpose I am biased towards keto or animal based. This is because these two diets provide more of a variety of foods, along with sufficient fat and cholesterol intake, and it is also possible to get some carb and fibre intake with these two approaches.

However the best diet by far for testosterone and for a balanced body is the omnivore diet, including a variety of natural whole foods.

When it comes to dropping excess body tissue then eating low starch carbs from fruit, vegetables is going to be the best approach for most men. If you experience any form of energy crash at any time, then maybe add some potatoes, legumes or even rice a few times a week. Be aware of starch and insulin.

Warnings: When it comes to buying vegetables then research a commonly used produce coating called "Apeel." This is a layer of an acetate or silicone derivative used to prolong the life of fruits and vegetables and to prevent food waste. This coating contains hormone disrupting chemicals and should be avoided by everyone. This transforms a natural whole food into a processed food.

When it comes to buying meats then beware of lab grown meats as these are also packed with toxins. Again lab grown meats are processed food. If you live in the UK, US and many other western countries then there is a high chance that lab grown meats are in your marketplace right now. Much of the ground beef now available in western supermarkets is lab grown.

If you decide to use the keto approach, the usual strategy is to be aiming for around 10-15% of total calorific intake to come from carbs, 30-35% from protein and the rest of your calorific intake coming from fats. When combined with an intense physical training program the body will make use of all that fat.

When it comes to carbs and blasting away excess body tissue, the best approach by far is to get your carbs from fruits and vegetables.

3oz of watermelon contains 11g carbs.

3oz of strawberries contain 13g carbs.

1 peach contains 14g carbs.

3oz blueberries contain 21g carbs.

3oz cherries contain 25g carbs.

32 grapes contain 28g carbs.

3 oz raspberries contain 15g carbs.

3 oz of pineapple contains 22g carbs.

1 apple contains 25g carbs.

3oz of cantaloupe contains 13g carbs.

1 orange contains 15g carbs.

A large mango contains 25g carbs.

1 banana contains 27g carbs.

Vegetables tend to contain carbs at much lower quantities due to fruit having natural sugar content. However they do usually contain more fibre.

An average sized avocado contains 13g carbs.

1 medium sized potato provides roughly 33g carbs.

3 oz of sweet potato contains 21g carbs.

1 large carrot contains 6g carbs.

3oz of broccoli contains around 10g carbs.

3oz cabbage contains 6g carbs.

These are all natural whole foods.

Should you decide to opt for the carnivore diet then be aware that carb intake is very low or non-existent so just adding a few pieces of fruit or vegetables a day is going to make a huge difference. An animal based diet of course allows for this anyway.

In my opinion carnivore is probably most effective observed in a cycle if you want to try this diet. One month carnivore followed by a month of animal based with some carbs from fruits and vegetables included. During your carnivore period being aware of, and taking care of, any potential nutrient deficiencies. Nutrient deficiencies are an enemy of testosterone.

Now, if I was in the position of having gyno myself I would begin my campaign by utilising keto. But I would also include three days per week where my carb intake would be increased a little to avoid energy crash from carb deficiency. Four keto days and 3 increased carb days per week.

On these increased carb days I would consume foods such as potatoes, legumes or whole grains with my evening meal.

This would be combined with exercise, and observing an effective conditioning strategy. This is the best approach to reducing the excess tissue in the chest and in reducing the appearance of gyno. A keto approach can be a very useful tool to use for this purpose.

Connected to diet and certainly worth your consideration is inter-mittent fasting. Doing an intermittent fast maybe once or twice per week will also be very useful for combating gyno. But be careful not to ever put your body into a state of severe calorific deficit for long periods of time. This can negatively affect testosterone production. The section about the T-boosting diet offers some guidance in weight loss while avoiding severe calorific deficit.

When I fast I usually do a 16:8 fast. On fasting day I wake up early at 6am and consume breakfast. I then train and at 11am eat another small meal usually with moderate to high fat content. I then take a high calorie lunch at 1pm. This includes adequate protein, fat and moderate carbs. My fast begins at 2pm and lasts until at least 6am the following day. During the fast you can drink water, or tea and coffee with zero milk or sugar. Adding a weekly fast to your routine will be very beneficial.

Regular consumption of foods such as extra virgin olive oil, ginger, garlic, nuts and chillies are also really good for promoting testosterone production and should be included in your diet.

Increasing or optimising your testosterone production in every and any way you can is also going to help you to reduce estrogen and lessen the effects of gyno. Include as many testosterone friendly foods into your diet on a regular basis.

Now the next thing to consider is your training. This is going to be an approach aimed at total body conditioning. At this stage you should avoid any attempt at bulking. Also when bulking and packing lean muscle mass onto the chest area this can lead to the gyno becoming more pronounced and noticeable. Body conditioning is most effective for reducing the appearance of gyno.

Provided you are getting enough protein and sufficient nutrients in your diet and exercising to a higher level of intensity you will still see muscle development happening.

But for the purposes of reducing and eliminating gyno, an approach aimed at body conditioning and becoming a lean machine with a physique like the well known influencer David Goggins is going to be very effective for this purpose.

It is advisable to observe a normal routine of resistance training, for full body development. My usual routine is a 4 day split. Workouts dedicated to each muscle group. My own workouts focus on conditioning, stamina and endurance anyway so would be also good for this purpose. My split consists of:

Day 1. Full leg workout, including exercises for quads, hamstrings, calves and glutes. My training equipment consists of a weighted vest, a bench, a pull up bar, kettle bells, dumbbells and resistance bands. I usually do an abs workout after that and then finish with 30 minutes of bag work for cardio.

Day 2. Chest, biceps and abs. Again after this I usually do 30 minutes of bag work.

Day 3. Rest day. We will get to rest days in a minute.

Day 4. Delts, Traps and triceps. Finishing with a quick obliques session and 30 minutes of bag work.

Day 5. Lats, rear delts and abs. Again ending with 30 minutes of bag work.

Days 6 and 7 are also rest days. On rest days I usually go mountain biking, rucking, hiking or walking. While we are on the subject of walking, always walk or cycle if you can. Unless I am travelling a long distance or am time restricted I will usually walk or cycle. Get used to walking as often as you can. All those steps will add up and its helping to tone and condition you.

HIIT, high intensity interval training, and circuit training are also very effective for body conditioning and even callisthenics, using bodyweight exercises at a high intensity is also an effective training method for this purpose. I often implement all of these training methods into my own routine.

But if you have gyno it is also going to be highly beneficial to add some extra sessions that would be a daily routine to be carried out separately from usual resistance training. This extra routine is 7 days a week and should also be done on rest days.

For this extra side routine, this would consist of exercises focused on very high reps and using movements that are effective for toning the whole chest, also the lower chest area where gyno is most commonly found.

These extra sessions would consist of sets of 50 to 100 reps, or a minimum daily number. For example 100 push ups. 100 dips etc. Also consider mixing it up and including both incline and decline push ups as well as regular push ups. Also butterflies holding light dumbbells or using a light resistance band can work well. Adding in movements such as pull-ups, bodyweight squats or lunges in high reps are also great for blasting away excess tissue.

These routines can be performed in sets of fewer reps when you begin. Just make sure that you set a target number, 100 of each movement is a good place to begin. And then just be certain to get all of those reps in every day.

As you get more used to doing this it will become easier as you get more used to doing it. It will be far more beneficial if you can reach a stage where you can do the total number of reps in just one or two sets. And over time, be looking to also increase the number of reps performed per day. Those high rep movements are excellent for toning and conditioning. These sessions will ideally be between 15 to 30 minutes per day. These are short sessions and to be most effective you should be breathing heavily by the time you have finished the session!

The main principle is to become as active as you can, as often as you can, in any way that you can. Take the stairs instead of the elevator, take those steps two or three at a time with each step. Walk to the store and carry your groceries home. Walk instead of using your car, motorbike or e-scooter. The more active you are the more conditioned you become.

Even consider adding some form of intense cardio to your routine. This can be running, cycling, swimming, rowing machine, cross trainer or bag work. Anything that gets your heart rate elevated will do for cardio. The more conditioned you become the more you will be able to blast away any excess body tissue.

But whatever you do please be sure to avoid steroids, pro-hormones and SARMS, because all of these mess with your natural hormone production. It can be tempting to enhance your performance in the gym, with a view to getting the job done quicker, but this kind of approach will exacerbate the problem in the long term and highly likely cause you other health problems.

Performance enhancing drugs can cause gyno in guys that didn't previously have gyno. If you have gyno then they will make the problem worse.

If you have gyno or any form of hormonal imbalance you should be taking some precautions against ingesting toxins or chemicals. This of course is good advice to any guy considering our modern chemical laden environment. As we know already many products etc contain hormone disrupting chemicals. These should be avoided as much as you possibly can if you have gyno.

When trying to reverse gyno the primary focus is balancing your hormones and anything that could affect or disrupt natural hormone production in a negative way should be avoided wherever possible.

Be selective over the products you use. When using chemicals to clean the house, or using any chemicals at work always wear gloves and avoid direct contact with these chemicals. Be aware that contact can also mean inhaling the fumes from chemically loaded products. After cleaning the home with these products rinse all surfaces thoroughly with water to minimise your exposure to chemicals.

When you wash your clothes use chemical free washing powders etc. Your clothes spend a lot of hours in contact with your skin. Also look to find good chemical free deodorants, shower gels and skincare. Completely avoid all sun products. All sunscreens are high in endocrine disruptors. This includes after sun products.

If you have to use any after sun treatments then opt for tallow balm, pure aloe vera or coconut oil or other natural moisturisers.

I make a 100% chemical free, home-made skincare that I use and the details of this are in a different section of this book.

You should also take care to avoid any hormone disrupting supplements. The obvious ones are steroids, SARMS and pro-hormones, but also supplements such as DHEA, pregnenolone and enclomiphine can affect natural hormone production.

Before introducing any supplement to your routine always carry out a little research into the affects that supplement will have on natural hormone production. If it can negatively affect NATURAL hormone production then reject it. Preferably read all ingredients lists before buying supplements. You would be surprised at how many things are added to these products. Always consider the positives and negatives to anything before jumping in.

If using supplements that come in silica based gel caps then best to remove the powder into a glass of water. Quite often these gel caps can contain chemicals. In fact do this with any supplements that come in gel caps, including natural or vegan gel caps.

Another thing to consider is using a liver detox supplement like milk thistle. This is going to help you to flush more toxins from your body. And make sure you are drinking enough water. Water also helps in flushing out toxins from the body. It is extremely difficult to completely avoid toxins so flushing out your system is a useful practise.

Lemon juice is a natural diuretic and adding some lemon juice from a freshly squeezed lemon will make you pee more frequently and this will also help in flushing away toxins. Lemon water is also good for weight loss and for helping to blast away excess tissue from the body.

And of course always filter all of your drinking water.

The best rule to apply to toxins and chemicals is that if you are ingesting it or absorbing it through the skin then avoid it.

A common tactic used by many guys looking to increase their testosterone and also guys with gyno is blocking or regulating estrogen. In cases of low T or gyno guys often have elevated estrogen levels so blocking or suppressing estrogen is something that should always be considered. This in particular applies to guys with gyno.

Some foods are particularly useful for suppressing estrogen synthesis.

Cruciferous vegetables such as cauliflower, broccoli, cabbage, carrots and brussel sprouts, have high amounts of glucosinolates, which help to flush out excess estrogen through the liver.

Mushrooms, red grapes, whole grains, flax seeds and a diet including lots of fruits and vegetables, high protein foods, legumes, meats such as organs, beef and chicken, high iodine foods such as eggs, fish, seafood, dairy and grains, also cottage cheese and yogurt and turmeric are foods that are known help to reduce estrogen levels in men. Don't forget to moderate your intake of dairy. Too much can help to increase gyno.

With turmeric, it can be taken either in supplement form, or you can use powdered turmeric in hot water and consume it as an infusion. To get the best effects with turmeric higher doses are more effective. When taking turmeric, combine intake with black pepper as this can enhance the effects of the turmeric.

Many guys with gyno often consider estrogen blocker supplements. These can be effective and a natural alternative to the pharmaceutical medications often prescribed for gyno.

These usually consist of a stack of natural herbal ingredients and are less likely to cause the unwanted side effects that come with medical prescriptions.

Using these supplements as a way of kick starting the process of reducing estrogen can be very effective.

A word of warning about blocking estrogen. Cycle. Stop using them completely when the gyno has been significantly reduced or has disappeared and avoid completely when a state of hormonal balance has been achieved.

Blocking estrogen can lead to disruptions to natural hormone pr oduction.The best approach is to cycle these supplements. You could do one month on followed by one month off. Or a week on followed by a week off.

Be aware that intentionally blocking estrogen can also lead to disrupted hormone production.

Normally I advise guys not to try blocking estrogen. But in the case of gyno, often lowering or regulating estrogen levels is going to be helpful. Particularly in the beginning to help kick start your recovery.

DIM, or diindolymethane, supplements are also useful for this purpose. This compound is found in cruciferous vegetables. DIM works by supporting good estrogen metabolites and reducing bad estrogen metabolites.

DIM has also been shown to inhibit aromatase, which converts testosterone into estrogen. DIM has also been shown to be effective in helping to support healthy testosterone levels. This supplement can be useful for men looking to balance out their estrogen, and should be considered if you have gyno.

This is pretty obvious but another thing you should be doing is everything you can to optimise your testosterone production.

Another thing to consider is to optimise pituitary functioning. The hormones secreted in the pituitary are used to help make testosterone and also HGH is also produced here. HGH is involved in the regeneration of healthy cells and is an important factor to consider in optimising your body for hormone production.

Paying attention to this is going to be very helpful in treating gyno. Because optimised pituitary function helps to induce balanced hormone production.

Reducing sugar intake, preferably cutting all intake of refined sugar, taking meals at the same times each day, eating glutamine rich foods, such as eggs, intermittent fasting, L-arginine supplementation, reducing body fat, improving sleep quality, staying well hydrated, not only fluids but electrolytes too, high intensity exercise and managing stress effectively all contribute towards improved pituitary functioning.

Another thing you can do alongside the natural estrogen blocking supplements to kick start the hormonal balance process is to take a T boosting supplement. These are commonly used by body-builders to help recover natural T production after a steroid cycle.

In the many studies that suggest that these supplements increase testosterone levels, the increases to testosterone were recorded in men with existing low T. In guys with good baseline T levels these supplements are unlikely to make any significant difference. Something the manufacturers and those marketing these things neglect to say.

It is more accurate to call them T maintenance supplements rather than T boosters. I use this type of supplement once per week for T maintenance purposes.

As they have a track record for helping to restore natural testosterone levels, particularly in guys suffering with low testosterone and hormonal imbalances they will be useful to guys with gyno. Again they are best cycled.

One thing you can consider trying is to cycle the T booster alongside the estrogen blocker. For example, a week on the estrogen blocker supplement followed by a week on the T booster supplement. Do this for 4 weeks and then take a week or two off before resuming the cycle. This is just a suggestion.

The important thing is to avoid blocking estrogen too much. This will have a negative effect. When you are seeing results then maybe try reducing the doses of each supplement.

Your end game with this should be naturally optimised and balanced hormone production.

If you have gyno then there are a few other supplements that you may find particularly useful.

Taurine. During exercise and exercise recovery levels of taurine are depleted quickly when this happens exercise related fatigue is more likely to occur. Because of the high activity regime you need to follow this can help you to combat tiredness.

Also I would recommend supplementing with vitamin D, but be aware that you can also increase vitamin D by eating fatty fish, eggs and mushrooms. Also fish oil supplements combined with vitamin D can help.

An often neglected thing when it comes to vitamin D is that taking a vitamin D supplement alone will not work. You need to combine that supplement with natural sunlight to get the full benefits.

Yes a vitamin D supplement helps if you live in a colder climate and when there is less warm sunny weather. It is advisable to use a supplement during the colder months too.

But you also need to go outdoors, preferably every day. If it is daytime then the sun is up and the UV rays are still getting through. Even if it is cloudy. Even in cold weather. The only time the sun isn't available is at night time when it is dark.

So to get the best from your intake of vitamin D get outside and expose your skin to the sunlight. Even if it is behind the clouds. Even if you are wearing clothes. A t-shirt exposes the arms, neck and face. Not wearing a hat exposes more of the face. All of this helps.

Another very important supplement to consider if you have gyno are adaptogenic herbs such as maca, ginseng, ashwagandha, fenugreek, rhodiola rosea and mucuna pruriens are very effective in helping to balance hormones. The get their name, adaptogens, because of their ability and effectiveness in helping to restore and maintain balance in the body. I would highly recommend including adaptogens in your regime to help in combating gyno. In my opinion, panax ginseng and ashwagandha are among the most effective.

Mucuna pruriens has also been found to increase testosterone while at the same time suppressing prolactin. Prolactin is something that could contribute towards gyno so this supplement is certainly worth considering.

Zinc and magnesium are also important. Zinc and magnesium supplements are best consumed with a meal for better absorption. ZMA supplements are well worth your consideration, these contain zinc, magnesium and vitamin B6. Vitamin B6 is said to help in suppressing estrogen synthesis in men.

A complete vitamin B complex along with vitamin C. These are all water soluble vitamins, which means any excess gets flushed from the body and is not stored for later use in fat cells. Supplementing will help prevent any deficiencies.

Also consider using vitamin K, L-arginine, L-carnitine, omega 3 fish oils, and maybe boron. These will all be helpful. Boron is another micro that is said to help suppress estrogen. L-carnitine boosts androgen sensitivity.

But always look to getting as many micro nutrients as you can from natural food sources. If you are eating a lot of meats and avoiding dairy then a calcium supplement will be very useful to help prevent iron overload. Don't forget to remove the supplements from the gel caps, the more supplements you are taking the more important this is.

Improving androgen receptor levels and androgen sensitivity is very important for treating gyno and restoring hormonal balance. Androgen receptors determine how well the body reacts to testosterone and optimising your androgen activity is going to be essential for guys with gyno.

DHT, or dihydrotestosterone, is a hormone created from testosterone that helps to give men more masculine features. This hormone is more powerful than testosterone and helps us men maintain sex drive and our masculine characteristics. It also helps significantly in reducing gyno.

DHT is also effective at controlling blood sugar, improving memory and cognitive function, preventing anxiety and depression, improving sexual function, heart health, increasing strength and muscle mass, improving bone growth and bone density and even helps to prevent auto-immune diseases.

Some men try to suppress or block DHT because it has been associated with male pattern baldness. And it is. I strongly advise against blocking DHT as this can and does have a negative effect on testosterone. Given a choice between testosterone or hair I choose testosterone. Hair we can live without.

If you have gyno or any hormonal imbalance then any attempts to block or suppress DHT could prove to be a disaster. You want to be promoting masculine features and suppressing feminine features not the opposite. Blocking DHT is effectively attempting to block your masculine features.

If you have gyno then this is the worst and the most counter-productive thing that you can possibly do. Consider that roughly 10% of your total testosterone is converted into DHT so the higher your testosterone levels, the higher your level of DHT will tend to be.

But increasing or optimising your DHT is one of the best things you can do if you have gyno.

Of course exercise and in particular sprinting can be effective for increasing DHT. Also losing any excess bodyfat.

Increasing intake of dietary fats and cholesterol can also increase levels of DHT, no surprises there. And taking a zinc supplement with a meal can help.

Other supplements that are shown to be effective in increasing DHT production are tribulus terrestris, tongkat ali and caffeine.

DHEA supplements have also been linked to increases in DHT. But these supplements are synthetic hormones and can have an affect on natural hormone production. In another section I cover some things we can do to increase DHEA levels naturally.

Diosgenin supplements have also been shown to be effective in increasing DHT.

But the best supplement, in my opinion, for increasing and optimising DHT is creatine. In studies it was shown to increase levels of DHT in young athletes. It is also a very good supplement to consider for weight training purposes and this is pretty well known.

Before implementing any changes to your life carry out research and judge for yourself whether or not this will be good for you.

The last thing to consider is your own self belief that you can do this. If you believe you can then you will.

9

How Do I Know I Have Low Testosterone?

The Symptoms of Low Testosterone.

The effects of having low testosterone can be quite devastating. Usually men will notice a decline in energy and vitality that is usually put down to getting older. For most men they only ever get tested when a problem occurs. This is now becoming more frequent and common among younger men.

Low testosterone levels in men are considered to be anything below 300ng/DL.

It can be helpful to be familiar with the known symptoms of low testosterone. Usually when one of these appears it is a sign from your body that you might need to pay attention to a few things. Never assume the worst and just jump onto TRT. If you do everything in this guide that probably won't ever be necessary.

The signs that you might be experiencing low testosterone levels are numerous and could be indicators that you have a problem.

Low sex drive. Testosterone plays a key function in your libido and sexual performance. Any decline will naturally be a cause for concern for any man. This will be often accompanied by low semen output.

Difficulty maintaining an erection. Your hormonal levels play a key part in achieving and maintaining an erection. With low testosterone levels you might experience difficulty getting an erection before sex, or find that it takes more effort to achieve an erection. A good indicator here are the spontaneous erections that usually occur when we are asleep. If you have a problem with sex drive or sexual functioning it will usually be that the cases of morning wood will become less frequent or even stop altogether. An aspect to note here is that if you have regular morning wood then the problem might be psychological or a relationship problem. It may not necessarily be a testosterone issue.

Fatigue. If you are constantly tired or feeling a sensation of tiredness and a lack of energy, this could be down to low T levels. You will also find it more difficult to become motivated even if you are getting plenty of sleep.

Difficulty in gaining muscle mass. Men with lower T levels often find that they cannot effectively gain muscle mass, or have difficulty maintaining lean muscle mass. The more testosterone you have, the more active your muscle cells are and the more they grow. Take away that testosterone and increasing muscle mass can become really difficult.

Reduced exercise tolerance, strength or stamina.

Increased body fat. Considering that you need testosterone to burn fat and grow muscles, any deficiencies are likely to result in excess calories you eat being stored as fat. Fat cells produce an enzyme which converts more testosterone to estrogen. Excess fat results in falling T levels, which in turn leads to further weight gains.

Gynecomastia. This increase in fat cells can also cause man boobs and is a common result of increased body fat.

Hair loss. Often men with low T levels will have lower facial and body hair when compared to guys with higher T levels. Testosterone plays a significant part in the production of facial and body hair. In older men the reduction of under arm or pubic hair or needing to shave less often occurs with reducing T levels. In younger men the inability to grow a full beard, or having a patchy beard can be an indicator of lower T levels.

Cognitive functioning. Having lower T levels has an effect on the health of our brain and mental clarity. This means that you could start forgetting things or start to experience difficulty in concentrating. Low T levels have also been linked to irritability, depression and low moods, and even anxiety. Also be aware that your mental state can have an influence on your T levels.

Excessive sweating or night sweats. It is normal to sweat profusely during vigorous exercise and during hot weather, but if this is also accompanied by hot flushes this could be an indicator of reduced T levels.

Keeping an eye out for any of these signs is our first line of defence against declining T levels.

If you are not experiencing any of these issues then don't worry about how many ng/DL you have because everything is probably fine.

These are warning signs that there might be a problem it doesn't necessarily mean you have a problem. The body is a complex organism and it usually gives you a sign if its balance or equilibrium is affected.

With all this in mind we should explore all the possible causes to be better equipped to finding a solution. It does however, in conclusion, seem that the tests did not comprise entirely of normally functioning and healthy subjects so the results could be a little misleading and they failed to state a definitive answer as to why T levels are falling.

We shall now look at all the things to avoid or be aware of to help prevent low T levels.

We will begin with estrogenics. Should we be concerned?

10

The Hidden Dangers of Hormone Disruptors.

E strogenics. Cause for Concern?

Why Men *Need* Estrogen.

Before we dive into the subject of estrogenics we first need to consider why estrogen is so important to men. There seems to be a new movement of men who are of the opinion that estrogen is totally bad, and if at all possible, something to be blocked from entering the body, or its production suppressed in some way.

Truth is if you did manage to block all your estrogen, you would then have a severe hormonal imbalance and that would have a negative effect on your T levels. So if you are thinking of using an estrogen blocker (aromatase inhibiting drug) like Anastrozole or Tamoxifen, think again. Estrogen is essential to men. It only becomes a problem if your hormones get out of balance. And I will show you a highly effective little trick that I have used to maintain hormonal balance later in this guide.

Estrogen plays a role in many of the normal functions in the male body. These include controlling sex drive, enabling erections, sperm production and the regulation of fat tissue. Estrogen is basically fundamental to testicular function!

Around 80% of the estrogen present in the male body is made from testosterone. Most of the estrogen in the male body is testosterone that has been converted to estradiol, a form of estrogen, by an enzyme called aromatase. Many men think that blocking aromatase is the answer to all estrogenic issues. In fact the estradiol present in men plays a role in some masculine functions, as listed above, and is of great benefit to testicular functioning.

The truth is that the balance of estrogen production to testosterone production is the key to the correct hormonal balance that takes place in a man's body. If that balance is lost, in either direction, then a number of different problems can arise.

So if you have low testosterone levels then you will have a low supply of the raw material needed, which is testosterone, to make the estradiol in sufficient amounts. So if your T levels are low, chances are that your estradiol levels could be low too.

The symptoms of low testosterone, low estradiol or estrogen, and hormonal imbalances are all pretty much the same. Low or no libido, erectile dysfunction, poor fat metabolism, loss of muscle mass, tiredness, poor moods and poor sleep patterns.

So estrogen is pretty important to the normal functioning of the male body. To block it out entirely or to even suppress it is going to leave you with a hormonal imbalance and you will probably experience symptoms associated with low T levels.

So now lets get into estrogenics now that we can see how important it is to have *some* estrogen in our bodies. So what exactly are these chemicals the estrogenics guys have been warning us about?

The chemicals are collectively known as endocrine disruptors and are found in many commonly used household items and in many health and beauty products. Most of our food packaging and pretty much all plastics contain them. These chemicals have been found to have an impact on hormone levels and have been linked to declining testosterone levels.

Some of these chemicals have been found to imitate and increase natural hormones like estrogen. Some have the effect in that they disrupt metabolic pathways to suppress the production of testosterone. In effect they have the potential to affect the balance and equilibrium in many of our bodily functions.

So essentially this means that these endocrine disruptors are capable of either blocking or amplifying the hormonal messages which are sent to and from your immune system, your neurological pathways and your reproductive system. Research has also demonstrated a link between these chemicals and learning disabilities and even DNA damage. I'm concerned already and I bet you are too.

And the really bad news? These endocrine disruptors are literally everywhere. Their use is so widespread that to completely avoid them altogether is going to be extremely difficult. To list every product and item that they can be found in here would take up a whole book on its own!

And there is even more bad news. These chemicals are many and it would be difficult to memorise them. A full list, which is by no means complete, can be found at this site:

https://edlists.org/the-ed-lists/list-i-substances-identified-as-endo crine-disruptors-by-the-eu

Here are 4 of the most dangerous, which are also the most commonly used. It is these in particular that you need to be aware of. Chances are you are already being exposed to these on a daily basis.

Phthalates.

These are estrogen imitating plastic softeners and they leak out of plastics. They enter your body by being ingested, inhaled or absorbed through the skin. These have been linked to the inhibition of testosterone production and the damage of sperm in men.

They are commonly found in plastic bags, food packaging, in buckets, plastic tools, garden hoses, plastic shower curtains, waterproof raincoats, soaps, hair products and skin products. This list is nowhere near complete.

To combat against these chemicals ensure that you thoroughly clean your home, phthalates can escape from plastics and and become mixed in with dust in the air. Always remove any food or drink from plastic packaging before heating or eating. Avoid plastic packaging if you can. This is going to be pretty difficult I know. Good luck with that.

Always rinse any meats, fish etc thoroughly with water before preparation and cooking. The tap is OK for this but if you are super concerned you might want to take that a step further and use filtered water. Always put on gloves when handling plastics to limit the amount that is absorbed by the skin. Not always practical but when it comes to the garden hose or cleaning the house it should be OK. Just don't use plastic or rubber gloves!

Another thing you can do is to search for phthalate free grooming products there are many companies now producing this kind of product. Always read the ingredients before buying and if in doubt don't buy it. Even some products labelled as 100% natural have endocrine disruptors in them. Phthalate free products could have other alternative chemicals present in them. Always check the ingredients list!

Persistent Organic Pollutants.

These chemicals are produced during industrial or manufacturing processes. They disrupt testosterone production and lower free testosterone and can make free testosterone inactive.

They can be found in non stick pans, meat, fish and dairy products from industrial farms, paints and industrial oils.

You can combat these by avoiding the use of all non stick pans, don't heat food in plastic packaging or plastic wraps. Wherever possible try to source hormone free meats and dairy products and wild line caught fish. Generic obvious advice I know but it will be difficult, especially for city dwellers. Difficult also because packaging can be misleading. Just because the packaging might claim hormone free doesn't necessarily mean that it is. And what was hormone free? The animal itself or the feed that it was given? Or both? It is very very rarely both. Grass fed cows often are given growth hormones. The cows fed grains are usually given hormone fed grains.

Growth hormones increase profits and save time. These are commercial businesses. Think about it.

Organic products are not fed with chemical plant foods, they are claimed to be 100% naturally grown. Yet they are mostly sprayed with chemical insect repellents to prevent crops being damaged or destroyed. So technically they are neither organic nor 100% natural. But it's a great way to sell products, and nobody ever checks up on these claims. Wash all fruits and vegetables before use.

Parabens.

Parabens are commonly used as preservatives in many grooming products. This is one to be particularly aware of because even in natural organic products made with natural plant based ingredients they often use parabens as the preservative element to increase the shelf life of the product.

They are known to decrease testosterone and damage sperm production.

These parabens have names including ethyl, butyl, methyl, propyl, or benzyl. Always check the ingredients on the products you buy. Look out for plant based organic products and ensure that these products do not contain parabens as the preservative element.

Parabens are found in soaps, body, hand and face creams, toothpastes, pharmaceutical medications and products, and even some food and drinks.

A surprise is that these chemicals are also found in many supplements. Beware of supplements with a shiny surface, often this will be listed in the ingredients as hydroxy-propyl methyl-cellulose. Also commonly found in gel caps too.

While on the subject of gel caps, if you are Muslim then be aware that many gel caps are made from gelatin which comes from the pig. Always source gel caps that are vegan friendly if this applies to you. If it does not specifically say 100% vegan friendly or similar on the container then assume that they contain gelatin derived from pig fat.

BPA.

BPA, or Bisphenol A is a chemical that blocks or suppresses the normal effects of testosterone within the body.

BPA is even found on till receipts. They are thermally printed and by handling the receipt the BPA is absorbed through the skin into your body. You have probably seen many cashiers wearing gloves to protect themselves from the harm of BPA as their work involves a lot of handling of till receipts.

BPA is also found in the plastic liner that food and drinks cans are lined with. It is also found in plastic baby bottles and even water pipes and water storage tanks.

To combat against the effects of BPA always go for fresh food instead of canned. Also reusable glass or stainless steel drinks bottles to store your drinking water. But bear in mind that some of these steel drinking bottles, especially the cheaper ones sometimes have a plastic liner inside them.

Use some kind of water filter in your home especially for drinking water. Carbon filters are effective at removing hormones and are relatively cheap. Reverse osmosis filters are very effective but expensive as they need to be installed into your water system. I use a carbon filter system for all my drinking water and then store that drinking water in dark glass bottles. This is because direct light can degrade the water and affect water quality. Dark glass helps to prevent this.

Always decline till receipts if you can, and avoid heating any foods that came in plastic packaging in the containers they were sold in. Also avoid plastic containers, such as Tupperware, that are typically used to heat food in a microwave oven. Whenever possible rinse the food with water to remove as much BPA as you can and always heat foods in microwaves in a ceramic dish.

Even with all the awareness and preventative measures it would be nearly impossible to remove endocrine disruptors completely from your life. Even with a well balanced healthy diet it would prove a nightmare to find everything you need without that involving plastic packaging. Practically everything now comes in plastic packaging.

Washing the food and rinsing off as much as you can is all you can do. How effective that is I do not know, but its better than nothing. With some foods of course rinsing would be completely impractical. When it comes to any foods, wash them before use if practical, whether they came in plastic or not.

So in light of all this it is a good idea to stay well hydrated. Drink plenty of (filtered) water to flush out your system. Use a liver detox supplement such as milk thistle as your liver has to process many of the toxins we ingest this includes many of these chemical toxins mentioned above.

Regular use of saunas can help too by sweating out as many of the toxins as we can. Always be sure to rinse off the sweat as some of these toxins can be re-absorbed by the skin if they are left on the skin for any length of time. If you do not have a local sauna then consider investing in an infra-red sauna blanket. Many gyms also have sauna facilities these days.

They say that an ounce of prevention is worth a pound of cure so becoming more aware of these chemicals and what we can do to combat them is certainly going to help, even if it does not completely eliminate the threat.

The threat is real, and there is a lot of truth to this estrogenics theory and the data confirms the effects these toxins can have on testosterone levels. In my case I discovered all of this only a year or two ago. I had been consuming unfiltered tap water, buying foods in plastic packaging and no doubt been unwittingly contaminated along the way.

But I am 50 and still have reasonably good testosterone levels. Now that I am aware of these endocrine disruptors, and am also at an age where my T levels are naturally going to be on the decline anyway, I have now adopted a prevention regime following many of the precautions that I have laid out above.

So as I have been undoubtedly exposed to these hormone disruptors, how have I managed to maintain good natural T levels? I have used many of the products containing these hormone disruptors and my T levels are OK, and my free testosterone levels are above average for my age. So do we really need to be so over concerned?

An important thing is to not be anxious or to fret over this too much. Just adopt the precautions that I have discussed above and this is a good enough preventative strategy. This is something that is largely beyond your control anyway. To completely avoid these chemicals would prove to be almost impossible, and to even try to would take up a lot of your valuable time.

So considering that I have been exposed to endocrine disruptors as much as anyone why are my T levels good? What did I do to make this happen? I have an explanation for this which I will share with you later in this guide when we get to the relevant section.

Think of the prevention against these chemicals and other testosterone disruptors as a defence strategy. The optimisation of your T levels is your attack strategy.

Now before we move on it is important to remember that some estrogen is essential to us men.

Estrogen is naturally found, in small but absolutely essential quantities, in men and it plays an important role in men's health. It needs to be balanced with the rest of your hormones, including testosterone. Many guys are now looking to block or lower their estrogen levels. This could cause hormonal imbalances and can have a corresponding affect on T levels.

This might be difficult for some guys to grasp but low estrogen can contribute towards low T levels.

The male body produces estrogen and this is a totally normal and necessary process. It performs many functions within the healthy body including erectile function and libido and the regulation of fat mass as opposed to lean mass. Lean muscle mass of course is regulated by testosterone. Balance. The master key to so many things!

Normal total estradiol (estrogen) levels in men are usually in between 10 and 55 pg/ml, or 1.0 to 5.5 ng/DL. Free estradiol levels are considered to be around 0.3 to 1.3 pg/ml, which is 0.03 - 0.13 ng/DL. Now an important thing to note is that these normal ranges are not agreed on by everyone in the medical community. Human bodies vary so much, what could be a normal range for one guy could be either too much, or too little for another.

But as with testosterone the magic number is not important, your levels are only low if you are experiencing any symptoms. If everything is working fine and you have no symptoms then everything is probably OK.

Now looking at these amounts you can see that normal estrogen levels in men are such a small percentage of total sexual hormonal output, so there is nothing to worry about. Being in possession of *some* estrogen is not as bad as some would have you believe.

So next time you hear someone telling you how they have lowered their estrogen levels or advising you how to block your estrogen then you should take this advice with a pinch of salt. If these claims are true then they have probably also blocked some of, or lowered their testosterone to maintain the balance within their hormonal system at the same time.

If you take an aromatase inhibitor of any kind to lower your estrogen this will have an effect on T levels too. Not many testosterone gurus understand this. A naturally healthy body will always maintain balance to compensate.

Also any method that involves artificially increasing T levels, such as steroids, TRT, prohormones or SARMS can cause increased estrogen production because the body attempts to balance out hormone levels and compensates for the excess testosterone introduced into the system by producing more estrogen.

But also consider that if you increase your T levels naturally there will still be a reactive increase in estrogen too. Accept this. It is a good thing. You have more testosterone!

Blocking or suppressing estrogen production and aiming to lower your estrogen levels in any way is going to also cause your T levels to lower too, as your hormonal messaging system adjusts to maintain the balance.

Always consider this fact. Its all about the balance. A healthy body is efficient at maintaining inner balance. An unhealthy body becomes less efficient at maintaining balance, and this is when unwanted raised estrogen and hormonal imbalances are more likely to occur. Maintaining a healthy body and practising healthy lifestyle habits are the best ways to keep estrogen under control.

Here are some important additional points on estrogen.

Stress is a big factor involved in the production of estrogen in men.

Some foods, medications and all alcoholic drinks can increase estrogen in men, especially beer.

Eating unhealthy foods and gaining weight can increase estrogen in men.

Unhealthy lifestyle choices and a sedentary lifestyle can increase estrogen in men.

Here is a list of some of the foods that have been attributed to an increase of estrogen in men. These include alcohol, grapefruit and its juice, limes, lemons, oranges, sunflower oil, vegetable oils, flaxseed, sesame seeds, walnuts, celery and strawberries. Bear in mind that many of these foods are also packed with micro nutrients needed for a complete well balanced diet.

Another thing to bear in mind is that all of these foods have the potential to trigger aromatase, leading to the conversion of testosterone into estrogen. This belief is based upon the presence of phytoestrogens, which mimic the behaviour of estrogen. However, since phytoestrogens act as estrogen and mimic its behaviour, then the body doesn't need any additional estrogen and it doesn't need to convert any testosterone into estrogen. If it is present in the correct amount the hormonal system does not need to produce more?

This is a statement that many will vehemently disagree with. But steroids mimic testosterone and so the body doesn't need to make more additional testosterone. So why would something that mimics estrogen not do the same? If you are concerned then avoid these foods. Simple.

Now before we get into the attack phase, there is another preventative measure to consider. Testosterone killers. Things to avoid if you want to optimise your testosterone production.

11

The Importance of Cholesterol and Hormone Production.

We all know that having a medically high cholesterol level is when you have too much bad cholesterol present in your blood. This puts us at increased risk of certain illnesses. For example heart disease, some circulatory conditions, and an increased risk of having a heart attack or a stroke.

This can have a profound effect on your lifestyle and your mobility and a very negative impact on your testosterone production. It is a very important aspect to consider in trying to maintain good health and healthy T levels into our older years.

The problem in terms of our hormonal health arises when this advice is misunderstood. Many have taken this medical advice to keep our cholesterol low literally, and have adopted the approach of trying to cut out all cholesterol from their diets, and to observe a low cholesterol, and in some cases, particularly with those following a plant based or vegan diet, a no cholesterol diet. This is a grave error in terms of hormonal health and testosterone production.

Among the plant based community there is a false belief that the body can produce all the cholesterol that it needs for normal bodily functioning, without the need to ingest any cholesterol from foods. This is simply not true. Consuming no cholesterol will not only harm your hormonal health but also your sexual health and physical performance along with it.

The truth is not enough cholesterol is equally bad for our health as too much.

There are two different types of cholesterol. High Density Lipo-proteins, or HDL cholesterol and LDL cholesterol, Low Density lipo-proteins.

HDL, is called good cholesterol. This is because it cleans the bad cholesterol out of your blood. The cholesterol that is not needed by the body is broken down by the liver so that it can be passed out of your body.

LDL is called bad cholesterol. It becomes bad when there is too much of it. It can build up inside the blood vessels and arteries. This can lead to the build up of fatty material, which makes it harder for blood to flow. This will result in depleted circulation and increased risk of related diseases. This commonly leads to cases of erectile dysfunction.

So first let us consider why cholesterol is so important for normal bodily functioning. And also why we cannot function at our optimum potential in terms of testosterone if we do not consume cholesterol.

First and most importantly cholesterol is the building block of testosterone, which is vital to our T production. The body secretes hormones in the pituitary gland which then travel through the blood on route to the testicles and the collect cholesterol from the blood in order to enable the production of both sperm and testosterone, which we went over in more detail in a previous chapter. Without that cholesterol present in sufficient quantity, this process and the results achieved from this process are severely impacted.

This can result in reduced testosterone production. This ultimately leads to reduced levels of testosterone within the body, which in turn will affect libido and sexual performance and erectile functioning. One of the predominant side effects of low testosterone is reduced libido and difficulties in maintaining an erection. Not something that any man wants to happen to them.

Cholesterol is also essential for efficient adrenal functioning. Our levels of the hormone DHEA, which contributes to how we are effected by the process of ageing, this hormone is secreted in the adrenal glands and cholesterol is also the building block for the production of DHEA.

Also we need to consider production of the hormone pregnenolone, which is known as the brain hormone and this is fundamental to normal cognitive functioning, and it helps to maintain normal cognitive functioning and to prevent its decline during the ageing process.

Pregnenolone is synthesized from cholesterol in the adrenal glands and the testicles. It is also synthesized as a neuro-steroid in both the central nervous system and the peripheral nervous system, which is why it is known as the brain hormone because it helps to maintain the effectiveness of our neural pathways in the brain.

Eating more healthy fats such as avocados, olive oil, nuts, seeds, and fish helps the body to convert LDL into HDL cholesterol. Foods such as animal fats and eggs are great for providing enough cholesterol, and this is important. We need all types of fats in our diet. This includes saturated fats and it is important that these fats come from healthy whole foods.

When it comes to our levels of testosterone, it is important to note that both DHEA and pregnenolone are important pre-cursor hormones that are fundamental to testosterone production.

It is a complicated process, and the human body is a complicated organism. Put in simple terms, cholesterol makes pregnenolone, which makes DHEA, which in turn help to make and balance testosterone, estrogen and progesterone. And all of these hormones contribute greatly towards male sexual health and physical performance.

A deficiency in any of these hormones, including estrogen and progesterone, would be catastrophic to our sexual health and indeed our levels of testosterone.

In addition to this, cholesterol is also essential for the synthesis and absorption of vitamin D, which is also important for the maintenance of healthy testosterone levels.

Cholesterol is also very important for bile production, which helps significantly in the digestive process, the uptake of nutrients into the cells of our body and our metabolism, and with fat absorption. And of course fat absorption contributes towards keeping our cholesterol levels maintained for testosterone production.

Cholesterol is also important for the regeneration and repair of cells, and the building of cells within the body.

So you can clearly see just how important getting enough cholesterol is to our testosterone.

If we do not have enough cholesterol present within the body, this will lead to depleted pregnenolone production, reduced levels of DHEA and a decrease in testosterone levels.

We will also experience impaired cognitive functioning and brain functioning. This can affect the production of the hormones within the pituitary gland which initiate the production of testosterone. In addition to this it is highly probable that this will result in increased anxiety and stress, increased levels of mental sensitivity, agitation, confusion, poor memory, difficulty in focus or concentrating and the potential for sleep problems.

Consider that the testosterone production process occurs at night during sleep, so if you are not sleeping properly this can also negatively affect your testosterone production.

Increased stress results in the increased production of the stress hormone cortisol, which is also synthesized using cholesterol, so in effect stealing the ingredients needed to make testosterone. This is why poor sleep and increased stress can have such a detrimental effect on our sex lives and T production.

Other symptoms of low cholesterol include dry skin and skin irritation, joint pain, muscle pain and poor muscle recovery, the loss of muscle mass, depleted energy levels, reduced vitality and in extreme cases, especially in the event of long term cholesterol deficiency, even lead to an increased risk of heart attacks and strokes.

The Australian Heart Foundation says that:

"For those not at high risk of cardiovascular disease, or diabetes, or whom have not previously had LDL lowering treatments (drugs such as statins) *there is no limit to the amount of cholesterol that can be consumed in foods such as eggs and animal products.*"

Cholesterol is therefore vital to our production of testosterone and to male health, well-being and life quality.

High cholesterol only ever becomes a problem when the body does not use up that cholesterol and it is allowed to build up within the body.

Anyone can get high cholesterol and it can be caused by many different things. Some of these things you have control over and some you do not.

Focus on the things you can control like your lifestyle habits. Things like not smoking, regular exercise, not eating too much bad trans fats can all help you to lower your risk. Maintaining your body fat levels through exercise is an excellent way of reducing your risk which should never be overlooked.

Also consider that exercise is a form of good positive stress. Moderate to high intensity exercise provokes an increase in cortisol levels. When it comes to exercise and good stress practises, this helps the body to use up the cholesterol and to significantly help to prevent the build up of excess cholesterol in the body. It is prolonged stress that results in a continuous cortisol production having a negative effect on T production. Periodically planned stress events, such as physical training, can be very beneficial to helping to balance out our cholesterol and improving our performance.

By focusing on what you do have control over and what you can change you can give yourselves the best possible chance to improve your body condition and performance.

Here are some tips for you to follow and things to try to help lower your bad cholesterol levels and to help keep you in top form.

Foods. Eating the right sort of foods can reduce bad cholesterol.

The healthier fats are those which consist mostly of polyunsaturated fats and mono-saturated fats. But also remember that you still need some saturated fats.

Polyunsaturated fats are in fish and fish oils.

Oils which are rich in mono-unsaturated fats are olive oil and avocado oil. These types of oils are the best ones to go for to help keep levels of harmful LDL in the blood to a minimum. The good thing with these oils is that they can help to lower LDL and raise HDL which for our purposes here is a good thing.

Saturated fats are also an essential part of our diet. Animal fats contain saturated fats also eggs and dairy are a healthy source of good saturated fats.

Choose a diet based on eating whole foods. Meats, fish, fruits, vegetables, legumes, unrefined carbohydrates. Avoid all processed foods and sugary drinks and sodas.

High fat foods are considered to contain more than 17 grams of fat per 100 grams of food. High saturated fat is more than 5 grams per 100 grams of food. Foods with higher levels of bad saturated fats are;

Milk and white chocolate. Cakes, puddings and biscuits.
Pastries, pizza and pies.
Processed meats like sausages, burgers, bacon and kebabs and most takeaway foods.

Fat is essential for our energy levels. Too little fat in our diets can leave us feeling tired. It is recommended that men should eat at least 90 grams of fat per day. Saturated fats should make up no more, or less, than a quarter of this.

Look to different methods of cooking foods such as baking, steaming, boiling or grilling instead of frying. Avoid using spreads like margarine and seed oils altogether.

Increasing fibre intake can help to reduce the absorption of bad cholesterol into your blood. But remember that too much fibre can be bad for you and your digestion. A good range to aim for is no less than 10g fibre per day from good clean whole foods and never more than 25g per day.

Whey protein taken as a supplement helps to lower bad cholesterol and blood pressure.

Lower bad cholesterol levels are attributed to healthier blood flow and better cardiovascular performance into old age. It is important for our health to maintain good blood flow. Lowering bad cholesterol levels is an excellent place to start.

But at the same time always ensure that you are getting enough cholesterol to ensure healthy hormone production. Taking care of this will have great benefits to your T levels.

12

Balancing Cholesterol Levels.

Not enough cholesterol can be detrimental to hormone production. But too much cholesterol can lead to clogged arteries and an increased risk of heart disease and circulation problems.

Let us consider a few ways we can help to balance out our cholesterol.

Now first thing to point out. You need some cholesterol in your diet. It not only plays a role in T production but also in the production of all of your body's hormonal output. So its pretty essential. A cholesterol deficiency will lead to hormone depletion.

But it is also important to consider that just consuming more cholesterol does not guarantee that the body will automatically use it to create optimised testosterone levels. Especially if the body is out of sync in any way.

Also, cholesterol only ever becomes a problem if an excess is allowed to build up within the body. This occurs when the body is not using the cholesterol up in sufficient levels. You do not need to get obsessive over this. A small excess and permanent levels of present cholesterol are beneficial.

However this has lead to many believing that increased consumption of saturated fats will lead to higher testosterone. Again if the body is out of sync in any way this is not guaranteed. Too much saturated fat is unhealthy and leads to numerous health problems. But saturated fat is essential and we need some sat fats in our diet. And we also need some cholesterol.

So how much cholesterol do we need? Difficult question because we are all different and we all have different nutritional requirements. A general guideline is that a bigger guy will need more than a smaller guy. Probably but not necessarily. Also higher levels of activity result in varying nutritional needs. Also consider your metabolic rate, your body type all these things affect your ideal optimal nutrient intake.

Recommended daily intake is 300mg per day. Now based upon the fact that mainstream suggests low cholesterol intake this is probably not enough for most people. So I suggest aiming for around 2000mg per day. But this is just a suggestion. I urge you to find your own sweet spot for your own personal requirements. That could be more than 2000mg for some and less than 2000mg for others.

Also consider your previous habits. If you have been leading a sedentary lifestyle and consuming a lot of processed foods or takeaway then you may already have high blood cholesterol levels.

So a good bit of advice to anyone is before starting to optimise your cholesterol intake, is to get a blood exam to determine your current levels. This will give you insight into how to conduct your strategy and where to begin and it can be a real time saver too.

A good thing to consider with cholesterol intake is to consume cholesterol from foods which are high in cholesterol but not so high in saturated fats. You need some saturated fats in your diet but excessive consumption of saturated fats can lead to higher levels of LDL cholesterol. Think long term here. Consuming a modest amount of saturated fats every day isn't a bad thing. Eating avocado helps to balance this as they naturally help in the conversion of LDL into HDL cholesterol. This is why it is important to observe a well balanced diet.

Foods that are high cholesterol but low in saturated fats include eggs, shellfish, liver and other organ meats. These foods can be a great way of getting enough cholesterol in your diet while at the same time avoiding too much saturated fat.

If you are someone that has previously consumed a lot of processed foods then I would highly recommend that you start here. Replace your consumption of processed foods with these foods.

As a means of general advice always consume cholesterol rich foods from whole food sources such as meats and dairy products.

Now for the balancing out of your cholesterol. By this I mean that you are encouraging your body to use up most of the cholesterol you are consuming, while also at the same time, maintaining healthy cholesterol levels. Consuming enough cholesterol is only one side of that state of balance.

Now there is one thing that is absolutely effective for inducing your body to consume cholesterol. Now this might seem counter-productive to some but that is stress.

But this is planned stress events. Stepping out of your comfort zone and being challenged. Not prolonged unhealthy and detrimental stress. Stress induces cortisol production, and cortisol is made using cholesterol. High stress can harm hormone production as it can steal the ingredients needed to make hormones. Which is cholesterol. But used in moderation it can be highly effective in preventing excess cholesterol, helping to maintain a balance and preventing an excessive build up.

The best way of doing this is high intensity physical activity. This stresses the body and induces a cortisol spike. But remember to consider not too much and not too little. Again this will be different for everyone.

Drinking coffee also spikes cortisol. But moderation again is the best approach here. Also drinking green tea helps to lower LDL and reduce total cholesterol levels.

Another drink effective in reducing cholesterol is golden milk. This is milk with turmeric added to it and its great for lowering total cholesterol levels. You can also add turmeric to dishes as well. Golden milk also does not spike cortisol nor contain caffeine so is great for later in the day.

Another thing is high cocoa chocolate, also fish high in omega 3 fatty acids, olive oil, pears and apples and foods high in plant sterols.

Avocado is the food richest in plant sterols. This is why it is effective at reducing LDL while increasing LDL. Other foods include nuts and seeds, sage, oregano, thyme, paprika, legumes and fruits and vegetables.

What I do is I consume moderate to high cholesterol. I balance my diet to include meats, fish, fruits, vegetables, legumes, whole grains and this strategy has worked because blood tests confirm my cholesterol levels are not a cause for concern and my hormone levels are really good. I frequently add paprika or turmeric to my dishes.

I usually eat meat or fish at every meal. I consume at least 4 eggs per day and my diet includes plenty of organ meats. I also eat a small piece of pure fat each day.

My evening meal is usually high cholesterol. This is because all hormone secretion takes place overnight during sleep and I ensure my blood will have sufficient levels to make this take place as efficiently as possible. Often this meal would be meat instead of fish.

An obvious trick for balancing cholesterol is the optimisation of your T levels and doing all that you can for obtaining the balance of all your hormones will help your body become more efficient in utilising cholesterol. All of your body's hormones are made from cholesterol. Balanced hormones utilise cholesterol effectively.

Another thing to consider is that at around 2 to 3am your cortisol levels will rise as well and this also helps to contribute towards using cholesterol.

On waking I consume a coffee. This further spikes cortisol. About an hour after breakfast I usually train. This consists of 2-3 hours of resistance training followed by 30 minutes of bag work. High stress activity to stimulate more cholesterol use. Sometimes I go mountain biking in the afternoon but most of the time I don't get to do this as I have responsibilities and commitments.

Usually from midday onwards I begin my wind down towards the evening. My regular routine takes into account the need for my body to utilise the cholesterol effectively to keep my body in sync.

The aim is to reduce cortisol toward the end of the day to promote better sleep. I meditate and relax at the end of the day. My last meal of the day also includes moderate carbs as this also helps reduce cortisol.

All these little things combined together will help you to balance your cholesterol and this all helps to optimise your hormonal output.

Optimised cholesterol levels will significantly benefit your testosterone levels. Remember to balance everything out. Treat your body as an entire organism this will give you better results.

13

Balancing Cortisol Levels.

Cortisol is usually something that many consider to be bad for us. This is due to cortisol being the stress hormone and many view stress as something that is negative.

We now know that at least a moderate intake of cholesterol is essential for healthy hormone production.

Cholesterol only ever becomes a problem when the body is not using it all up effectively and an excess builds up within the body which can end up causing health issues, such as clogged arteries and circulation problems.

Cortisol is also made from cholesterol. So any cholesterol not used up in testosterone and hormone production can be effectively used up by balanced cortisol production. Planned stress events such as physical training are useful for this purpose.

Cortisol production is therefore a highly effective way of managing our cholesterol levels and keeping our cholesterol under control. A healthy balance of our entire bodily organism optimises testosterone production.

But, what is not often known or understood by many is that cortisol, the stress hormone, is essential for energy and health. The only problems with cortisol are that when it is out of balance so are you and so is your body.

Too much cortisol and of course hormone production will suffer. Too little and you could be suffering with adrenal exhaustion. This is when the overworked adrenal glands have effectively shut down. This will leave you with feelings of having to drag yourself through each day, feeling sluggish, and devoid of energy. Or you may find it takes a lot of coffee to pick you up in the morning but it doesn't last very long. It can also cause hypoglycaemia, it can make it more difficult to fight off infections, you could be more prone to aches and pains, reduced sex drive, and increased cravings for sugary foods.

When this happens it can be often mistaken as insufficient testosterone production and many guys could be jumping onto TRT or steroids and other PEDs without realising the root cause.

Energy depletion, poor post exercise recovery, low libido, feeling like crap, are often cited as reasons why some have started TRT use. It could have been adrenal exhaustion.

And adrenal exhaustion will also have a negative effect on your bodily balance and your hormonal production so there could be a lot of truth to this.

Cortisol is produced when we are under pressure or if we perceive difficulties or threats. The pituitary gland determines how much cortisol the adrenals should release to help the body cope, and for how long that cortisol will continue to be produced.

The production of cortisol is like a bodily alarm system in effect. In today's fast paced culture many are overworked and under rested. And this will cause that alarm to be over active.

In this state the cortisol production goes into overdrive leading to a whole host of problems.

But what is not often considered is that cortisol is not only produced in response to stress. Chronic stress puts cortisol into overdrive. But normal balanced levels of cortisol are critical for maintaining energy throughout the day.

And cortisol orchestrates the performance of other key hormones, such as thyroid hormones and testosterone. Cortisol is effectively the control system for hormones. Cortisol gets your blood pressure up when it needs to be up. During intense exercise for example. Cortisol raises your blood sugar levels only when you most need it. Again during intense exercise when your body needs to tap into your glycogen stores for energy. Cortisol also moderates your immune system. So cortisol, although labelled as something bad, is essential for optimum bodily functioning. And balancing cortisol is highly beneficial to T levels.

In a balanced individual, cortisol should ideally be following a regular cycle. It should be at its highest level upon waking and then taper off throughout the day so that we are left feeling relaxed just before going to bed.

In an unbalanced person the body spikes cortisol constantly at all hours. The cycle turns into a roller coaster and excess cortisol causes that person to develop a reactive an uncontrolled hair-trigger response to any stressful or challenging situation. And this ultimately leads to adrenal exhaustion and hormonal imbalances and potentially, reduced testosterone.

Continuously elevated cortisol is seriously detrimental over time. It ends up depleting serotonin, makes it difficult to sleep properly, it can also leave you more prone to storing fat and can also lead to poor moods, inflammation, thyroid issues and low sex drive. And unless you understand the importance of treating the whole bodily organism as a whole, you are likely to make the mistake of jumping onto TRT unnecessarily.

So how can we maintain or restore our cortisol cycle?

One way is to cycle carb intake. A low carb diet can support weight loss but it is not ideal for those with disrupted cortisol.

In a 2014 clinical trial, subjects with cortisol issues were able to reset their cortisol cycle by eating low carb breakfasts, moderate amounts of healthy carbs in the afternoon and higher amounts of healthy carbs in the evening.

Endocrinologist Alan Christianson, author of the book, The Adrenal Reset diet, directed this trial. He now prescribes carb-cycling to his patients who are suffering with any type of cortisol disruption. His book is also a very interesting book and I highly recommend it.

Higher carb meals drop cortisol. Lower carb meals cause cortisol to stay higher. Carbs elevate blood sugar, this causes the pancreas to make more insulin to manage that increase. Insulin decreases cortisol output. As blood sugar goes up, cortisol comes down.

Avoiding carbs altogether can cause cortisol to stay elevated when you need it to come down. When you are too low on carbs, you raise cortisol because the muscles are being pulled apart for that glucose. In turn this raises cortisol and this becomes a big problem in the evening when you need cortisol levels to drop in preparation for sleep. This leads to an increase likelihood of disturbed sleep patterns.

Supplementing can help. Of course there is no single supplement that can lower cortisol levels but there are 3 essential nutrients that can help.

Omega 3 fatty acids can be helpful. In a 2010 study, subjects took 2400mg of fish oil daily for 6 weeks lowered their morning cortisol levels, and recorded improvements to their cortisol cycle.

Vitamin B5 helps to reduce the hyper-secretion of cortisol. Vitamin C has also been shown to be effective in lowering cortisol levels.

Staying hydrated can also be of great benefit. We are more likely to become dehydrated under stress. Feeling anxious raises our heart rate and triggers faster and heavier breathing both of which lead to loss of fluids.

The practise of regular meditation and relaxation techniques can also help fix your cortisol disruption. Any practise that helps you to feel calm and centred will be ideal. These practises will be especially useful in the evenings as you prepare to become relaxed for better sleep induction.

Avoiding training or intense physical activity in the evenings can also be very beneficial. Training spikes cortisol levels and is useful in the morning or afternoon.

Try using adaptogenic herbs. Ginseng, ashwagandha and rhodiola are very effective in balancing hormones and relieving stress. And this includes helping to balance and restore cortisol levels to their normal level.

And when it comes to cortisol, sleep is vitally important. Your sleep patterns will support a healthy lifestyle. Getting enough rest, both physically and mentally, will make it easier to avoid bingeing on coffee in the mornings, and help to keep you focused and less likely to feel tired during the day and needing to sleep.

COMPLETE GUIDE TO TESTOSTERONE

Cortisol and melatonin, a hormone which regulates sleep and waking cycles works in tandem with cortisol. When cortisol drops to normal levels, melatonin makes you feel more relaxed and sleepy in the evenings. When you are asleep, lower levels of cortisol allow your cells to repair and heal. If your cortisol levels stay elevated, your body can't make those repairs properly and you wake up feeling fatigued.

When your cortisol levels are balanced you will have the energy your body needs all throughout the day and you will get the rest you need by sleeping better.

And this in turn will help with production of all of your hormones and help to keep them all balanced. Including testosterone.

If you want to optimise your T levels, recognise the importance of balancing your cortisol levels out.

14

Androgen Receptors.

A ndrogen Receptors and Androgen Sensitivity.

Androgen receptors and your own levels of androgen sensitivity are important things to consider when it comes to optimising and maintaining your testosterone levels.

When it comes to the functioning of the male body without androgen receptors your testosterone is unable to perform its many roles and purposes within your body. Androgen receptors help with the processes that carry out these functions.

Decreased androgen activity will produce symptoms of low testosterone. Maintenance of your androgen receptivity is fundamental to the long term maintenance of your T levels.

Now, androgen receptors are a type of protein found in the cells throughout the body. They activate and control the expression of human genes by binding to androgen hormones such as testosterone. They play the same role within the female body.

They help to control the effects of androgens and DHT in the male body. They also play a role in the balance of hormones within the male body. They play a significant role in the development of sexual characteristics, which for us men is our masculine features, and help to increase our libido and reproductive function, and also to play a role in the functioning of the nervous system and the adrenal glands, which are also a part of the endocrine system.

The androgen receptor gene, part of our human DNA, are effectively genes that instruct the body to produce the protein that eventually becomes the androgen receptor itself. Once they become bound to their specific hormone, they interact with other proteins, which result in the necessary changes in the functions of those cells.

When it comes to our testosterone androgen receptors are designed by nature to react to testosterone. When the testosterone becomes bound to these receptors the hormone initiates the bodily process that interprets the gene instructions that will carry out the biological functions within the body such as building muscle mass, bone density, hair growth, testicular functioning and libido along with energy levels and our mental states.

The number of androgen receptors present in the cells determines how sensitive the cell is to the effects of testosterone. The more androgen receptors present within the cells the more androgen sensitive you are. Androgen sensitivity correlates to a stronger and more effective response to the hormone.

If the cells have lower numbers of androgen receptors present, these receptors will be less sensitive and will not respond as effectively to testosterone. Testosterone relies upon androgen receptors to make the male characteristics, so increasing androgen receptors will enhance the effects of testosterone on the body.

Any deficiencies in androgens means that the body has lower levels of testosterone. Good levels of androgens means that you will tend to have higher testosterone. Increased androgen sensitivity means that your levels of free testosterone will be elevated.

Care and maintenance of your androgen receptors and your androgen sensitivity are therefore vital to having optimal T levels and maintenance of your androgens will play a significant role in maintaining healthy T levels as you get older. So this is very important and it needs your full attention.

Fortunately there are some methods and habits we can adopt into our lifestyle to promote the production of androgen receptors. Research has shown that testosterone levels and androgen sensitivity do not suffer any drastic decline in healthy older men. The truth is, the age old myth that its all downhill after the age of 40 is not completely true. Provided you pay attention to leading a healthy lifestyle.

By far the most effective way is engaging in intense physical activity. And the most effective exercises are resistance training and weight training carried out in an intense manner resulting in an elevated heart rate. These types of training are more likely to result in an increased number of active androgen receptors. More on exercise in a later section.

Eating a healthy well balanced diet is very important for testosterone and we will be diving deep into the subject of nutrition later on but increasing your protein intake can also help to increase androgen receptors.

Eating more protein can help your body to increase the activity of androgen receptors. High protein consumption, which correlates to around one third of total calorific intake, can help to decrease SHBG while increasing your free testosterone levels and androgen sensitivity. It can also help to control your insulin response. As a result your body reacts by increasing the number of available androgen receptors.

But at the same time care must be taken to avoid decreasing SHBG levels too drastically as this could have a negative effect. Not too much and not too little. And this sweet spot of course will be different for everyone.

When it comes to diet it is also necessary to ensure that we include all macros and micros in our diet. Consumption of fats and carbs is also fundamental to androgens. Any deficiencies in our diet can lead to reduced testosterone. Diet is also something that should be highly personalised to be tuned in to our bodily organism. We all have different needs. There is no such thing as a special diet that suits everyone. This is why it is important to consider diet in relation to testosterone in some detail further on in this guide.

Connected to our diet and another great way to boost androgen receptors is intermittent fasting. There is some evidence that suggests that prolonged fasting can have a negative effect on total testosterone but it seems that regular fasts can boost androgen receptor activity. The typical intermittent fast involves fasting for 16 hours during a 24 hour period. A fast once per week is a good consideration to observe and very beneficial not only to our T levels but also has many other health benefits.

Supplementing with l-carnitine can also be highly effective for androgen receptors. Research has shown that taking 2-3g of carnitine per day for 3 weeks resulted in increased sensitivity of the androgen receptors. When supplementing with l-carnitine be sure to also supplement with a fat soluble antioxidant such as vitamin E, because l-carnitine can possibly increase the production of free radicals within the body and fat soluble antioxidants help to deactivate the free radicals before they can cause oxidative stress within the body.

Ginseng is also beneficial to androgen receptors. It has been used in traditional Chinese medicine for centuries. It is known to be very beneficial to health and it is known to increase blood flow and erection strength, boost circulation, aid cognitive functioning as well as having anti-ageing, anti cancer and anti diabetes benefits.

It is also beneficial to helping to improve androgen receptor sensitivity.

Ginsenosides and ginseng polysaccharides upregulate androgen receptor mRNA expression levels and promote testosterone. Panax ginseng in particular can be very beneficial to maintaining healthy levels of hormone receptors which in turn ensures proper functioning of androgens. This correlates to increased androgen sensistivity and this will help to ensure sufficient and consistent levels of free testosterone.

Vitamin D is also beneficial to androgen receptors because it has been shown to work directly with the endocrine system. Vitamin D is known to be fundamental to testosterone. Vitamin D also has its own receptors throughout the body and these are linked to androgen receptors. Vitamin D deficiency is associated with inhibited testosterone production and the effects of testosterone on androgen receptors and has been linked with directly causing low testosterone.

It is also widely believed that increasing your vitamin D intake will also increase your androgen receptor activity and as a result, increase testosterone levels. The optimal dosage is somewhere between 800-2000 UI per day. Beware also of the possibility of toxicity in higher doses.

Sleep is important to androgen sensitivity. As part of our natural circadian rhythm, most of our testosterone is secreted at night, and our testosterone levels naturally increase during the night. Many studies have shown that sleep deprivation can significantly reduce testosterone production and result in reduced testosterone levels. Sleep deprivation also has a corresponding effect in reducing androgen sensitivity. More on promoting good sleeping habits in a later section.

Capsaicin, which is an active element found in chillies and hot peppers has also been found to increase androgen receptor sensitivity. Eating spicy foods is also great for testosterone levels and good for the circulation.

When it comes to destroying our androgen receptors alcohol comes in at no 1. Just one drink can cause a reduction to testosterone in just 30 minutes.

Now this is not going to be what many guys want to hear but sexual activity, and by this I mean just one ejaculation, reduces androgen sensitivity. Semen retention of course is claimed to boost testosterone which is not entirely true but a fact is that having too much sex, or ejaculating too frequently can crash our androgen receptor levels. Sure most men want to be seen by their woman as a guy that can provide sexual satisfaction and it has commonly been perceived that a guy with a high sexual appetite is desirable. But one fact remains. Ejaculating every day is going to tank your androgen receptors.

But there is more to this. Regular sexual activity is also known to promote testosterone production. The build up of sexual desire is caused by the activation of the androgen receptors. Abstaining from sex promotes this activation resulting in an increased desire. Indulging in that desire too frequently can cause deactivation of the androgen receptors, which in turn can have a negative effect on desire and sexual hunger. Therefore the best approach is again not too little and not too much. We must observe a level of balance in all things.

Now many of our dietary choices can also have a negative effect on androgen receptors. These we will cover in a later section. All testosterone killers will of course have the same effect on androgen receptor levels and sensitivity.

So eliminating as many of these from our life will have great benefits to us and our testosterone.

15

DHT.

DHT, or dihydrotestosterone, is an androgen hormone that stimulates the masculine characteristics of a man. Your body naturally converts around 10% of your testosterone into DHT each day. This principally takes place within the testicles and the prostate.

The more testosterone you have the higher your levels of DHT tend to be. DHT is created from testosterone but is more powerful than testosterone. It is also important for maintaining healthy balanced hormones.

DHT is principally responsible for male characteristics and normal male bodily function. Facial hair, body hair, a deeper voice, muscle growth, strength, bone density and sexual function are all determined by having good healthy levels of DHT.

DHT is also responsible for male pattern baldness which is why many guys often try to suppress or block the conversion of testosterone into DHT. There are even supplements available for this purpose. Many hair loss treatments such as minoxidil and finasteride also help to block DHT associated with hair loss.

Having low levels of DHT can result in decreased testosterone levels. It will result in the development of a hormonal imbalance. When you attempt to block or suppress DHT, this can lead to a deficiency of 5-alpha reductase the enzyme that helps to convert testosterone into DHT.

Having low levels of 5-alpha reductase can cause underdeveloped genitals, namely the penis and testicles. It can also prevent the conversion of testosterone into DHT and make you develop reduced testicular functioning. This can possibly negatively affect testosterone secretion.

DHT helps to activate androgen receptors. Androgen receptors are important for how testosterone is utilised by the body. DHT is also essential for maintaining a sex drive. DHT is crucial to libido and erections in men. Next to testosterone it is an important androgen hormone for men and it should not be suppressed or blocked.

DHT also has an effect on many other bodily functions. It can help to regulate blood sugar levels. It does this by regulating glucose metabolism. DHT is also involved in memory and cognitive functioning. Conditions such as senile dementia, which result in age related cognitive decline are affected by hormone levels within the body. DHT helps to prevent cognitive decline.

Higher levels of DHT have been associated with lower amounts of fat deposits in the heart. Elderly men with higher levels of DHT have lower probability of death from heart disease compared to men with low levels of DHT.

DHT has been linked to increases in strength and muscle mass, and increased bone density in men, which is no surprise, and it also offers some protection from auto-immune diseases. It is said that healthy DHT levels result in overall enhanced immune response, and stronger immune responses are thought to be possible by stimulating increased nitric oxide production.

It is quite well known that testosterone plays a role in moods and mental state. DHT has been linked helping to suppress anxiety and depression and this has been shown to be a result of the actions of DHT in the brain.

The no 1 biomarker for how well we age in so many different ways is natural hormone production and healthy hormone levels. DHT is one of those hormones and it has many benefits for the male body.

There are also some possible negative effects of DHT. As we have already mentioned it is associated with male pattern baldness. In studies it has been shown that in men with premature baldness occurring at a much younger age, they had higher levels of DHT.

DHT can also trigger acne. This is primarily associated with higher levels of DHT during puberty. However low levels of DHT during puberty have been linked with the development of genitals and adult male features being retarded.

Higher DHT levels can also increase a man's risk of developing prostate cancer and also increase the risk of developing an enlarged prostate. Low levels of DHT however mean that it is even more likely that you will get prostate cancer, and have a decreased survival rate for prostate cancer. In reality this just means that having healthy balanced levels of DHT will reduce the risks of that cancer being fatal. Best chance of not ever getting prostate problems lie in optimised balanced hormones.

Exercise, in particular activity that involves short intense bursts of activity will help to optimise levels of DHT. Also maintaining healthy levels of body fat. The optimum level of body fat for men, and indeed for testosterone, is thought to be between 10 and 20%. Body fat that is too low can negatively affect testosterone production, and body fat that is too high can encourage or promote estrogen production, or in men, the conversion of testosterone into estrogen.

The best foods to consider for optimal DHT levels are dietary fats and meats. If you are involved in optimising your testosterone levels and you are observing a well balanced and complete diet then you should be getting enough meats anyway. We will go into diet in detail in later sections.

Supplements thought to be particularly beneficial to DHT are zinc, tribulus terrestris, diosgenin, caffeine, tongkat ali and DHEA. However DHEA supplements are known to affect natural hormone production and should only ever be considered by older guys suffering from problems with their testosterone levels.

By far the best supplement, in my opinion, for optimising DHT levels is creatine. It is a highly beneficial supplement for guys who workout and is certainly worth considering.

For guys with abnormally high levels of DHT, adaptogenic supplements such as ginseng and fenugreek can help to balance out hormones.

Consumption of flaxseed, and black tea are also said to inhibit the conversion of testosterone into DHT. But black tea is particularly effective in helping to prevent iron overload from high meat consumption so it does have benefits to helping to balance out iron levels.

Spinach, kale, pumpkin seeds, soy, green tea, beetroot and bananas are also thought to inhibit DHT production.

Blocking or intentionally reducing DHT levels is not recommended. It should only ever be considered if you have levels which are abnormally high. And this is quite rare. There are many possible negative side effects associated with blocking DHT. These include impotence, reduced sex drive, difficulties maintaining an erection or achieving an orgasm, an increased risk of depression and also an increased risk of developing gynecomastia.

DHT is a powerful sex hormone and it is essential to normal healthy male bodily functioning. Although associated with some negative aspects it is an important factor to consider when optimising and balancing your hormonal output.

16

Nitric Oxide Production.

N itric Oxide is important to our testosterone production because it plays a role in efficient circulation and optimising our natural levels of nitric oxide will be beneficial to us in many ways.

Nitric oxide is a signalling molecule in the body that helps our cells communicate. It plays a part in the body's signalling process used to secrete hormones and in the production of testosterone.

Nitric oxide also relaxes the smooth muscles on the outer lining of the arteries allowing them to widen making room for oxygen and nutrients to flow easier throughout the body. This also improves our blood flow and circulation. This also improves the process of secreting testosterone.

When the lutenizing hormone and follicle stimulating hormone travel through the blood collecting cholesterol on route to the testicles, increased blood flow helps to improve this process.

A deficiency in nitric oxide is known to cause difficulties in sustaining an erection and it can also have a negative effect on testosterone production.

This is why is important to treat the whole body as an entire organism when we are optimising our T levels. There are many different things that can contribute towards testosterone production. Nitric oxide levels are one of those many things.

Nitric oxide helps to regulate blood pressure, it helps to prevent erectile dysfunction, it helps to prevent plaque build-up in the arteries, it helps to enhance exercise performance, it helps to boost the immune system, all of these things can also either harm or help testosterone production so it is important to consider.

You can buy nitric oxide supplements but by far the best approach is to be looking to increase your nitric oxide levels naturally.

One of the best ways to improve nitric oxide production is to engage in regular physical activity. Another effective method is with correct breathing. Simply breathing in via the nostrils will increase nitric oxide production. This process is augmented if this is combined with deep breathing. The full breath is the best method by far and it far more effective than belly or abdominal breathing as it utilises the entire lung and it also increases blood oxygen levels.

The humming breath is reputed to be very good for this. You inhale a full breath and then make a humming sound as you exhale its very simple.

Regular dedicated breathing exercises are recommended for optimising nitric oxide production. My book, The Full Breath, contains many breathing exercises which are great for this purpose.

Good dietary sources of nitric oxide are nitrate rich vegetables such as kale, spinach, beetroot, cabbage, cauliflower, broccoli and carrots. Research has demonstrated that eating nitrate rich meals on a regular basis can increase nitric oxide and lower blood pressure and even aid cognitive functioning.

Chillies, garlic and ginger are well known for their circulation boosting effects and they are also very good for nitric oxide production.

Citrus fruits such as, lemons, oranges, limes are also great for boosting nitric oxide levels. Pomegranate is also very good as its loaded with anti-oxidants that can protect your cells against damage and help to preserve nitric oxide.

Meat, poultry and seafood are all good sources of a co-enzyme called Q10 which is known to help preserve levels of nitric oxide within the body. Organ meats, fatty fish and muscle meats like beef, pork and chicken contain the highest concentrations of Q10.

Nuts and seeds are high in L-arginine, an amino acid that is involved in the production of nitric oxide. Eggs are also a great source of L-arginine.

Supplementing with L-arginine can also be very beneficial to nitric oxide and it has been shown that supplementation can boost nitric oxide after only 2 weeks. Supplementing with ginseng has also been shown to be very beneficial to improving nitric oxide production and it is great for improving blood flow and circulation.

Salty foods, sugary foods, vegan meats, pre-packaged foods, fast foods and high consumption of alcohol can deplete nitric oxide levels, but we already know to steer clear of these.

This is why we need to consider a well balanced diet. Everything must be balanced in order to optimise not only nitric oxide levels but testosterone production as well.

There are benefits to eating animal based AND plant based foods and limiting your diet to either one or the other is not the best approach as either can lead to nutrient deficiencies.

If you want to optimise your nitric oxide levels then eating a varied diet containing whole foods from both animals and plants will bring you the best results.

And this in turn will help to optimise and maintain healthy levels of testosterone.

17

Testosterone Killers.

The Biggest Testosterone Killers Known to Man.

Often guys are looking to improve their physique and athletic performance and increase their testosterone. They can be inclined to search for easy options with fast results. They want a competitive edge, or bigger muscles and more mass, or even just for attention and to be noticed. There are many reasons that guys will consider using performance enhancing drugs. This however can have a detrimental effect as all of these options will harm your natural testosterone production and are certainly never going to be the best long term option.

When considering low T levels you must be aware that there are also some supplements and pharma solutions that are always on offer and for some there is no other option. These should ideally be used only in extreme circumstances and only as a last resort. You have tried absolutely everything and it hasn't worked for you. And to be honest this scenario is highly unlikely in any fit and healthy guy.

The reason for this is that any supplement that increases testosterone levels can also potentially disrupt or even stop natural hormone production altogether. A great reason to investigate and research any supplements before diving in.

The objective is to optimise and maintain testosterone levels naturally, and to keep our natural T levels up. This can be a challenge because many of the supplements available can have a negative effect on natural T production.

Always conduct thorough research into any supplements before taking them. Even the ones that I am going to recommend to you! They may work great for me but may not be suitable for you. Look into any negative side effects as well as positive benefits from *any* supplement. Many supplements can interact with or aggravate certain medical conditions or interact with some medications. Always seek to get your nutrients from food if you can but sometimes supplementation is going to be necessary to get the required amounts.

Lets consider some very common solutions that men resort to when trying to increase their T levels. These offer fast results and are very effective but at the same time are in fact the biggest testosterone killers.

Anabolic Steroids.

With many guys now working out and wanting to increase their muscle mass and size and achieve an aesthetic physique, this often leads to steroid use.

Now it is a fact that if you are attending the gym on a regular basis then you will be offered steroids at some point. You will be told that you will get excellent results, and you will get far better and far quicker results and more efficient recovery than will ever be possible taking the natural route. This of course is all true.

You will also probably be told that they are safe in smaller doses and if you don't abuse them. I was also told that everyone is on it here (my gym) and that was a real eye opener. After receiving this insight it dawned on me that more than more than half of that gym's users were using steroids and this was across the board and not just confined to one gym. And to look at most of these guys it was not obvious by looking at them that they were using steroids.

I almost said Fxxk it I will give it a go but something inside me held back and I decided to research and find out as much as I could before diving in. Had I just dived right in I have no doubt that I would not still be in the game training and with a good physique and good T levels at 50 years old. What a life changing search phrase that turned out to be, "steroids side effects." This is the best and most effective decision I ever made when it came to training and fitness.

We all know that steroids can cause a whole host of health problems and I wont go into that here but one thing that people do not talk about when it comes to steroids is the effect this has on your hormonal and sexual health.

With each steroid cycle, the increases in testosterone caused by the steroids has an effect on natural T production. The body stops producing natural testosterone because it is getting all it needs and then some from the gear. Also the body produces excess estrogen to compensate for the elevated T levels. The body adapts and attempts to compensate for the hormonal disruption that has been introduced.

Body builders usually cycle their steroids and then use post cycle therapy to try to recover their natural testosterone levels. What tends to happen though is that the off cycle periods become shorter and the doses higher as tolerance is built up, or a plateau in physical development is reached. And the longer the off cycle period the more likely you are to lose those gains.

Their only solution therefore is to increase the dose to continue making progress and seeing visible results. And to keep the off cycle periods to a minimum.

The longer you continue using steroids the greater the damage is done to your natural testosterone production. It can even stop completely with prolonged use. The time it takes to achieve these results varies among individuals and the doses used. Also the higher the dosages the greater the damage to natural T production and the greater the risk of that damage becoming permanent.

When it comes to your natural testosterone production, even in smaller doses steroids will still cause harm. You are elevating your test levels unnaturally and natural production will still be disrupted. There is no safe dose to prevent this from happening.

So great is this effect that it is possible, in fact highly probable, to cease to function hormonally as a man by using steroids. You can destroy your testosterone production to the point that it will *never* come back. Seriously consider this.

Pro body builders who have taken steroids long term often need to be prescribed TRT, testosterone replacement therapy, for the rest of their lives, as they can no longer produce testosterone naturally and cannot restore their natural testosterone production. Steroid abuse is known to completely suppress the production of gonadotropin and testosterone. Not partially, completely.

There is a lot of advise out there stating that it only takes 4 months to recover natural T production after prolonged steroid use. This is highly unlikely. If you are lucky enough to be able to restore your natural testosterone production at all, it would probably take between 9 months and 2 years.

In a detailed study involving 100 athletes they observed the effects of anabolic steroids before starting a cycle, during the cycle and up to a year after ceasing use. It was a requirement for this study that candidates had not used any steroids for at least 3 months prior to the testing. It was observed that some of the men, 37 of them, had low baseline T levels indicating possible previous steroid use. There were no instructions on how to cycle or what dosage to use, this was left up to the men themselves to decide.

The findings during the cycle discovered that: "Irrespective of androgen (steroid) dose and duration of use, androgen exposure resulted in complete suppression of the hypothalamic-pituitary-gonadal axis, as demonstrated by undetectable Lutenizing hormone and follicle-stimulating hormone concentration in nearly all subjects." Pretty conclusive. Testosterone production was shown to completely stop for most candidates.

When it came to sperm production they found that: "Testicular volume declined during androgen abuse and spermatogenesis decreased, with two thirds of subjects having oligospermia or azoospermia by the end of the cycle."

Spermatogenesis refers to the production of sperm. Oligospermia is when sperm count is significantly reduced. Azoospermia is when there is no sperm present at all. You will produce semen that has no sperm present.

In conclusion it was found that in the men who had normal baseline levels at the beginning of the study, most of them restored their T levels in between 3 and 12 months. Just one cycle bear in mind. It took these same guys an average of 45 to 55 weeks to fully recover their sperm production. This is just one cycle.

The researchers also stated that the evidence available indicates that cumulative (long term) exposure to androgens reduces the chance of recovery.

So if you are using steroids stop immediately. Start repairing the damage. If you can. The end game of steroid use is that you will destroy your natural testosterone production. If you are in the life game for the long term then this will no doubt have a detrimental effect.

TRT, Testosterone Replacement Therapy.

The pharma industries' solution to low testosterone is TRT, or Testosterone Replacement Therapy. There are many fitness influencers using TRT as a fast track route to an aesthetically pleasing body. They are under pressure to please their audiences and their physique is their marketing image. The products and services they sell are geared towards gaining a physique like theirs and a lifestyle like theirs so naturally they feel inclined to cheat. For guys in their 20s and 30s this is a form of instant gratification and of taking the easy way out to impress people.

But the same thing happens on TRT. Natural T production is disrupted and can even cease with long term use. The singer Robbie Williams took TRT for a year as part of his treatment for depression. A years use led to him suffering from erectile dysfunction after he stopped using. You have been warned.

A lot of young guys absorbing testosterone related content seem to think that for guys in their 30s using TRT is acceptable and inevitable. This is being defeated at a psychological level before the battle has even begun.

Whereas it is acceptable for guys in their 70s and beyond to be using TRT, for guys of under that age, and with no medical issues, it is a performance enhancing drug, synthetic injectable testosterone, and a way of getting a pleasing physique by a much easier route. Instant gratification. And of course they will pay a heavy price for that further on down the road.

If you are considering TRT please ensure that it is only as a last resort and that you have tried everything you can to improve yourself naturally first before travelling this path. Remember that TRT is a drug that will treat the symptom of low testosterone only. It will cause imbalances in all other hormones and will not restore or maintain natural levels of pregnenolone or DHEA. These are likely to decline more rapidly over time. It is also highly likely that you will also experience increased estrogen levels.

Prohormones.

With all the bad press and health risks associated with steroid use, this often leads to guys seeking out less risky options. However when it comes to testosterone, many of these alternatives will also disrupt your natural T production.

Prohormones are supplements that contain ingredients that convert to testosterone after being ingested. The effects are usually quite quick making them a tempting option. Prohormones basically provide the raw materials to induce the body to produce testosterone.

Steroids are synthetic testosterone, this means once you have ingested them you have no control in how much testosterone is made. With prohormones they provide the ingredients and the body controls the T production meaning that the body will only use as much pro-hormone as it needs. This feature is often used in marketing to suggest that they are a natural healthier alternative to steroids and they will not affect natural testosterone production in any way.

Prohormones can be harmful to health and these risks increase with long term use. They are classed as banned substances by many different athletic associations. Once ingested you are no longer a natural athlete.

There are also many side effects associated with prohormones use. These include shrinking testicles, acne, mood changes (similar to roid rage) fatigue, breast enlargement, or gyno, hair loss, infertility and reduced sperm production, liver toxicity, kidney disease, heart problems and an increased risk of some forms of cancer, such as prostate and pancreatic cancers. They can also raise bad cholesterol levels, which is bad for T levels, and raise blood pressure, which is great for raising cortisol levels.

They contain toxins which must be processed by the liver, and this can affect adrenal function, which could have an effect on hormone production. They are often marketed as safe alternatives to steroids that will give you gains without side effects associated with steroid use. This is simply not true. You will experience quicker gains than you would naturally, but the side effects are similar to steroids.

When it comes to T levels you are artificially raising your testosterone levels. As a result your body sends the message that the body is fine and does not need to make its own testosterone. So it stops production.

When you finish your prohormones cycle, usually 30 days, you are then in trouble. Your body has shut down testosterone production and your T levels crash. Instantly. Just like with anabolic steroids. Your body has become used to the artificial testosterone. Your hormonal balance is also out of sync, meaning that your body has been into es-

trogen production overdrive to try to maintain the hormonal balance!
And it has now become used to doing this!

You will also feel like shit and have no energy and those gains in
muscle mass will slip away quickly. Consider this. It takes 2 months
of post cycle therapy to repair the damage of just one 30 day prohormones cycle. In those two months you will probably lose most, if not
all of those gains. This is similar to steroid use. The off cycle periods
for the user become shorter and shorter and the natural T production
becomes harder and harder to restore. This happens because they
don't want to lose those gains. Keep that up and you wont be able to
keep IT up!

SARMS.

SARMS, which are Selective Androgen Receptor Modulators, are
another supplement often falsely plugged as a safe alternative to
steroids. It is often claimed that you will get all the gains but without
the side effects. This is not true. SARMS are absolutely devastating to
T levels and manhood.

All the risks and effects of SARMS are similar to prohormones so I
will not repeat myself. With SARMS there is also an increased risk of
heart attacks, strokes, psychosis and sleep disturbance.

They also cause testicular shrinkage, and can have a negative effect
on natural T production. In an article in Men's Health magazine in
2019, they interviewed 3 guys who had used SARMS. All reported
negative experiences. One of the guys, after just 4 weeks use noticed
that his balls had gotten considerably smaller. He ceased use immedi-

ately. Then he tried all the post cycle solutions that he could find and to no avail. He was quoted as saying "I tried everything and they (his balls) just wouldn't come back." The damage was permanent. He had to go onto TRT.

Smaller testicles amount to less testosterone production. You will probably get big muscles, but with balls the size of petite pois and no sex drive to go with that.

And as with steroids, SARMS can switch off testosterone production abruptly and completely. You have been warned.

Another thing to note is that prohormones and SARMS are not natural as many believe. The false claims made in the marketing of these supplements would lead many guys who are using them to consider themselves as being natural athletes. This is not true. Using these supplements amounts to being enhanced.

So great care must be taken when supplementing to ensure that whatever supplements you are using do not disrupt, or shut down, your natural testosterone production.

Now we shall look at our diet and how it can harm our testosterone levels.

18

How Your Diet Could Be Killing Your Testosterone.

Dietary T Killers.

In truth we need to be doing all we can to improve and maintain our testosterone levels. This includes our diet as what you eat will have an effect on your health and well-being and also your hormones. There are many foods that have been cited as T killers but often there is little research to verify these claims.

However the secret to diets and testosterone as we all know is to consume a well balanced diet. I will go into more detail on that in a later section. So therefore the biggest T killing foods are the ones that contribute towards bad health, and poor dietary choices, much more than specific foods. Keeping your intake of these to a minimum, or at the very least under moderation is the best approach. Lets go over these here.

Alcohol.

As far as food and drink goes alcohol is certainly one of the biggest testosterone killers. Drinking on a regular basis will harm T levels, but alcohol can even have short term immediate, affects on your T levels. Drinking heavily can even destroy T levels and this damage can be permanent.

Research has shown that testosterone levels can drop after only 30 minutes after consuming just one alcoholic drink. With only one drink T levels were restored by the following day. When the amount of alcohol consumed was increased to simulate a typical evening at a bar, this was considered to be 5 drinks, it was noted that recovery towards baseline levels took 3 days.

In one clinical study determining the effects of alcohol on testosterone the researchers compared the T levels of healthy men to the T levels of men who were alcoholics.

It was no surprise that the alcoholics had extremely low testosterone compared to the healthy men.

The test went further. The healthy group of men were given a pint of whiskey to drink per day for 30 consecutive days. After only 72 hours this group began to show a significant decline in T levels. By the end of the 30 day trial, the healthy men group had T levels similar to those of the alcoholics.

So from this we can surmise that regular drinking habits will cause a decline in testosterone levels, and that it will result in a noticeable decline in only a short period of time.

If we consider how testosterone is produced we can see clearly why alcohol is detrimental to T levels. In men there are 3 glands responsible for our testosterone production. The hypothalamus, the pituitary gland and the testicles.

The hypothalamus releases a hormone called gonadotropin which acts on your pituitary gland. Then the pituitary gland releases Lutenizing hormone. In response to the release of this hormone the testicles then synthesise testosterone.

Alcohol disrupts and interferes with all three of these glands. This disruption takes place as soon as the alcohol enters the bloodstream and continues to disrupt until the alcohol has passes through our system and the toxic by products have been completely eliminated.

The damage achieved and the time it takes to recover will be determined by how long you have been drinking for, and the amount you have been consuming.

Of course quitting alcohol can help reverse the damage. In the case of long term drinking, or alcoholism, recovery can take months, years or even be permanent.

Back to our study it was reported that in the healthy male group who were given a pint of whiskey per day for 30 days, recovery in this group to baseline levels, and the reversal of the effects of the alcohol, took 10 weeks after alcohol consumption was stopped.

If you care for your testosterone levels keep your drinking to a bare minimum or eliminate it from your diet entirely.

Dairy Products.

Now dairy is an essential part of any well balanced diet as I will reveal later but there is a potential dark side that you need to be aware of.

Milk effectively comes from pregnant cows and their milk contains estrogens and progesterones. Most dairy products are made with milk of course such as cheese and yoghurt. Progesterones can affect testosterone by suppressing the release of the gonadotropins, which are needed for the secretion of the follicle stimulating hormones and Lutenizing hormones. These hormones then travel to the testicles to help make testosterone. If the testicles don't receive these hormones they cannot synthesize testosterone.

But dairy and milk in particular also happen to be packed with essential micro-nutrients that help to make up a well balanced diet. For example milk is a great source of vitamin A, vitamin K2, calcium, iodine, potassium and it is also a good source of natural DHEA.

All these nutrients are needed to help the body maintain its balanced state and deficiencies in any of these micro-nutrients can have an adverse effect on testosterone.

Another dairy product made from milk are protein powders such as whey protein. They are in effect milk protein isolates. And this also potentially means estrogen isolate too. Potentially. This has yet to be proven. Estrogen is inevitably present in milk. But remember that in relation to T levels most estrogen in the male body comes from testosterone that has been converted into estrogen. Consuming some estrogens in your diet can mean that your body has enough estrogen and doesn't need to produce more.

Excessive consumption of these protein supplements is something to be aware of. You don't ever need to consider cutting them out completely, they are a very useful dietary supplement, just be aware.

One of the fundamental rules of a well balanced diet is to consume a wide variety of foods. Dairy is essential but moderation is the key. Too much of anything can be bad.

Processed Foods.

Processed foods are catastrophic to T levels. They are usually high calorie, high in sugar and high in unhealthy fats such as trans fats, or trans unsaturated fatty acids. They can also contain many other additives, sugar, salt, preservatives and chemicals which are added during the manufacturing process.

Examples of processed foods include processed meats, such as sliced deli meats, ham, bacon, sausages, salami, paté, burgers and hot dog sausages. Also some cheeses like cheese spreads and the sliced plastic looking cheeses that are present in cheeseburgers are processed.

Tinned fruits and vegetables are also processed and they are then put in a liquid that contains salt, sugar or even both, to preserve them. They are then placed in metal cans which are lined with a thin film of plastic that contain endocrine disruptors.

Also many popular savoury snacks such as potato chips (crisps in the UK) sausage rolls, pies and pastries. If you want to consume these foods it is best to make your own and avoid the ready made processed options.

And of course this also means many popular sweet snacks such as cakes, biscuits and even many breakfast cereals. Not only are they processed, they are also packed with sugar.

Avoid any ready made foods and microwave meals. Sure they are convenient but they are processed, have had all kinds of crap added to them to preserve them for longer and are packaged in plastic dishes which they tend to be heated in and then eaten from. Never a good idea.

Learn to cook your own meals. If you are not a great cook just look up some recipes and follow the instructions. It is not that difficult. It's a great skill to have and you will be able to choose exactly what goes into your food.

Consider that it is common knowledge that processed foods are associated with poor health, both physical and mental, along with their associated nutritional deficiencies, and obesity. And all these things will affect testosterone. Poor health affects hormone production and upsets the body's finely tuned system of balance. Any nutritional deficiencies left unattended for too long will have the same effect. Obesity also encourages the conversion of testosterone into estrogen.

There have also been some studies that suggest that consuming trans fats on a regular basis, and trans fats are abundant in many processed foods, can reduce testosterone levels by as much as 15%.

Convenience saves time right now, but destroys your health and crashes your T levels.

Trans, or Hydrogenated Fats.

It seems to be common knowledge that trans fats are bad for you and contribute to many diseases but that doesn't seem to prevent many people from consuming them on a regular basis.

They are abundant in many popular takeaway foods for example. Uber eats might save you time but take out will potentially tank your T levels.

They are also called hydrogenated fats because of the process used for producing them. The raw materials are usually cheap low quality oils such as soy-bean, corn oil and canola oil, and they are then subjected to hydrogen atoms passing through the oils under extremely

COMPLETE GUIDE TO TESTOSTERONE   147

high pressure and nickel is used as an alkaline catalyst for the process involved to harden them.

This means that there will no doubt also be traces of nickel present in these fats. Nickel is an endocrine disruptor. Exposure to nickel can harm the stomach and kidneys and also can contribute to many forms of cancer.

Once the process is completed the unsaturated molecules in the raw oils then become fully saturated and they become hard at room temperature. Like the lard or ghee that is used in cooking.

When cheap low quality oils are hardened and zapped with hydrogen, trans fatty acids, or trans fats are formed. This is effectively a shitty grease, and margarine is pure trans fat. It has had synthetic colouring added to it to make it look like butter. So avoid using margarine for anything. If you must spread anything on your toast butter or even jam packed with sugar would be more healthy.

Trans fats are particularly bad because they lower good cholesterol and increase bad cholesterol. Good cholesterol is used to make testosterone. Bad cholesterol clogs the arteries and reduces blood flow.

Trans fats also cause inflammation in the body. Inflammation harms the body in many ways, including the production of hormones. Trans fats increase oxidative stress and help to increase cortisol, the stress hormone. Trans fats also negatively affect the proper function of all the glands used in the process of producing hormones. And trans fats also increase the risk of heart disease and clogged arteries, which will affect blood-flow and increase the risk of erectile dysfunction.

And of course studies found that those who consume trans fats on a regular basis were found to have testosterone levels up to 15% lower than those who moderated their intake.

They have no potential health benefits. At all. So why bother to consume them? Complete elimination is an excellent strategy here.

Pastries and Baked goods.

In many baked products and pastries, which are usually made with processed ingredients, trans fats are usually present. Trans fats are known to be linked to reduced T levels. Trans fats are created when vegetable oils are chemically processed. This is done to give the products a longer shelf life. We already know why trans fats and processed foods are bad, and for those same reasons, so are pastries and baked goods!

Diet Soda.

Now these sugar free options are considered by many to be a healthy alternative to sugary sodas but these diet drinks can have a negative impact on your T levels. It will be hard for many to believe but the full sugar versions of these drinks are actually more healthy. However this is not a recommendation for you to drink more sugary sodas, I am just stating a fact. I would recommend removing *all* sodas from your diet.

The main problem is with the artificial sweeteners they contain. In particular aspartame, which has been shown to do significant damage to the testicular tissue and levels of testosterone.

One study showed that men who drank diet sodas had lower T levels than the men who didn't. This difference remained when compared to subjects who drank sugary sodas. Also the men who drank diet soda also had abnormally high levels of a hormone called SHBG, which binds to testosterone making it unavailable for use in the body.

To put that into context you could have good total T levels. But with abnormally high levels of SHBG this will mean much lower free T, meaning testosterone that is available to use right now. And low amounts of free testosterone can lead to symptoms associated with low testosterone.

Aspartame is an artificial sweetener that just happens to be used in a wide variety of products today. The real hidden danger here is that it is often found in products that are labelled "diet" something or other and are taken for granted to be a more healthy option.

It is commonly used in diet sodas, energy drinks, sugar free fruit juices, sugar free sports drinks and also in many processed foods. It is literally everywhere.

The bad news is that it is toxic. Even the World Health Organisation have labelled it a potential carcinogenic. Aspartame is what is known as an excitotoxin. Too many of these toxins can cause nerve cells being damaged or even killed completely because of excess stimulation by neurotransmitters.

Of course neurotransmitters are pathways that have an influence over many bodily functions. Put simply when toxins enter the body it is signals from neurotransmitters that kick-start the process of processing these toxins and eliminating them from the body.

What also happens is that these toxins bind themselves to various brain receptors causing problems, and as we know brain receptors play a significant role in not only testosterone production, but in many other vital bodily processes. Excitotoxins have even been associated with neurological disorders. Any neurological disturbances of course can also affect our hormonal system.

With more and more mounting evidence of the effect of aspartame on T levels it is a good idea to completely eliminate them from your diet. Always check the ingredients before buying anything you are not sure of. If it says "artificial sweeteners," chances are it is aspartame, so reject any food that includes this phrase too. It can also be referred to as E951. Food manufacturers will do their best not to draw your attention to toxins.

Sugar Sweetened Beverages and Sugar.

Fizzy drinks are becoming one of the more popular beverage choices for younger men. Sales of these drinks generate huge revenues and they are often the first beverage of choice for many.

However in studies it has been shown that men who consumed these drinks on a regular basis were found to have lower sperm counts and T levels than men who did not drink them, or the men who moderate their intake. And these studies also observed that when increasing the amount of intake it became more likely that T levels would become even lower with increased intake. The more calories per day of intake, the greater the reduction in T levels seems to occur.

Now most of these sugar loaded drinks, that are not limited to just sodas, contain corn syrup and many other dubious ingredients that sound like chemicals of some kind. These drinks include energy drinks, sports drinks, fruit juice concentrates, fruit punch and those chilled ready to go coffee drinks.

Too much soda intake, and sugar intake as well, can lead to negative effects on hormonal balance in men and also affects overall health. Sugar consumption causes spikes in insulin production.

Medical evidence clearly points out that excessive consumption of sugars, sugary foods and sugary drinks can lead to an increased risk of various medical conditions. These include not only low T levels, but also obesity, inflammation, diabetes, gout, cardiovascular diseases, metabolism problems and premature ageing of the skin.

Now many of these other conditions are of course known to have a corresponding effect on hormonal balances and endocrine function. Sugars also amount effectively to useless calories, and much of this gets stored as fat, leading to excessive weight gain of course. Focus on belly fat and man boobs rather than muscle gains!

This excessive weight gain often leads to abnormal functioning of the testicles and increases the risk of activating the hormones that convert testosterone into estrogen.

Excessive consumption of sugars also leaves you with an increased likelihood of experiencing nutritional deficiencies as these foods and drinks lack any vitamins, minerals and other nutrients.

So there are many ways that consuming sugary foods and drinks can lead either directly or indirectly to decreases in testosterone.

A study into the intake of sugar sweetened beverages in men aged between 20 and 39 found that excessive consumption led to lower total testosterone levels.

Another study found that men who consumed 442 kcal of sugary drinks per day had lower T levels than the men who limited their intake to 137 kcal per day. It was also found that excessive consumption of sugar sweetened beverages caused insulin spikes because the body must produce more insulin to manage the sudden sugar overload.

So the evidence seems pretty unanimous that sugary drinks do not correspond to high T levels.

I was amazed therefore to discover many headlines appearing in February of 2023, in many different publications such as the Daily Mail and the New York Post, suggesting that sugary drinks increase testicle size and T levels! The New York Post published an article with a headline, which stated that, "Drinking Coke and Pepsi leads to larger testicles and more testosterone." going on to say that the study was attempting to determine the impact of carbonated beverages on fertility and sex organs in men. The study in fact was carried out on mice, which was stated much further down the page.

In the Daily Mail it was said that, "The country's most popular drinks might refresh the parts that other drinks cannot reach - by giving men bigger testicles and making men more masculine." Making *men* more masculine. A suggestion that this also applies to human men as opposed to just male mice.

Lets face it. The differences between male and female mice are not easy to spot. The only obvious difference is the genitalia. So this statement obviously does not imply that the mice grew longer beards, had deeper squeaks, hairier legs or more muscle mass than their female counterparts! More masculine? And what about the female mice than consume Coke? Bigger tits and fuller lips with increased fertility? I am almost disappointed that they didn't test on female mice too just to see if it had the same effect. Think of the money women could save on lip and boob jobs and fertility treatments!

It then states that research on mice showed adult males who drank Coca-cola or Pepsi had higher testosterone levels and larger genitals than their peers. Now I wasn't aware that lab mice had peers so this article was highly suggestive that this new ground-breaking study's findings applied to human males, or men as they are more commonly known.

If I pointed to a male mouse and said "that man over there has a long tail.........." So that's a pretty definitive term, the word "man." And if you had 10 mice in a cage would it be possible to single out the coke drinking mouse among his peers?

On the day this article appeared in many mainstream news outlets and all of them were suggestive towards implying that these results applied in particular to men as well as mice. None of the articles stated categorically that as this was only a study of rodents, there were no human test candidates, and that it should not be assumed that the same results would apply to humans. The small minority of articles that did only divulged this vital information at the very end of the articles.

I am not insinuating that these publications were attempting to mislead the public in any way, disclaimer, but taken literally how many men caught sight of that headline and then rushed off to the local store to stock up on coke? After all most people read headlines and then scan the first few lines before moving on?

A lesson to be learned from something like this is to not believe everything you see, hear or read. Further research involving a phrase such as "sugar sweetened drinks and T levels," entered into any search engine would have quickly delivered pages of evidence that shows these claims are not true. At least for men anyway. Seems to work wonders for mice though. However if you are reading this I assume that you are not a rodent? Of course I could be wrong. The power that Coke or Pepsi has.

Low Quality Meats.

We all know that meat and animal fats have a positive effect on our health, testosterone production and muscle development. However the quality of the meat is a thing to consider.

In low quality meats there is usually a high content of omega 6 fatty acids, and usually a higher fat content which can contribute to inflammation. Think of those really fatty pork strips that many people put on BBQs here as a great example.

Inflammation can impact the body's hormones including testosterone. Omega 6 and omega 3 fatty acids are both essential to a well balanced diet. Excessive omega 6 has been linked to reduced T levels. Considering that the average modern western diet typically has an omega 6 to omega 3 ratio of 10:1, and in those with poor diets and sedentary lifestyles as much as 40:1, low T anyone?

Omega 6 fatty acids are inflammatory. Omega 3's are anti-inflammatory. Balance is the key to a healthy diet of course. Recommendations are to never exceed a ratio between omega 6 and omega 3 of 4:1.

But ideally you should seek to balance that out a bit more and try to aim for a ratio between omega 6 and omega 3 of between 2:1 and 1:1. The ratio of these fatty acids in the human brain is between 1:1 and 2:1 so these seem the obvious parameters for optimal health and optimal hormone health. If you are concerned about saturated fats and cholesterol then take that to 3:1.

Soy.

Soy has a reputation of being a testosterone killing food. It has been a widely held belief in modern times that it contributes towards the feminisation of men and that it can lower testosterone and increase estrogen and affect erections and sperm quality.

The issue of soy being a T killer or not has split the fitness industry with some being advocates of avoiding it at all costs and others insisting that it does not affect T levels so I will be fair and present both sides of the argument and let you decide for yourselves.

Not being vegan I do not consume soy on a regular basis and have never considered soy as part of my diet. It is a nutrition packed food, a good source of protein and it contains nearly all of the essential amino acids, and it is packed with many essential micro-nutrients so makes an excellent source of these nutrients for vegans.

I do not consume soy. Not because I believe it to be a T killer, but simply because I am getting all the nutrients it contains from other food sources. I will just give you the facts as I have discovered them through extensive research.

Soy contains an active ingredient called isoflavones, which are phytoestrogens. These are believed to be responsible for interfering with hormonal levels by raising estrogen, which will have a corresponding impact on T levels. It is worth it to note here that eggs, also contain phytoestrogens, and are of course good for T levels because they are an excellent source of good cholesterol.

A thing rarely considered is that phytoestrogens mimic estrogen in much the same way that anabolic steroids mimic testosterone. With steroid use the steroids mimic testosterone. This then means that the hormonal system detects that there is already enough testosterone present in the blood and the body doesn't need to make any more.

Natural production then shuts down and the body then produces more estrogen to try to compensate for the excess testosterone provided by the steroids.

As phytoestrogens mimic estrogen it would be fair to suggest that as they mimic estrogen, the same hormonal system would carry out its natural processes? That being the phytoestrogens mimic estrogen. The endocrine system detects that there is enough estrogen present and signals to the body to stop converting any more testosterone into estrogen? And even to possibly increase testosterone production to compensate?

According the laws of nature and our understanding of the endocrine system this of course is highly possible. If steroids, which mimic testosterone can shut down T production and produce more estrogen then there is no reason why the presence of phytoestrogens, that mimic estrogen in the same manner, cannot shut down estrogen conversion. Many medical scientists believe this to be the case, some don't, but officially the jury is still out on this at the time of writing and further investigation is needed.

There have been numerous studies that suggest that soy is responsible for lowering testosterone levels but more than 95% of these results have been recorded in animals. A few human studies have delivered similar results so lets take a closer look at these because after all, we are humans.

A 2013 study showed that men who consumed 20 grams of soy protein every day for 2 weeks were found to have lower T levels than another group of men who consumed 20 grams of whey protein over the same period.

Another study by Godin et al, in 2007, studied 12 men who were given 56g of soy protein for 4 weeks. Serum testosterone decreased by 19% and increased within 2 weeks of discontinued soy protein. Lutenizing hormone levels decreased during the 4 week period of soy protein use and then increased after they stopped using the soy protein but it was stated that the changes "did not reach statistical significance."

They concluded that soy protein powder decreases serum testosterone levels in healthy active men. Soy protein powder is basically a protein isolate derived from soy products, similar in nature to the way that whey protein is a protein isolate derived from milk.

And in most of the human studies supporting the opinion that soy is a testosterone killer, involved testing which observed the consumption of soy protein isolate. Soy proteins contain significant amounts of phytoestrogens, and this could be a factor that has influenced these results.

But it is only fair to mention that the studies that suggest soy affects testosterone are flawed. Many are lacking a control group. In a scientific study the control group are not given the treatment, or are given a placebo and their results are then compared with the treatment or experimental group, those that have received the element being studied.

Most of these studies focus only on a small number of participants and therefore do not represent the majority of men. Most of these studies also failed to collect what would be considered to be crucial data in this argument. The studies did not record estrogen levels.

So the evidence, which would support claims that soy feminises men, by raising estrogen levels in men, has not been collected in these studies. The evidence in human trials that suggest consumption of soy lowers testosterone levels, could be limited to consumption of soy protein powders, and raw soy foods were not considered. And the studies that support this are isolated studies and not numerous.

When researching the effects of soy on T levels it seems that the majority of the evidence, and the human studies, support the suggestion that eating soy has no affect whatsoever on testosterone levels.

The best example is an analysis carried out which evaluated the data from multiple studies into the effects of soy on T levels. In 2010 in a journal, Fertility and Sterility, JM Hamilton-Reeves et al published an analysis of more than 30 studies involving over 900 men. They reported that in all of these studies it was recorded that "neither soy foods nor isoflavone supplements alter measures of bioavailable testosterone concentrations in men."

The objectives of this research were pretty detailed. They sought to, "determine whether isoflavones (phytoestrogens) exert estrogen like effects (the feminisation of men) by lowering bioavailable testosterone through evaluation of the effects of soy protein and isoflavone intake on T, sex hormone binding globulin, SHBG, free T and free androgen index in men."

There were found to be "no significant effects," on any of these measures. These studies correlate to studies taken over varying durations of between one month and more than four months of soy consumption.

It is interesting to note that the above mentioned study involving Godin et al, which found a 19% decrease in T levels in healthy men consuming soy protein was included in this analysis. The conclusion of the study is pretty adamant that no significant effects occurred. To me a 19% drop in T levels in only 4 weeks is pretty significant and something that I would like to avoid if possible.

They did mention this result in the report to be fair and they confirmed the 19% decrease in T levels. They also confirmed that it was only a small study involving 12 subjects. They also mentioned that one of these subjects had abnormally high baseline T levels, which were outside normal ranges at the start of the study. This candidate continued to experience a significant decline in T levels even after the soy intake was stopped.

In references made to this study by supporters of the suggestion that soy lowers T levels, they do not mention this exceptional candidate. The researchers themselves offered no explanation as to why his baseline levels were abnormally high.

However the other studies included in the analysis did all correlate to their, the researchers' conclusion. Apart from Godin et al in 2007, all the other studies found that no affects on hormone levels were observed after consuming soy.

Another analysis was published in 2021 that confirmed the 2010 analysis, was published in another journal, Reproductive Toxicology.

This report resulted from the analysis of 41 studies which took place between 2010 and 2020. This analysis involves data recorded on observations of more than 1700 men.

They also reached a conclusion that they did not find any link between soy consumption and testosterone levels. That amounts to 71 human studies involving over 2600 men.

In one recent study in China in 2021 monitoring the effects that increasing intake of soy-bean oil had on synthesis of testosterone in Leydig cells, concluded that increasing intake of soy-bean oil can actually lead to elevated testosterone levels. Now before you go rushing out the door to the store, that study involved only mice and that does not necessarily mean that the same result applies to men!

In my opinion unless you are vegan it is highly likely that you can get all the nutrients you need from other sources. So it is not going to be a problem at all if you want to skip soy ingestion altogether. If you are vegan then it can be a highly nutritional food source packed with protein, amino acids and many other micro-nutrients that will benefit your diet.

It seems that there is only a small amount of evidence that confirms that soy is a T killing food, and no available evidence confirming that it feminises men.

A story that went viral in 2008 concerned a man who got gyno and this was attributed to him consuming soy. This guy however was overweight, led a sedentary lifestyle and consumed take away foods on a regular basis. But he also happened to drink 3 litres of soy milk per day. It is highly possible that this story went viral without being fact checked, which led to many advising men to avoid all soy products may have contributed to the belief that soy is a T killer.

If you are concerned about soy then just don't include it in your diet. As a meat eater you will be fine without it. In any event it would be a good idea to moderate your soy intake and not go overboard. Balance is the key with diet.

Vegetable Oils.

Vegetable oils contain high quantities of polyunsaturated fatty acids that have been linked with negatively affecting testosterone levels. But remember that polyunsaturated fats also include omega3 fatty acids found in fish so it is necessary to include this type of fat in your diet.

The reason that vegetable oils are considered bad for T levels is that they are very high in omega6 fatty acids and high intake will negatively affect the ratios that were advised earlier on in this section.

The real dark side to vegetable oils, and the best reason to avoid them is in the way they are manufactured. Vegetable oils are a collective term that refers to oils such as canola, soy-bean, peanut, rapeseed, and sunflower oils.

These oils are not derived from the plant materials themselves but from the seeds of these plants. During the manufacturing process these seeds are subjected to a high pressure pressing to extract the juices from the seeds, which make the oils. To maximise the amount of oil that is obtained from this process involves the use of substances such as hexane. The oils are also bleached and deodorised to give them a more pleasant taste and appearance.

Hexane is an industrial solvent that is also used as an industrial cleaner and degreaser. It is easily ingested by inhaling or by being absorbed through the skin. Hexane has been linked to long lasting and even permanent nerve damage, and is an irritant that can affect the eyes and the respiratory system. It has also been suggested to be carcinogenic. And there is no doubt that traces of hexane will still be present in any vegetable oils because it is involved in the process of making it.

High intakes of vegetable oils have been linked to diabetes, irritable bowel disease and cardiovascular disease.

They have also been linked to depleted testosterone levels. And these oils probably contain traces of industrial solvents in them. If I recommended ingesting industrial solvents you would think I'm crazy right?

Avoid using oils such as soy-bean oil and palm oil and any vegetable oils for your cooking. Avoid eating any fried foods if you can, as these lead to obesity, which in turn can raise insulin levels and affect T levels.

Refined Carbohydrates.

Carbohydrates are an essential part of any well balanced diet. Low carb diets such as keto have been linked to lower T levels in men. But carbs are a confusing subject for many and it is all down to the foods that you get your carbs from.

There are 2 different types of carbs. Refined carbs and complex carbs, each type has its own nutritional properties.

In addition to these 2 carb types there are 3 separate sub-types to consider. The first is sugar. This is often added to foods such as breakfast cereals and surprisingly these are also added to many pre-prepared savoury foods. A typical small frozen pizza can contain as much as 7g of sugar.

There are many natural sugars which occur in things like honey, fruits and vegetables. When considering your diet it is important to note that these elements do also contribute to your sugar intake, despite being natural.

Foods containing natural sugars, such as fruits, are a better option as they also contain many vitamins and minerals that will be beneficial to us.

The next sub-type are starches. Starch is derived from plants and is present in foods including bread, potatoes, rice and pasta. These starchy foods give us a source of energy that is released slowly throughout the day to help keep us energized.

The third sub-type is fibre. Fibre also is derived from plants. It is essential to include dietary fibre in your diet, as it improves digestion, and contributes to a healthy digestive tract.

Foods rich in this sub-type include fruits and vegetables, whole-grain bread, rice, pasta and many legumes such as beans, chickpeas and lentils.

The human body can survive without sugar. But it cannot survive without carbs because we need them for fuel. When it comes to carbs therefore we should be aiming to eliminate the sugary carbs and to be concentrating on the starchy foods that contain fibre.

Many dieticians advise to lower carb intake as part of a weight loss diet. However these starchy foods can in fact help to maintain a healthy weight because they give us a sense of feeling full and they fill us up for longer so you are much more unlikely to binge on unnecessary snacks.

So we want to be aiming to consume only complex carbohydrates, and limiting our intake of refined carbs. Refined carbs are the enemy of testosterone. Why?

Refined carbs relate to sugars as I have already mentioned. These are glucose, sucrose, fructose, dextrose and anything made from grains that has had the wheat-germ or bran removed from them. In other words they have been "refined" to the extent that they have had many of their nutrients removed during the refining process.

This means that they will give you very little nutritional value or benefits. They are also digested quicker by the body leaving you more likely to feel hungry and resort to snacking. This will have a negative effect on the body. You are effectively consuming negative calories, which can contribute to energy loss, low moods and low sense of well-being, while of course aiding in weight gain. Especially around the waistline.

Another downside to refined carbs is because they are rapidly converted to energy, glucose, in your body this will cause a sudden spike in blood sugars and the body will then spike insulin secretion. The insulin enables this glucose to enter the cells and be used for energy.

Of course raised insulin levels has an affect on testosterone. Do this over any length of time and the results can be a disaster.

Because the more frequently you induce these insulin spikes, and this could amount to several times per day if you consume refined carbs regularly, your body will develop the habit of producing too much insulin, which will lead to insulin resistance over time.

Insulin resistance means that your body no longer recognises insulin. This is the ultimate strategy for getting diabetes. Diabetes is of course associated with erectile dysfunction and declining testosterone production and hormonal imbalances.

Now when it comes to refined carbs there are many foods and drinks that are really obvious. Fizzy drinks, potato chips, sugar sweetened foods, many breakfast cereals and many ready made foods.

But some are not so obvious. Sports drinks, which are said to increase energy levels during exercise are one of the worst offenders. That energy is coming from sugars with added electrolytes to help convince you that its great for sport. Flavoured yoghurt. Yoghurt is seen as a healthy and beneficial food but it is often stuffed with sugar.

The stealthy ones are things like rice and pasta. Wait! These are good sources of carbohydrates right? Well yes and no. White pasta, white rice, white flours and white bread are all refined and can contain more sugars and have often been leached of many nutrients during the refining process. If you want to keep those T levels up into old age, give yourself a massive head start by choosing, brown rice, whole wheat pasta, brown bread, or whole wheat bread over their white counterparts.

White breads have been made with white flours. Which have been bleached. Yes you have been consuming bleach! During the refining process they use bleaching agents including potassium bromate and chlorine dioxide to remove the slight yellowing, to make it white, and to improve its baking qualities. But baking qualities of course do not correlate to nutritional qualities.

White rice contains arsenic. This was a common poison used in times past to murder an unwanted spouse! A great way to do away with an unwanted husband or wife but not a great nutritional element!

Ncbi states that, "Arsenic disrupts male reproduction by direct effects on the male gonads or modulates pituitary activity, which causes disruption of androgen secretion from Leydig cells, decrease testosterone levels within the testes and spermatogenesis in seminiferous tubules."

If that wasn't enough to convince you here are the differences in the nutritional values of white and brown rice.

A cup of white rice contains 205 kcal, it provides 44g of carbs, 0.6g of fibre and 4g of protein. A cup of brown rice contains more kcal, 216, but also provides 44g of carbs but has a much higher fibre content, 3.5g, and slightly more protein, 5g. But brown rice also has double the amount of manganese, 88% of the daily value. It also has more phosphorus, more than twice the amount of iron, three times more vitamin B3, 4 times more vitamin B1, and 10 times more vitamin B6.

Complex carbs are far superior in terms of digestive health and in fuelling your body with the required energy it needs to function in a healthy way. These carbs are also superior in nutrients that is not limited to fibre but essential micro-nutrients too.

For the optimisation of T levels they are far superior too. And without the T depleting potential of refined carbs.

So that is what you need to consider to help prevent declines in T levels, and to keep those T levels optimised as you age.

Now lets dive in and consider all the things you can do to potentially raise your T levels and to keep them optimised.

19

T Boosting Lifestyle.

T Boosting Lifestyle Choices.

A lot of what I am going to tell you in this section is pretty well known, you only need to go to any search engine and ask "how can I increase my T levels," and this generic information will show up.

There is an abundance of sites giving you this generic info but no full guide to testosterone would be complete without covering all of this. The downside to this generic content is that you will not get anywhere near a full guide, because they keep repeating just those same generic things. I will be as brief as possible and just list these things for you, along with a few explanatory notes. I will place the greater emphasis towards aspects to these things that are not so well known.

In my younger years I did not intentionally set out to increase my testosterone. I had no concerns about T levels, my interest was purely for fitness and training purposes. My energy levels were satisfactory along with my physical performance. And guys were not so concerned about testosterone as they are today. Now that it has become an established fact that men's T levels are declining its a good thing really because being aware of this will give you a better chance to fix this than being completely unaware. Every cloud has a silver lining.

In this half of the book I will share with you everything that I discovered, and have done, in the last 2 decades to maintain my T levels. I will also show you my exact routine, what I do, what I don't do and why I do or don't do these things. In this part of the guide you will discover absolutely everything you can possibly do to augment your T.

Now the medical world states that a good supply of testosterone is fundamental to pretty much every aspect of your body, its function and your quality of life. This is widely agreed upon. Your muscles, libido, heart health, cognitive functioning, your overall mental health, moods and even your testicle and penis size do require enough of this hormone to be functioning efficiently.

If you suffer with low testosterone then these generic commonly known things in this section must always be your primary consideration. Get all these things down first, more often than not it will be something here that you might need to fix. Always examine yourself as an entire organism when trying to determine what the problem might be.

It is important to have all the things in this section down first. Before you try anything else. If you think or you already know you might have a problem, then again look at and address these things listed in this section before you do anything else.

Why? Because if you were to implement absolutely everything I am going to show you right away, all at once then you are not going to know what exactly it is that was wrong. You will not be able to clearly see what it is that is working for you, or not working for you. Knowing the reason for the problem is going to pay off. You can ensure it never happens again. It could be something as simple as tweaking your diet or adding an extra rest day to your training routine.

It is a good idea to carry out self observation to determine whether there could be underlying causes to your low T levels such as bad lifestyle choices, bad diet, bad habits or your mental health or even your environment. Self observation is going to be necessary because as individuals we all have different personal requirements. This part I cannot do for you.

Being stressed, suffering with depression or anxiety, being miserable in your life circumstances or job, bad relationships, all these things can also have a negative effect on your natural hormone production.

But the good news is that the things in this section are all things that are all largely within your control and you can influence these factors and have the power to change them.

Just go through this list and by just changing things up a little in each department in turn, if you feel you need to, you are more likely to see a problem or any room for improvement here.

A study published even linked low testosterone with an increased risk of premature death. So if you think you might have low T levels, get checked out and then start doing something about it.

A fair warning here. If you do get checked out and discover that your levels are below the threshold for being considered low then it is highly likely that you will be offered a pharmaceutical solution to your problem. The medical industry is quite naturally biased towards their own products and solutions. These pharma solutions generate revenue after all.

Western medicine traditionally treats symptoms rather than the root cause. This is probably why so many prescriptions are now handed out for the slightest conditions. Doctors are very busy and often overworked. Often they only have the chance to quickly scan your file briefly before you see them. You are just one face out of the many that they will see that day. I hope that you don't need to see a doctor that often and that they hardly know you.

For this reason they rely upon a quick 2 minute scan of your personal file and they then consult medical books and also their knowledge to give them an idea what to do for you. And the treatment they will prescribe and any options they will consider is based upon this. Bear in mind also that most doctors have their own specialist element in medicine. The doctors that many of us see may or may not be a specialist in that particular field of medicine.

Testosterone replacement must only be considered as an extreme last resort. This means that you have tried everything and the problem still remains.

Take 10 patients all of whom have depression. The root cause of their depression is likely to be different for each individual. Therefore it will take 10 different strategies, each tackling the root cause of each individual case of depression, to cure all of them effectively. In reality even the same group of pills that medical journals recommend for this condition are unlikely to work for all of them.

This principle works for T levels too. The underlying root cause will be different in each individual case.

Always seek to discover the root cause of your problem. Always analyse your lifestyle and habits first otherwise you could end up popping pills or consuming treatments that you don't really need and end up causing more harm than good.

The most important things to address first are your sleep habits, your stress levels, mental state and physical activity along with your body-fat percentage. Establish mental, physical and dietary balance and harmony. If the root cause were to be down to any of these things, then anything else you try, such as supplements are likely to have only a minimal effect.

The main aim of this whole guide is to put forward viable solutions that are an effective alternative to TRT.

Exercise.

We already know that physical exercise is very beneficial to our health and it has been widely accepted that exercise can have a positive effect on your T levels.

One study in 2015, the subjects being obese men, found that increased physical activity was more effective in raising T levels when compared to those just observing calorie restrictions to their diet and taking solely a dietary weight loss route.

Another study, which involved a year long observation, discovered that in a group of men who had never exercised before, their T levels had increased by 15% over that period.

A 2012 study, using a direct comparison of men who did regular exercise compared to a group of men who did not exercise at all, discovered that the group who engaged in regular exercise had T levels ranging from 20-35% higher than the group who did not exercise.

The evidence to support the fact that training does have a correlating effect on raising T levels is abundant. But something that is not so well known is that not all exercises affect T levels in the same way.

The best type of training for boosting T levels by far is resistance and weight training. Using what are known as compound movements being the most effective. Compound exercise examples being squats, dead-lifts, bench press, military press etc. It has been proven by research that this type of training gives increased T levels in both the short term and in the long term.

One study concluded that after just one 30 minute weight training session, T levels increased by up to 21.6%. They then subjected the men to strength and resistance training 3 times per week for 4 weeks and noticed increased T levels ranging from 15-30%.

Various studies have concluded that with regular resistance training that these increases in T levels could be sustained over long periods of time.

Another very effective exercise method proven to raise T levels in men is HIIT, or High Intensity Interval Training. Basically this is training involving short bursts of intense efforts followed by brief rest periods. It can be done using many different movements and forms.

One study discovered that 90 second sprints followed by 90 seconds rest, then repeated multiple times over a 45 minute period was far more effective at elevating T levels, than just running for 45 minutes non stop.

Another great training method for boosting T levels is circuit training. This type of training involves doing a circuit of different exercises one after another. When you have completed the group of exercises you then take a brief rest and then repeat the circuit.

It is similar to HIIT, but the idea is to build a circuit combining sets of exercises that work different muscle groups, which provides more of a complete body workout.

A simple example would be 20 pullups followed by 50 pushups, then 50 dips, finishing with 50 squats. Then rest for 60-120 seconds and then repeat. The set is the completion of all the exercises in the circuit. In a typical circuit training session you would be aiming to complete between 7 and 10 sets. The variations are limitless you can increase the number of exercises in each set as you become more proficient and also you can do this using resistance bands or weights too.

It might be surprising that research shows that most types of cardio exercise such as running and long distance cycling do not have much effect on T levels. The most effective training methods all seem to follow a principle of short bursts of very intense activity followed by brief rest periods before repeating the burst of activity.

A word of warning about training. We all know there is a lot of benefit to training but there are some who believe in training every single day and who promote skipping a day as something to be ashamed of. This is bad advice and will have a detrimental effect over time.

Taken to excess, over training will actually LOWER your T levels. Even if you are training using the methods that are proven to work best. And this has been proven by research. Rest and recovery are vital elements to training and vital in maintaining T levels. More exercise volume does not result in bigger T gains.

Over training often leads to prolonged fatigue, disturbed sleep and depression and irritability, which ironically are also symptoms of low testosterone. If you are over training and have decreased your T levels by doing this, then addressing your approach to your exercise regime should redress the balance.

My own regime consists of training two consecutive days followed by a rest day, this being repeated in a continuous cycle. In addition, once every 3 months or so I will take a full week off and fully abstain from all training. Allowing the body to recover is absolutely vital to maintaining T levels.

This is observing a balance. Now from this you can deduce that I am training only 4 times per week and there will be many that will say that I am not grinding hard enough and disagree with this regime as not being enough.

But a detailed analysis of all the studies into the effects of exercise on testosterone levels reveal that it is a little more complicated. Yes training can benefit testosterone production but training every day will have the opposite effect.

Regular exercise is recommended for improved health and for effective weight management. And it is these elements, or benefits, of training that contribute to more efficient and balanced hormone levels.

There are certain training methods and intensities that can lead to increased T levels. But there are also training methods and intensities that can crash T levels. And everyone is different and the corresponding results and effects will be different, depending on the individual. There are many factors to consider.

In the case of individuals who have not engaged in exercise before who then begin to do so, there has been noted an overall improvement to T levels. Many of the studies into the effects of exercise on testosterone have involved candidates who were overweight, or who previously led sedentary lifestyles. So for these individuals in particular they can and have increased their testosterone production.

And it was also confirmed that dietary improvements, combined with exercise, was far more effective at raising T levels than just dietary considerations alone. Improved health, the diet and training combined, and effective weight management, the diet and training combined, are the underlying factors that resulted in increases in T levels.

So this means that it would maybe be more accurate to say that: "Improved health and effective weight management obtained through improvements to diet and engaging in physical exercise improves T levels, in those not previously engaging in exercise and observing a healthy well balanced diet." This would be far more accurate than just saying that exercise raises T levels.

And the studies seem to correlate to that statement.

A study on elite athletes in 2018, suggested that some elite athletes had low testosterone levels and that could be attributed to higher blood cortisol levels from working out. It was observed in these men that the training did boost T levels, but that increase did not last long. Their levels returned to their normal baseline levels after no more than a few hours. This study also observed that their training did not "significantly change testosterone level."

These subjects are obviously guys with a well established habit of already observing a good diet and training hard on a regular basis. And in the case of elite athletes it can be presumed that they train most days, and that the training involved is at a very high intensity? A different set of results when compared to overweight men and men who lead a sedentary lifestyle?

These candidates were all observed to be in excellent shape, and had no obvious symptoms of low testosterone levels. And the researchers stated that having no symptoms of low T is more important than your actual T level.

In fact it is the guys who have high body fat percentages that are overweight who are more likely to actually experience symptoms of having low testosterone.

So keeping your energy levels consistent, developing muscles and having good bodily function, having a balanced metabolic rate, and effective weight management, is going to *prevent* all the health issues associated with unhealthy living. And it is these factors that are going to keep T levels good.

The reality is this. If you are leading a sedentary lifestyle then training will increase your T levels. Continuing to train will help you to maintain and keep those gains.

If you are observing a bad unhealthy diet and you switch to a healthy well balanced diet, then this will increase your T levels. Keeping to this healthy well balanced diet will help you to maintain and keep those gains.

Combining these two factors together will give you the best results and optimum T levels. Sticking to this combined regime will allow you to maintain those gains for years to come. Once you have reached this level then it is unlikely that you will see any further significant gains to your T levels. At this point just keep maintaining that rhythm.

The concept is similar to weight training and developing muscle mass. You will reach your full genetic potential. When this happens you will likely plateau and further gains are going to be hard. In effect you have optimised your physical body and the best strategy from here is to maintain those benefits. Your T levels are the same.

This is contrary to popular belief but it is a fact. Once you are at your optimal the best most effective strategy is to keep that up and keep it going.

Eating a healthy, well balanced diet.

Attention to diet is usually observed by anyone engaging in physical training. Diet is an important part of training, which also correlates to T levels. It is so important that this gets further attention in detail in the sections further on in this book. For now I want to bring to your attention to lesser known things about dieting that can actually harm T levels.

Your diet is one of the things commonly associated with improving your T levels. It is well known that having a body fat percentage that is too high can result in lower T levels. Keeping this in check can no doubt improve T levels, but what is not often considered is that low body fat, which is too low, can have an equally detrimental effect.

And for those who pursue an aesthetic physique and maintain low body fat percentages over time this can have a catastrophic effect on T levels. And of course optimum body fat percentages will vary among individuals according to size, body type and genetics. This only serves to confuse matters even further.

When it comes to achieving a lean, ripped and conditioned physique, the guys with a slim linear body type will have the advantage. These men are naturally inclined towards being able to function and to keep energy levels optimised with lower body fat percentages than bigger bulky guys.

So what is the optimum body fat percentage for maintaining good T levels?

The average "healthy"man's body fat tends to be somewhere in between 10 and 20%. Of that, 3% is considered to be essential, meaning anything less and you would simply die.

Anything below 5%, regardless of body type, is considered to be too low and is a sign of poor health. And this includes athletes. It just isn't biologically viable for a human to sustain extremely low body fat over extended periods of time. Combining that state with intense physical activity is a recipe for disaster.

In the case of competing body-builders, leading up to the competition day they will be aiming to achieve less than 5% body fat in order to give the best, most aesthetically pleasing appearance of their musculature and muscle definition that they possibly can. They are judged on their entire physique and just the difference of just 1 or 2% extra body fat could have a detrimental effect on how they place in the competition.

I have spoken to many body-builders and they all state that leading up to and on competition day they feel like crap and are pretty run down. But realise that they do not stay in this state off season. They all told me that after the competition is over they binge on calories for a few weeks in order to recover. Considering the extremes that they are going to, this comes as no surprise.

In a particular study, observing (natural and not enhanced) subjects during preparation leading up to body-building competitions, the average competitor's T levels dropped by up to 75% during the cutting cycle leading up to the competition.

Without enough body fat your endocrine system, your reproductive system, your central nervous system, your cardiovascular system and skeletal system are not able to function normally.

In the same study it was also noted that these same competitors also experienced decreases in heart rates. In most of the subjects, their resting heart rate dropped to below 30 BPM.

Having an extremely low body fat percentage does affect the cardiovascular system's ability to function normally and consistently. If your heart rate becomes too low, a condition called bradycardia, this can lead to spells of dizziness and even passing out and heart attacks.

Also consider that the nutritional and calorific deficit often required to maintain extremely low body fat percentages can cause cardiac arrhythmias and can even cause sudden death.

This could be what occurred to the You Tube influencer Alex Eubank. He is well known for having an amazingly chiselled physique and had maintained very low body fat percentages over quite a long period of time. One day, while he was observing a fast, he felt unwell during a training session and had to be rushed to hospital. Fortunately he survived.

Taken to this kind of extreme the pursuit of the perfectly aesthetic physique can have a detrimental effect on your health. Alex is just a young 20 something. Taking your fitness to an extreme can often have the opposite effect it can even be hazardous to your health.

Another side effect of low body fat is the depletion of energy levels. Without any stores of fat your body, in effect, has little or no reserved energy. Without sufficient energy stores your body cannot function at optimal, or even normal levels over prolonged periods simply because it is being starved of energy. Think of an elastic band. You stretch it and stretch it, it becomes overloaded and then it will break. Your body is the same. And consider that getting your body fat this low often involves going into a calorific deficit and this will ultimately lead to nutritional deficiencies.

Nutritional deficiencies have also been linked to drops in thyroid hormone production. And thyroid activity is known to have a corresponding affect on T levels. Nutritional deficiencies in themselves are known to lower T levels in some cases.

According to the National Library of Medicine, "thyroid stimulating hormone is known to affect the metabolism of testosterone and all androgens through mediating sex hormone binding globulin levels, which alters levels of free and bound (total) testosterone."

Many different sources agree that a healthy thyroid function is fundamental to helping to maintain good T levels.

Depleted thyroid hormone production also plays a part in fatigue and energy levels.

Nutritional deficiencies are also associated with poor health. They can contribute to diseases and health issues just as much as nutritional overload.

And of course with a nutritional deficiency, your workouts will then suffer. And your muscles will struggle to recover from the exercise.

This is because when your body fat is too low, your levels of glycogen are also very low. Glycogen is effectively carbohydrates that are stored in your muscles and liver. This glycogen is absolutely vital to enabling your body to recover from exercise.

To fuel the body and aid recovery these stores must be replenished and maintained. We all know that exercise takes up energy. Recovery also requires energy.

Another problem with low body fat, and the corresponding nutritional deficiencies, you will probably be left feeling hungry all the time.

What happens is that all the constant dieting required to get your body fat down to these levels will also decrease your levels of leptin. Leptin is a hormone that is produced by body fat cells.

Low leptin levels trigger the hypothalamus, a gland involved in the production of testosterone, to sense this drop and to initiate an increase to your appetite to compensate. This results in you feeling hungry.

Via signals in the brain the hypothalamus and pituitary glands, on detecting low leptin levels, then signal to your testicles to produce less testosterone. Without addressing the nutritional deficiency, the body naturally goes into survival mode. In survival mode the body is concerned with survival and not in making testosterone. All resources are re-directed towards essential and immediate survival mechanisms.

So the ultimate effect this all has is, any muscle gain becomes extremely difficult in men who have extremely low body fat percentages. The muscles become weaker and muscle mass effectively drops. This constitutes the main reason for many guys jumping on TRT, steroids or other PEDs in an attempt to counter the problem.

But the real problem lies in the obsession of pursuing an aesthetic physique. The sense of never being satisfied and always seeking visible improvements. This psychiatric condition is know as body dysmorphia. Their physique looks amazing to everyone else but they themselves cannot see that.

And if this wasn't bad enough, if your leptin levels become too low, and thus your testosterone levels also become too low as a result, this can lead to hypogonadism. This effectively means that the body's reproductive system can be disrupted, or even shut down completely. This of course is a worst case scenario, but it is almost a certainty that your T levels will crash.

By starving yourself of enough calories, ignoring your appetite and depleting your energy levels further, you are instructing your body to go even further into survival mode. The body is no longer concerned with reproducing so your sperm count will drop and you may develop problems in getting or maintaining an erection.

Very low body fat and energy levels has also been linked to higher cortisol levels, which as we know can have a detrimental effect on T levels. All of this creates additional stresses on the body. High cortisol levels also have an effect on our immune system, leaving us more susceptible to becoming sick. This can also hamper your body's ability to absorb vitamin D, which also plays a significant part to your T levels.

Body fat is also important for cognitive function. Having low levels of essential fatty acids could result in an increase in irritability and poor moods and can even be attributed to mood swings. This can lead to having difficulty in concentrating and mental fatigue, or brain fog.

For those of you concerned with your appearance, your looks or the natural effects of ageing, the fats in your body are also important for maintaining healthy looking skin. There is a tendency in people pursuing low body fat percentages to not be eating a lot of carbs. Low carb diets also cause low T levels. More on that later.

Consuming carbs enables the body to store water. Without enough carbs in your diet you can become dehydrated. Your body compensates by drawing water from your skin. With your body effectively in survival mode the water is re-directed to your vital organs and your skin then becomes dry and more prone to blemishes.

So we can see that having body fat that is either too high or too low can have a negative effect on our T levels. So what is the ideal body fat percentage for men?

This of course varies between individuals as determined by size and composition as we all have different requirements. The trick is to be able to fine tune our body function to its own individual optimum levels.

Now I am a guy who is quite short and lean. I am 55kg and 165cm. I am of below average size and mass. Although capable of going a bit lower, I tend to maintain my body fat at between 10 and 15%. I do this because at this percentage my energy and vitality levels are optimised.

At this percentage I have a flat, hard abdomen. On waking in the morning after a good nights sleep, and not consuming food for the previous 8 hours, my abs are usually quite visible. However they usually disappear after eating something.

Lets say that I wanted to do a photo shoot and to be looking my best. This doesn't happen often at my age! For me I could observe a high protein low carb diet for 3 to 5 days and my abs would become pretty well defined. I have a fast metabolic rate, which of course reduces the time needed to make this happen.

But I would also notice a slight drop in energy and motivation levels when it comes to training. Not a great difference but enough so that I would notice it. I have discovered that after increasing my carb intake, it enables me to redress the balance in no more than a couple of days. But please bear in mind I have been training a long time and my body is fine tuned to my own personal requirements and that it has taken some years to figure out and to achieve this state.

For you it will no doubt be different as chances are, your personal requirements are not the same as mine.

To help explain all this better let us consider exactly what is meant by body fat.

Fat is an organ that is essential for human life. There are different kinds of fat and each serves its own purpose and has its own function. For our purposes here we shall focus on two kinds of fat. Visceral fat and subcutaneous fat.

Visceral fat is the fat that is stored around your vital organs. When you first begin a weight loss regime this is the fat that you tend to lose first. This explains why you might initially see a decrease in weight without appearing to look any slimmer.

This harmful fat if allowed to accumulate around the organs is what ultimately contributes to all the health problems associated with being overweight.

Subcutaneous fat is the fat that is stored between the skin and musculature. It is our layer of insulation and this is the fat that serves the role of stored energy. In the case of an individual with a sedentary lifestyle these stored fats are likely to accumulate and thus are what give an overweight person the physical appearance of being obese. This occurs by simply failing to efficiently use up the store of fat.

Our ancient ancestors, who were hunter gatherers, did not always have access to food. It would have been these stores of fat they would have relied upon to survive until more food could be acquired. Basically something that is hard-wired into us by nature as a survival mechanism. Of course in the modern western societies in which we live, for most of us, we have easy and constant access to food so our stored fats are hardly ever relied upon in the same way as they were for our ancestors.

So the fundamental principle of developing a lean athletic physique is the consuming of these fat stores and the energy they provide, in order to fuel the workouts required for muscle development and conditioning. In order to keep that going, the stores must be continually replenished and maintained. The optimum being neither to little nor too much. The secret sauce is finding that harmonious balance that works best for you.

This is why body fat is important. For you as an individual it is important to find your own optimum functioning level of body fat. And this will be different for everyone.

Knowing your own optimal body fat percentage is a good measurement to gauge your real level of fitness and function. And real fitness amounts to having sufficient and consistent energy and vitality and this energy and vitality be naturally aspirated and not coming with the help of performance enhancing drugs or other unhealthy practises.

There are so many institutions giving different numbers for different age groups when it comes to body fat percentages. It can cause confusion because these do not take into account lifestyle and fitness levels. They are just guidelines and general recommendations. These are obviously a good place to start. I cannot give you a magic number because we are all different. But I can offer some guidelines.

To give you an idea, here are the recommended percentages for men that are quoted by the American Council on Exercise. I feel that of all the versions that I came across this one seems to be the best for our purposes here because it has an emphasis on individuals who engage in physical training. And anyone interested in T levels will need to consider physical activity.

Essential fat - 2-5%
Athletes - 6-13%
Fitness - 14-17%
Acceptable - 18-24%
Obesity - Over 25%.

The same institution gives a range of between 6 and 10% as being the optimal body fat level to get your abs to show. Of course don't forget that this will fluctuate according to your weight, height and body type.

Often any issue with energy or T levels could be addressed by tweaking the diet, and a slight increase to body fat stores. Your training parter might function completely fine with 8% body fat. The same percentage for you could cause your energy levels to crash or for problems to show themselves. This is why we should be placing an emphasis on our own personalised body fat levels when seeking to increase and maintain good T levels.

Maintaining a healthy balanced diet is listed as one of the most important things men can do to maintain their T levels and this is absolutely true. I go into more detail on this later when we look at the optimal T boosting diet. I have included a section both on foods that kill T levels and T boosting foods separately to emphasise some do's and don't's.

Therefore it suffices to say here only that a nutritious diet based upon whole foods is best. Be sure to include a healthy balance of protein, carbs and fat. A balanced diet is fundamental to T levels and for your overall health.

A word of warning here. In a society that thrives on seeking quick results there can be a tendency when beginning a weight loss regime to attempt to drop weight quickly. Many begin with enthusiasm and set targets of so many pounds in the first month and think more of the numbers and the targets rather than long term plans.

This is the dark side of weight loss and T levels. Drop too much weight too quickly and it can cause your T levels to crash. Combined with exercise and that increases the likelihood of this occurring.

A number of studies have investigated the effects of rapid weight loss on testosterone levels and have come to the conclusion that a rapid fat loss causes a decrease in T levels. By as much as 63%. Think about it. If you are dropping weight to improve your T levels because they are a bit low causing them to crash could prove to be a disaster. A further crash will affect your exercise regime and you could experience symptoms of low T.

One study observed the levels of testosterone and Lutenizing hormone in the male participants. After 3 weeks of intense physical exercise and intense dieting, which helped them to drop weight quickly researchers discovered that their levels of testosterone and LH had significantly dropped.

Their levels were found to have dropped by as much as 63% and the underlying cause of this was undernourishment caused by severe dieting. And of course lower T levels will make it harder to drop weight effectively and to keep maintaining that weight loss.

Just something to be aware of. I am not trying to sink your weight loss plans, only to make you aware of what could possibly happen if you go about trying to drop weight quickly.

In the section on T boosting diet I put forward a suggestive strategy for both weight loss and weight gain (bulking) that will help to prevent this occurring. By gradually dropping the weight you are far more likely to keep the weight off long term and to effectively manage your weight much more efficiently.

Sleep.

It is quite common for sleep to be associated with male T levels. Medical science suggests that we should be getting at least 7 hours sleep every night.

When we are deprived of sleep this can, and does, lead to decreases in our testosterone. This can also have a detrimental effect on our energy levels and physical training too.

Why is sleep so important? Because the majority of your daily testosterone release happens during sleep. Testosterone production begins to increase when you first fall asleep. Production peaks during REM, Rapid Eye Movement, sleep. It will remain high while you sleep but tends to be depleted all the time you are awake. And of course T levels are usually higher in the mornings. This is a natural occurrence. T levels *rise* during sleep. Testosterone is *made* while you are asleep.

A thing to consider with sleep and testosterone is that a lack of sleep can contribute toward lowering T levels. Low T levels can cause insomnia, and difficulties in getting undisturbed sleep, which in turn, can further reduce T levels. As this can easily spiral out of control it is something important to consider for men and prevention seems to be the best course of action.

The effects of sleep deprivation, even over a short period of time, can lower T levels by a similar amount to that of ageing 10 to 15 years.

In one study involving 10 men in their early 20s all of whom had a similar body mass index were subjected to sleep deprivation for a week and they recorded effects this would have on testosterone. The additional criteria for test subjects were no history of endocrine or mental disorders, irregular sleep times or any sleep problems.

Prior to the commencement of the test the men were instructed to sleep for 8 hours, between the hours of 11pm and 7am at home. The subjects then spent 10 days in the lab under supervision where they were allowed to sleep for 10 hours for the first three nights, followed by a week of being deprived of sleep. Only 5 hours sleep per night.

In just one week the T levels in this group of men were seen to have fallen by 10 to 15%. Considering that as we age our levels are estimated to drop by 1% per year this is the equivalent to ageing by 10 to 15 years.

Another study demonstrated that T levels increase as the sleep duration increased. But this corresponding increase was only evident up to 9.9 hours. Any increases in sleep duration after this point resulted in testosterone decreasing. Again we seem to be finding that balance is the key. Not too little and not too much.

The best strategy for sleep is to get your body clock accustomed to sleeping and waking at roughly the same hours. Many guys obviously tend to sleep for longer on days that they are off work. Try to avoid doing this. The main benefit of having a structured and consistent sleep habit is that you increase the likelihood of getting enough sleep on a regular basis.

Irregular sleep hours, and going to bed or waking at different times, can play havoc with your body clock. This kind of habit is highly likely to initiate a sleep problem.

We can all appreciate having a thought out and prepared training routine and it is an excellent idea to adopt a similar approach to your sleep. It is best to have a sleep routine that you adhere to.

While we are on the subject of training it is suggested that getting plenty of physical activity can help you sleep better. However it is best to avoid any physical exercise before bedtime they say. Personally I train about an hour after waking. My reasoning behind this is that first and foremost you are physically replenished and refreshed after sleeping. Also your T levels tend to be higher in the morning and this I believe has a positive effect on exercise performance.

However not all forms of physical activity are the same. As we know traditional bedroom activities can help to induce sleep after climaxing, especially in men!

Going back to the ideal body fat concept, medical science attributes a healthy body weight being conducive to a good nights sleep. It has been found that being overweight can reduce the amount and the quality of your sleep. This is all interrelated of course.

Another consideration is your sleeping environment. A good quality mattress and pillows can make all the difference. If you are not comfortable then it stands to reason that this is going to have a detrimental effect on the quality and duration of your sleep. Other environmental factors to consider are that that the room you sleep in should ideally be as quiet and as dark as possible.

In cities especially, there is likely to be noise and almost certainly light interference from street lights. Light has been linked to the suppression of the sleep hormone melatonin so reducing light should be a priority in your sleeping area. If you have these kind of disturbances in your locale then they can be easily solved with black out curtains or blinds, and a set of ear plugs to filter out any noise.

Having an ideal environment and surroundings can play a big part in ensuring a good nights sleep. Sleep experts also say that the temperature is conducive to improving sleep and they recommend keeping the ambient temperature between 65 and 68 degrees farenheit.

This one is pretty obvious, to limit your caffeine intake, especially later in the day. Now caffeine has been linked to increasing T levels and I will get into that in another section, but avoiding any stimulants in the second half of the day is definitely the way to go.

Another obvious thing to avoid is eating too close to bedtime or consuming big meals very late in the day. The reasons for this of course is that it is never a good idea to lay flat with a full stomach and our digestive system relies on gravity for optimum efficiency and it improves digestive performance by remaining upright for at least an hour or two after eating. A full stomach can of course directly affect sleep.

Now I have been guilty of breaking a few of these rules at times and sometimes it cannot be avoided. I have lived in many different places and circumstances and these have come with frequent alterations to my schedule.

When this kind of thing occurs, and it often does, for example when changing job, or changing your working hours, then always strive to adapt to your new schedule quickly. Always get quickly back into a pattern of sleeping and waking at the same times. Even if that means changing the times you go to sleep and wake up. Consistency is the key.

I have spent many years volunteering overseas and often in adverse and challenging and even in sometimes dangerous circumstances. And at times this has led to me developing sleep disorders. When you are functioning in this way, and adopting a tendency to sleep with one eye open, then you end up after time training yourself to stay awake and aware even when you feel tired. And when you do sleep it is not of long duration and not deep sleep.

The best way of describing this is that you come to a position of going beyond tiredness. On returning to normal life it is extremely difficult to just revert back to your old sleeping patterns. For me this took a while to fix, the solution I devised was to consume chamomile tea, which is available with added melatonin.

Melatonin also happens to promote testosterone secretion in the Leydig cells in the testicles, and enhance the production of testosterone. Studies have shown that taking melatonin supplements before bedtime can increase morning testosterone levels by up to 20%.

Now, I am still doing this every night and it has proven to be an excellent remedy and cure for sleep disorders. If you are suffering with any sleep deprivation or sleep disorder I would highly recommend that you give it a try. Do not expect instant results and exercise a little patience. This method does not induce sleep in the same way that a sleeping pill does, but it comes without any adverse side effects, like drowsiness in the morning or being reliant on a pill to sleep.

I would of course highly recommend that you never get yourself into this position if you can, but sometimes it cannot be avoided. I am lucky because I was relatively accustomed to adversity and harsh living conditions but not everyone is suited to this kind of lifestyle.

I would like to make it clear that I am not recommending melatonin as a testosterone boosting hack. It is after all an artificial sleep aid. It is a sleep aid containing natural ingredients and melatonin is a hormone released naturally by the brain to make us sleep. But if you do not already have any existing sleep issues then I would highly recommend that you do not use any sleep aids at all.

Natural secretion of melatonin will boost your T levels when you are asleep anyway. So why take something you don't really need?

You have to work with what you got and this applies to me too. Being a person with a history of sleep issues I found a solution that works well. If I did not have any sleep issues I would have never considered taking melatonin even for T boosting reasons.

I now observe a rigid and ordered sleeping regime. I eat my last meal of the day at least 2 hours before bedtime. After this meal I relax and wind down both mentally and physically. This usually includes some contemplation, awareness and meditation practises.

At my bedtime, usually around 20:45, I will drink my chamomile tea with melatonin, then brush my teeth. I use bicarbonate of soda to avoid using toothpastes containing endocrine disruptors.

I then get into bed at 21:00 and read for an hour. A lifelong habit, being someone who enjoys continually studying and seeking to improve my knowledge.

Now one last thing that is commonly recommended by sleep experts and that is to keep screen time to a minimum before bedtime. This is because the blue light from device screens can affect your sleep patterns. Yes I break this rule because most of the books I buy now are e books and I use a tablet to read from. I do however turn off the blue light as this device allows me to do so.

After an hour of reading, around 22:00, I begin to feel tired and I sleep through until between 06:00 and 07:00 the following day. I am getting somewhere between 8 and 9 hours of uninterrupted sleep each night.

My bedroom has sliding shutters, which are all the way down to blacken out the room. The mattress I sleep on and my pillows are made from memory foam and are very comfortable and they mould to the shape of your form. They are very good for getting a good nights sleep, quite expensive but well worth the money considering the benefits.

Stress.

Stress is commonly known to cause raised levels of cortisol, which interferes with the normal functioning of the hypothalamus and pituitary glands and can have an adverse affect on T levels. This is pretty well known so no further explanation is really necessary.

What is not often considered is that there are different types of stress situations and some of these can be good and beneficial to us and some not so good.

Good stress can be something like rising to a challenge, taking a risk or stepping outside of your comfort zone and feeling rewarded or benefited in some way for your efforts. Physical training and any other kinds of physical or mental exertions or challenges are also in a way types of good stress.

This is positive so keep doing these things. This kind of stress is not usually harmful and in most people almost never causes a problem, only when taken to extreme excesses.

The more you engage in practising situations of good stress the more resilient you will be at handling and managing the bad stress situations.

Stress management is important because experts say that when stress is "potent and unresolved," this is the point at which it begins to play a role in reducing T levels.

COMPLETE GUIDE TO TESTOSTERONE   201

Stress is a powerful thing because it can cause the production of stress hormones, such as cortisol. These stress hormones can not only affect your testosterone levels but also affect other areas of your life such as sleep, energy levels, overall mood and mental health, which can then further reduce your T levels. This is the vicious circle that can drag you into trouble if you are not careful.

For an excellent and effective strategy to become more accustomed to managing stress and using it to your advantage see my book, The Art to Masculinity, which explains in detail the processes I used to no longer be affected by stress in any way.

Experts also agree that the best way of solving the issue is to manage your stress. This is easily said of course but not so easy to do. But solving this issue first will actually help improve symptoms of low testosterone.

And in a reversal of the vicious cycle described above, if you can get your T levels back on track, this in turn is going work wonders for your stress management.

Another important thing is to take regular rest. Recovery from stress is just as important as recovery times from training. And of course training stresses the body too. And don't forget that the best thing you can do is to allow your mind to relax, in order to restore its energy levels and effect its own recovery in just the same way as you do for your body and its sleep.

The best formula bar none for mental relaxation and mental restoration is meditation. Just 10 minutes per day can make a real difference.

Increase Vitamin D Intake.

This is not so commonly known but vitamin D intake or sun exposure can have an affect on your T levels. Research has indicated a possible correlation between low testosterone being linked to low vitamin D levels. This fact is well established by many studies. In general men's testosterone levels are usually higher in summer months when compared to winter months where sunlight exposure can be limited.

If you live in a warm sunny climate then problem solved easily. Just go outside for at least 30 minutes, preferably an hour, each day, and you will get enough vitamin D. That's all it takes.

If you live in a colder climate, or as most of us do, a fluctuating climate where sun is only available for a portion of the year then this is of course going to prove difficult.

In this situation you will benefit from taking a vitamin D supplement. I use a vitamin D supplement myself. I will dive into supplements and natural testosterone boosters in more detail in the next section.

One test in 2017, involving men with a vitamin D deficiency, found that by taking a vitamin D supplement every day, resulted in increased T levels and improvements to erectile dysfunction.

One scientific article that I came across agreed that sunlight exposure elevates vitamin D levels and that vitamin D is thought of as a testosterone booster this is widely agreed upon.

The article stated that exposing your testicles to a few minutes of direct sunlight a day can help T levels. It goes on to recommend doing this in the early morning or late evening to avoid any cases of sunburn! This one could prove difficult as most beaches tend to be busy when the sun shines. You could be accused of untoward behaviour by exposing your testicles in a public place!

Now while we are considering supplements let us now consider the many supplements that are reputed to boost testosterone levels which are now available.

20

T Boosting Supplements.

There are many essential vitamins and minerals that can be beneficial to our T levels and many of them can be obtained in the relevant quantities from our diet but sometimes it can be very beneficial to supplement these levels to ensure you are getting enough of them to be functioning at an optimal level.

When considering supplements always seek to source quality ingredients and avoid buying cheap products. Cheap supplement products often use poor quality ingredients. They often contain other dubious ingredients and sometimes lack purity and also the actual content of the beneficial element is often very small or only in trace amounts.

Good quality products using the best purest ingredients are always the better option.

I have experimented with many of these products and supplements. After many years of experimenting I have now got this down to a core of supplements that I use on a regular basis as part of my own personal regime. I will reveal my own recommendations based upon these findings in the final chapter.

Something that is very important to note is that many supplements are best cycled to get the best benefits. I have noticed that with many supplements, you can build up a tolerance to them with regular use, and they can then tend to lose their effectiveness. However this does not apply to *all* supplements.

Always carry out your own research into any supplement before taking it. Even the ones that I am going to recommend. This is because supplements often have side effects. They can also interact or interfere with medical conditions and medications. Not all supplements are suitable for everyone.

When you have conducted all your own research and then decided that a supplement is for you, always start with a smaller dosage and observe for any signs of unwanted side effects. Only increase the amount when you are satisfied that it agrees with you.

Also for the same reasons never introduce multiple supplements into your body at the same time. Introduce them one at a time. If you were to experience side effects you would not be sure which supplement was causing you the problem.

You would then have to stop them all and backtrack to single out the offender. It can save you time.

Testosterone Boosters.

For gym regulars you are probably already familiar with products, sold in many gym nutritional suppliers, which are collectively known, and marketed as, Testosterone Boosters.

These products are also used by pro body-builders when they are off cycle as a means of post cycle therapy, or PCT. PCT is a practise aimed at attempting to restore natural testosterone production after a steroid cycle. These products can also be very beneficial for the purpose of naturally increasing and also in maintaining natural T levels.

Another challenge is that because there are so many different brands and many of them have just as many different ingredient variations. Usually they consist of a combination of various supplements along with some beneficial vitamins and minerals.

This can cause much confusion as to which ones to buy and which one will work best for you. One thing to be aware of though is that much of the research and data on the actual effectiveness of these products is supplied by the supplement industry themselves. Naturally they tend to show favour and bias towards their own products. Also many fitness blogs and fitness channels will highly recommend supplements that they earn commissions on. Just be aware.

Another point to consider is that the models used in the marketing content for many of these supplements are often guys who are enhanced unnaturally. This can give a very misguided impression as to the true effectiveness and real potential of these products. In reality they are giving the impression that you can get a similar physique to the model in the advertising, which of course you cannot. Of course this is not categorically stated but it is implied suggestively. Otherwise why would they use these models? Because this sells more products. The customers want the physique of the models!

The model in the ads is probably using the products for post cycle therapy, if they are using them at all. His physique gains were achieved with PEDs.

Just bear this in mind. They are useful supplements but don't expect the results you see in the advertising.

But thankfully there has been a lot of research into many of the various core ingredients that are included in these products, so for our purposes here we shall focus on these ingredients themselves rather than specific brands or products that are available. This will help you to be aware of the ingredients to look out for should you feel that this kind of product may be of any use to you.

A word of warning here. With many T boosters of this nature they can, possibly, and only in some cases, cause natural testosterone production to slow down. This we want to avoid. Our aim here is to augment and optimise our natural levels in the long term and to keep this going as we get older. Any form of artificially hiking your T levels comes with the risk of disrupting your natural production.

We should be aiming for supplementation that will benefit us and provide results. That can also be used on a regular basis without causing any harm to our natural hormone production.

What we should also not be doing is seeking quick results that may well work wonders in the short term and have a marked and noticeable effect but which may result in a negative long term effect and an eventual reduction in T levels. Always keep this in mind when considering *any* form of supplementation.

Warning: Always conduct your own extensive research into any of these supplement stacks before diving in. Better still to research each ingredient. Most of these supplement stacks have a full ingredients list available to view.

Often these supplements are not suitable with people with certain health conditions and can often interact with any medication you may be taking. Another benefit of conducting your own research is that you can become aware of any possible side effects that could occur. Then you will know what to be on the lookout for.

In the case of T booster supplements it can be very beneficial to scan the user reviews that have been left for products to be aware of any positive, or negative experiences that consumers have had when using the product. For this I would recommend looking at 3rd party marketplaces like Amazon for these reviews, rather than the ones provided on the manufacturer's own website, which are naturally going to be biased in favour of their own product. Even supplement stores can be biased as supplement sales are their income. They are being paid to recommend them to you.

Usually these products are sold in quantities to give you a 30 day supply at their, the manufacturer's, recommended dosages. It is also recommended that these products should not be used continuously, but rather used in cycles of one month on followed by one month off. There is a good reason for this. You will build up a tolerance to them. And some can slow down natural testosterone production.

Another thing to consider here is that their recommended dosages are based upon a guy of average size and weight. So what this can mean is that their recommended dosages could be too much for smaller guys and not enough for bigger guys. Always bear this in mind when using any supplements. Fine tune your intake to your own personal requirements and circumstances.

To be honest in my own personal experience there is no one brand or product that I can say really stands out above and beyond all the others. Truth is many of them are equally as effective and will give you similar results. I have also found that you quickly build up a tolerance to them and they lose their effectiveness very quickly. I have found it is certain single ingredient supplements that make the real difference.

There has been some research too and the general consensus among medical experts is that these products can have a benefit to your T levels. But proceed with caution. This research concludes that these T boosters are most beneficial in cases where low T levels are the actual root cause of the problem. And that they are best employed alongside a good diet and exercise.

For guys who already workout, especially guys who have been working out long enough to have reached their full genetic muscle mass capabilities, do not expect much from these supplements. They will not increase your performance. They will not make you stronger or enable you to lift more. They do not make much of a difference to your energy levels. They certainly *do not* live up to the hype and marketing claims that are made about them.

On the plus side I did not experience any detrimental effects. No catabolic reactions or crashes of energy. Just a few days of feeling more energised and then quickly developing tolerance.

I have wasted a lot of money on these products hoping to break the plateau and make more gains. They are practically useless for this purpose. This advice comes after years of experimenting with them. Choose your supplements wisely. I wasted my time and money so that you don't have to!

My personal recommendation regarding these supplement stack products is that if you are under 40 then they are a complete waste of time and money. Unless of course you already have particularly low T levels. The reason for this is that if you are a young guy, you should currently have good test levels, artificially elevating your T levels might have a detrimental effect.

You could also get unwanted side effects such as acne, mood swings and even aggressive behaviour. They can possibly cause premature thinning of the hair in some cases. Now let us look at these ingredients individually, and all the other supplements that could possibly be useful to us in turn.

D Aspartic Acid.

D aspartic acid is an amino acid that is commonly found present in many T boosters and is also available as a stand alone supplement.

D aspartic acid is known to increase the release of a hormone in the brain that leads to testosterone production.

During research involving healthy men aged between 27 and 37 they observed the effects of D aspartic acid by giving the test subjects supplements to take over a period of 12 days. Out of 23 test subjects, 20 of the men were found to have higher T levels and the average increase was 42%.

After three further days of not taking the supplements their T levels were found to still be 22% higher compared to their levels at the beginning of the trial.

It is interesting to note however that 3 of the test subjects experienced no T level increases. It is important to note that it was not mentioned if these subjects engaged in physical training. If there is no mention of them doing so then they probably didn't.

Research has shown, based upon a comparison of various similar studies, that D aspartic acid seems to be most effective in men who already have low T levels, and in men who do not train regularly.

Also it has been found that there is no noticeable increase in performance and it does not seems to positively affect muscle or strength gains in men who train regularly. It has also been found that it is relatively safe to use in quantities of up to 2000mg on a daily basis for no more than 3 months.

Tribulus Terrestris

Tribulus is a natural herb, derived from a plant that has quite a reputation for its testosterone boosting qualities. As such it is one of the more commonly used core ingredients in T booster products.

Tribulus caught the attention of athletes in the 1980s when some Bulgarian Olympic athletes accredited tribulus as being the secret to some impressive performances that resulted in winning medals in weigh-lifting. It later transpired that they had been using steroids, but since then, there has been a belief that tribulus can enhance athletic performance and elevate T levels in men.

The research into the benefits of tribulus has been pretty extensive and there is an abundance of research to consider. But the problem arises in that there are many conflicting results and findings concerning clinical trials and lab tests.

Now the research does indeed conclude that tribulus increases testosterone levels in males. Male mice and rats. When it comes to humans though there seems to be solid and consistent evidence to suggest that tribulus does not significantly increase T levels in men.

In one particular test involving male athletes, tribulus was shown to indicate improvements in muscle performance, and significant increases in testosterone. But this only occurred for the first 10 days and then ceased. But in other similar tests it has been found to have no significant effect on T levels.

Even though the research seems to support the theory that tribulus does not raise T levels, there is evidence to support the claims that it can increase libido. Researchers discovered that men with libido problems who consumed 1500mg of tribulus per day for 60 days, they all reported an increase in sexual desire. Now as we already know, libido is connected to testosterone levels.

Tribulus has also been shown to have a positive effect on the immune system, to have anti-inflammatory properties and potential in lowering blood sugar levels.

Tribulus is therefore a very useful supplement.

For this reason it could have an effect on natural DHEA production, and DHEA production plays a part in T levels as I will explain shortly.

I have used tribulus and found it to be effective for the first week. For me, I found that I quickly built up a tolerance to it and that prolonged use didn't seem to pay off. But it is still well worth your consideration.

DHEA.

DHEA, or dehydroepiandrosterone, is a naturally occurring hormone produced by your adrenal gland. Because DHEA production declines with age it is considered by some to be an anti ageing supplement. But there is no evidence to support the claims of it having anti ageing properties.

Your natural production of DHEA peaks at around 20-25 years old, the same age that natural testosterone production peaks. By co-incidence your DHEA production declines by roughly 1% per year, which is the same as the natural decline in T levels caused by ageing.

This is because your natural DHEA production affects your testosterone production. Conserving and maintaining your DHEA levels is therefore fundamental to maintaining your natural T levels. DHEA levels play a part in your hormonal balance. Depleted levels of DHEA will probably have a negative effect on T levels.

DHEA is known to improve mood and cognitive function. It has also be shown to increase sexual function and libido and also improve sperm health. It has been linked with reduced body fat and improved skin health and immunity. Healthy levels of natural DHEA also play a fundamental role in the development of muscle mass.

DHEA is what is known as a precursor to testosterone. This means that the body can convert DHEA into testosterone. Studies do indicate that DHEA supplementation does increase testosterone levels in men. Most notably in middle aged men, however men of all ages were noted to have experienced noticeable increases in both total and free testosterone.

Interestingly enough many of these test subjects also reported an increased sense of well being and vitality, of feeling younger, and experiencing improved moods.

Please note that many governing bodies for competitive sports and athletics associations have categorised DHEA as a banned substance. This of course only confirms its effectiveness in boosting T levels. It has also been demonstrated to give an increase in muscle performance, to energy levels and in increasing lean muscle mass.

Another important thing to note is that regular use is extremely likely to have an adverse affect on natural T levels and can slow down or even stop natural testosterone production altogether with prolonged use. Beware of this. For this reason I do not recommend using it.

DHEA can be beneficial to men who have been diagnosed with having low T levels, and that low testosterone has been confirmed to be the root cause of the problem. This means that they have tried everything else first. They have addressed things like diet, activity level, sleep and all possible lifestyle changes first, with none of these things having solved the problem.

There have been some side effects associated with DHEA use. Acne, fatigue, insomnia, high blood pressure, heart palpitations and a reduction of good (HDL) cholesterol.

With the risk also of developing hormonal imbalances, you should probably avoid DHEA supplements completely. Unless you are already suffering with particularly low T levels. Their effectiveness does make them a tempting option.

However when it comes to DHEA, the best strategy is to be doing everything you can to maintain your natural production of this hormone. Balancing all your hormones rather than resorting to direct supplementation of a synthetic derivative of DHEA.

Lets briefly move away from supplements and focus on what we can do to preserve our DHEA levels. There are ways to improve naturally as much as is possible to prevent these levels declining.

Coincidentally, the same basic, generic things that are recommended for improving and maintaining our T levels also apply to our DHEA levels. Regular physical activity, good diet, good sleeping patterns, managing stress and lifestyle changes like keeping alcohol consumption to a minimum are all going to be beneficial to our DHEA levels too. The two are very closely interconnected.

Physical activity has been shown to be very effective at helping to maintain natural DHEA production. Again, resistance training and intense forms of exercise being the most effective, as in the case of with our T levels.

DHEA is produced in the adrenal glands by converting cholesterol and producing DHEA. *Cholesterol is also a building block of natural DHEA production.* The DHEA is then used by the body to produce testosterone.

However when the body is under stress, and by this I mean bad prolonged stress, and not good stress produced by physical activity or being challenged. This bad stress demands the production of cortisol, the stress hormone, and the production of cortisol in the adrenal glands reduces the amount of DHEA that can be produced.

It is a good thing to also avoid over training, because over training can cause a decline in DHEA production.

The shift towards cortisol production basically steals the ingredients necessary for DHEA production and channels them instead into producing cortisol. This explains why stress, especially long term prolonged stress, has such a detrimental effect on our T levels.

Poor diet choices such as high intake of sugar and consuming high amounts of refined carbs increases blood sugar levels and insulin levels. Increased insulin levels also cause reduced DHEA production in the adrenal glands. Insulin is secreted in the pancreas but the body is a very complex organism and all these processes are connected and have an effect on each other.

High blood sugar levels affect vitamin and essential mineral absorption, that also affect the adrenal, which will then reduce DHEA production. This same process also in turn, causes reduced T levels.

First and foremost focus on your lifestyle choices. Pay attention to reducing or eliminating your pharma medications, these can affect natural DHEA production. Get your stress levels under control, get your activity levels up, avoid any nutritional deficiencies, get your blood sugar levels down, hone your diet and fix any sleep problems that you may have.

Also you will want to consider an anti-inflammatory diet. This will play a significant role in de-stressing the body, which in turn will augment DHEA levels. An anti-inflammatory diet includes things like fish, fresh fruit and vegetables whole grains and good fats.

Healthy fat consumption plays an important role in producing good cholesterol, which is essential to producing DHEA. Things like avocados, omega-3 fatty acids and fish oils, some animal fats and olive oil. Keep red meat consumption to a minimum and focus instead on things like chicken, turkey, rabbit, fish and eggs for your protein intake. Remember your ratio between omega 6 and omega 3 intake. Omega 6 fatty acids are inflammatory. Omega 3 are anti-inflammatory. The lower the ratio, the better for DHEA levels.

Also consider that healthy fat consumption includes the maintenance of healthy body fat percentages and if this is too low or too high then this will also have an adverse effect on DHEA levels. The body is a highly balanced organism. All the different organs require their own balance to be able to contribute effectively to the whole organism.

There are also foods that contain DHEA and these are covered in the beneficial foods section. Eating foods that are rich in DHEA is another thing that can help with your natural levels.

Intermittent fasting is another thing that you can consider. This practise has many diet and health benefits, including reduced inflammation and it also aids in producing a healthy balance between stress hormones, sex hormones and ultimately also DHEA production. Proceed with caution because too much intermittent fasting can decrease T levels. Best approach with this is to do no more than once a week.

There are also some supplements that can help with maintaining healthy natural DHEA levels. And this does not include the DHEA supplements themselves. If only it were that simple, but it is not. There are health risks and unwanted side effects, and hiking up our DHEA levels unnaturally works in much the same way as does artificially hiking our T levels. It can slow down, or stop natural production altogether.

Vitamin D is known to play an important role in good DHEA levels. If you cannot get enough all year round sunshine then supplementation is a viable option. It is also a good idea to supplement alongside sun exposure to ensure that your vitamin D levels are consistent.

Especially if you workout on a regular basis. If you are in a warm climate, consider a smaller dosage of vitamin D supplement, if you are lacking in a sunny warm climate then obviously a higher dosage of vitamin D supplement is going to be necessary.

Another excellent group of supplements for optimising our natural DHEA production, and indeed our testosterone production too, are adaptogenic herbs.

Adaptogens are plant based natural supplements that can promote or restore normal functioning. This means that they can either reverse or improve a deficiency or help to calm down over production and stimulate under production. They adapt, hence the name adaptogen, depending on what the target body's needs are.

This makes them highly effective in balancing hormones and preventing hormonal levels that are too high or too low. This applies to testosterone, DHEA and estrogen. *And they are by far, the best form of defence against endocrine disruptors.* I highly recommend that you consider using adaptogens. They are great for optimising and maintaining T levels and balancing hormones, but they are very effective at combating things that harm testosterone production.

So if T levels are low, they can help balance everything out. Same with estrogen, DHEA, cortisol and blood sugar. Whatever needs the body has these herbs will adapt to the organism and help in restoring the balance.

Adaptogens can stabilise or inhibit cortisol production and potentially enhance adrenal gland output. For example encouraging our natural DHEA production. They can support or stabilise endocrine function and support adaptation to stress. This will help us in balancing out all of our hormonal functions.

During times of high stress or prolonged stress or worry the adrenal glands produce cortisol to help maintain blood pressure and blood sugar. However if the level or duration of the stress is too high, this can trigger the adrenal gland to go into overdrive and produce much more cortisol.

What then happens is that production of the stress hormone cortisol becomes too much. The production of this stress hormone effectively steals the ingredients necessary for producing DHEA and can affect production and this in turn can have a negative affect on testosterone production.

This means that these adaptogenic herbs can help to support optimal DHEA and in turn testosterone production. The most well known adaptogens are ashwagandha and panax ginseng. These adaptogens are both covered later in this section, along with a few others that are less well known.

Adaptogens are extremely useful to helping optimising and maintaining our T levels.

Fenugreek.

Fenugreek is a natural supplement that is made from a plant that is native to North Africa and India. It is commonly used in Indian cuisine. It is also a frequent ingredient in some T booster supplement stacks. It is also believed to have adaptogenic properties. It is well worth considering for that reason alone. Adaptogens are known to be very effective at balancing the hormones.

For centuries fenugreek has been used as a natural remedy for various conditions, such as digestive problems, increasing energy levels, and even erection and libido problems in men.

It contains nutrients like vitamin D, vitamin A and some B vitamins. It also has anti oxidant properties and many health benefits.

Fenugreek has been shown to increase T levels in men across many studies. The majority of the studies tend to support this conclusion.

Fenugreek supplements can increase T levels naturally, the plant contains saponins that are known to be effective at increasing testosterone. The good news is that fenugreek can be used on a regular basis without affecting natural hormonal production.

During studies it was found that men who took 500mg daily in supplement form over an 8 week period had a significant increase in testosterone production. 90% of the test subjects demonstrated increases of up to 46%. Also the majority of subjects also reported improvements in mood and well being, also increased energy and sex drive.

Another study focussing on older men aged 45 and upwards discovered that taking 600mg of a fenugreek seed extract for 12 weeks increased T levels and sexual interest significantly when compared to the placebo group.

One significant side effect of concern when taking fenugreek is that your sweat and pee pee will start to smell. I myself noticed that this was quite pronounced especially when working up a good sweat in the gym.

It can also cause stomach complaints, excessive wind, diarrhoea, vomiting and nausea.

I felt that fenugreek was a very beneficial supplement and I experienced increases in energy and physical performance. Because of the smell of my sweat, which for me was quite strong, I discontinued use. After ceasing use, I did not experience any adverse side effects or catabolic reaction.

A very useful supplement with very positive benefits.

Ashwagandha.

Another completely natural plant based supplement with many positive health benefits. It is an evergreen plant that is native to the Middle East, East Africa and India. It is another adaptogenic herb. These herbs are highly effective for helping to balance your hormones and to help combat against the things that harm T levels, such as endocrine disruptors.

It has been used in Indian Ayurvedic medicine, a form of natural healing, for centuries. It has been used to alleviate stress, improve concentration and in increasing energy levels. It has also been said to be able to improve stamina and boost sexual performance in men.

In my own experience I have noticed improvements to energy levels and athletic endurance. It is a supplement that I would happily recommend to anyone who engages in physical activity.

In clinical tests ashwagandha has been shown to be beneficial in maintaining T levels in men. In a study involving older men aged between 45 and 70 it was shown that by taking an ashwagandha supplement daily for 16 weeks T levels increased by an average of 15%. Interestingly there was also noted to be a corresponding increase in natural DHEA production in these men too.

This could help to explain its uplifting energy increasing properties.

It is recommended to take ashwagandha continuously over a period of time to be most effective. The above-mentioned test also noted that the gains to T levels and DHEA levels occurred after more than 8 weeks of daily use. The same is recommended for all adaptogens.

It is recommended to take a break after a years use. I was using ashwagandha for around a year without experiencing any problems.

It has been found to be safe to use daily for prolonged periods. Side effects are rare, there have been reports of upset stomach and digestive tract issues in some. There is also the possibility of drowsiness if used in higher doses.

I was using 1000mg per day without any problems. It is recommended to not stop taking ashwagandha suddenly but to gradually reduce the amount before stopping. I personally did not notice any adverse or catabolic side effects after discontinuing use. I reduced intake to 500mg for 3 days and then down to 250mg for 4 days, then I discontinued, and this worked fine for me.

An important thing to note is that there are references out there that suggest that ashwagandha can raise estrogen levels. There is some truth to this of course. Being an adaptogenic herb it will act differently depending on the individuals' body requirements. So in women it is entirely possible that it could raise estrogen production. Even in men too. If a man has a hormonal imbalance and low estrogen were to be the problem.

But bear in mind that in a guy who has higher estrogen than he should, then ashwagandha will probably lower his estrogen. Adaptogens help restore balance to the organism wherever that balance is required. This is what makes them such amazing supplements.

I highly recommend ashwagandha. It is a very effective supplement. I am using adaptogens that I have a stronger preference for as an alternative to ashwagandha, which I feel are more geared to my own personal needs.

Ginseng.

Ginseng is another natural plant based supplement that is known to have many health benefits. The supplement is made mainly from the root of the plant and usually comes in powdered or pill format. It is also possible in some countries to be able to source it in pure dried root form.

It is also a highly effective adaptogenic herb that has powerful anti-inflammatory properties and can be very effective in reducing all kinds of inflammation. It has also been associated with improved cognitive functioning, treating erectile dysfunction and libido problems and even lowering blood sugar levels.

It is known to have positive cardiovascular effects and improves blood-flow to the capillaries. The capillaries are the smallest and most abundant of the blood vessels and they form the connection between the arteries, which carry blood away from the heart, and the veins, which return blood to the heart.

Improved efficiency of the blood flow of the capillaries help to optimise the flow of oxygen between the blood and tissue cells.

The boosting of blood flow can contribute to a corresponding boost in physical endurance and cardiovascular performance and may help increase strength and muscle mass.

It has been used for centuries in traditional Chinese medicine to treat many different ailments. For example as a treatment for impotence and of course it can be very useful for low testosterone levels.

Ginseng can help to improve T levels due to its adaptogenic benefits in helping to maintain a healthy production of DHEA, a hormone secreted by the adrenal glands that is then converted into testosterone by the body. As an adaptogen it also helps directly to testosterone by helping to balance the body's hormonal output.

Studies have also shown that it has great potential for increasing Lutenizing hormone, which plays a role in testosterone production. Because of its adaptogenic abilities in stress resistance and its anti inflammatory properties this is also thought to contribute to aiding natural DHEA production, with a corresponding positive effect on T levels it was discovered.

It has also been shown to be very effective in reducing the production of a hormone called prolactin, which is a hormone produced by the pituitary gland. High prolactin levels in men inhibits testosterone production, so this effect of ginseng has a direct benefit to T levels.

Ginseng is also known to help regulate the production of dihydrotestosterone, DHT. The more testosterone you have in the body means that you will have more DHT. DHT is an androgen, which means that it does not convert to estrogen and binds to an androgen receptor for longer. The body converts roughly 10% of testosterone into DHT, this is a natural occurrence in healthy men.

DHT is the element of testosterone in men that is widely believed to be responsible for receding hairlines and baldness in men. Hair loss is a common side effect from using steroids and TRT to artificially raise T levels. DHT is also thought to be responsible for providing men with their masculine characteristics, such as deeper voices, facial and body hair.

The ability of ginseng to regulate DHT has been shown to have a positive effect on T levels and in natural T production.

Ginseng is safe to use on a daily basis and any side effects that you may experience are only mild. One of the most common side effects is that it can cause insomnia in some people. For this reason it is best to begin use with a smaller dose and to then increase with continued use.

The ideal dose seems to be between 200 and 400mg per day. It is safe to increase this to up to 1000mg if no side effects occur. It is advisable to periodically take a break from using ginseng to get the full benefits.

I would personally recommend using ginseng continuously on a daily basis for 3 months and then take a break for a week or two before resuming use again. I have been using ginseng regularly for more than 25 years without any adverse reaction or side effects. I believe ginseng and its adaptogenic qualities to be very beneficial to maintaining good hormonal balance and to testosterone maintenance and production.

Adaptogens are most beneficial when taken on a regular and consistent basis.

Other users have reported some side effects associated with long term use or usage in higher doses, such as headaches, stomach upset, diarrhoea and dizziness.

If any of these side effects occur you may want to consider ashwagandha as a good alternative to ginseng with similar benefits.

Creatine.

Creatine is a commonly used supplement that has been associated with strength, performance and muscle gains in men.

Some studies have found that it does not have any direct affect on T levels. Other studies found that it can potentially increase T levels.

One study published in Science and Sports in April 2015, investigating the effects of short term creatine supplements and resistance exercises and cardiovascular responses, found that more than 5 days of creatine supplementation combined with resistance training is sufficient to increase testosterone levels and in reducing cortisol concentrations.

The researchers divided the men into two groups. A creatine group and a placebo group. All candidates engaged in resistance training. The subjects all performed that training on days 3, 5 and 7 of the trial.

The creatine group experienced increases in T levels compared to the placebo group. There were no recorded changes in heart rate.

Another study found creatine to not have much effect on free or total testosterone levels but it was found to initiate an increase in DHT levels.

During a test in which the participants were college rugby players aged 20 years in South Africa, the subjects were given creatine in doses of 25g per day for a 7 day loading phase. This was administered with 25g of glucose. The placebo group just received 50g of glucose during this phase.

Then they followed a maintenance phase of 5g per day for 14 days, together with 25g of glucose and the placebo group receiving just 30g of glucose.

T levels were measured after 7 days and 21 days. In both instances T levels were shown to be unaffected. However DHT levels were shown to have increased by 56% after the loading phase and remained 40% higher after the maintenance phase.

So how does that correlate to our purposes here? Well DHT is a naturally occurring hormone and it plays an important role in the masculine characteristics that are prevalent in men. For example a deeper voice, body hair and muscle growth. It is also fundamental to maintaining your sex drive or libido.

However if your levels of DHT are too high or they have been elevated, it can contribute towards hair loss and baldness.

High levels of DHT have also been attributed to causing acne, and this could be why acne is common with steroid use. With more testosterone in the blood than the body needs naturally more DHT will be produced.

High levels of DHT have also been associated with an enlarged prostate and an increased risk of prostate cancer. Note here that it has also been found that having very low DHT levels can also affect the prostate in the same way.

It is widely recommended that creatine is cycled with a one month on, one month off basis. This will ensure that your DHT levels do not become too high and start causing you problems. Others recommend that it is OK to use creatine continuously.

Personally I use 5g of creatine four times a week on training days. I cycle creatine weekly and I am not engaged in daily use and am getting 3 days off per week anyway. I only use creatine on training days. Two days of training followed by a rest day. This is just my own preferred way. This way I never need to cycle off creatine. Most creatine users either cycle their use, one month on, one month off for example, or use continuously and both of these regimes seem to work really well. I just have my own preferred way and it is not necessarily better than the others. More of a compromise between the two.

I did find that creatine was the only supplement that made any difference to muscle mass gains after reaching my full genetic potential. Not significant gains but slight gains that were noticeable. Creatine also outperforms any T booster stack supplements for muscle gains in my opinion.

I have included creatine here because it is a very popular supplement with guys who train regularly and it can have positive benefits. But there are many who are of the opinion that it is safe to use continuously, without the need to be cycled. But the research shows that it is probably best used in cycles to prevent any unwanted side effects or potential problems.

L-Carnitine.

L-carnitine is naturally present in many foods. Especially foods from animal sources. It can also be taken as a supplement.

It is also synthesised naturally in the liver, kidneys and the brain from the amino acids lysine and methionine. It is an essential nutrient because the ideal requirements exceed the body's ability to produce this nutrient naturally. Regular intake of vitamin C can also help this natural secretion process.

The body needs around 15mg per day. Studies have shown that the typical balanced omnivore diet provides between 50 and 145mg per day for a person of average size and build. By contrast the typical vegan diet for a person of the same weight produces only 1.2mg per day.

For vegans in particular supplementation may be necessary. The best food source for carnitine is red meats. 100g of cooked steak typically provides 122mg. 100g of ground beef contains around 74mg, and 100g pork provides around 61mg. It can also be found in much smaller quantities in foods such as fish, chicken breast and cheese.

This is one nutrient that is particularly beneficial to testosterone. It is known to increase androgen sensitivity and androgen receptor levels as we discussed in the section on androgen sensitivity. Androgen receptors are necessary to bind to testosterone for the hormone to carry out all its bodily functions. And to perform this function, increasing androgen receptor levels, the recommended intake is at 2-3000mg so for this reason supplementation is highly beneficial for our T levels. And studies have shown that absorption of carnitine in supplement form is at around 18% this means that higher doses are required.

But bear in mind that there are some side effects associated with higher doses so it is always advisable to start with smaller doses and increase the dosage slightly in increments if no unwanted or adverse side effects occur.

The studies into carnitine have also demonstrated the potential of l-carnitine supplements for reducing lactate levels, regulation of heart rate and increased VO2 and blood oxygen levels. It has also shown to be very beneficial to weight loss and cognitive functioning and has shown promising results in patients with dementia and in the treatment of depression.

Carnitine is also fundamental to energy levels. It helps transport fatty acids into the mitochondria to be converted into energy. Studies have suggested that it can even increase mitochondrial functioning which can help to prevent diseases and improve life quality during the ageing process.

It is also known to be very effective in increasing exercise performance. However for this purpose to get the full benefits and best results long term consumption has been shown to be more effective.

It can help in improving exercise recovery, increasing the muscle oxygen supply, increasing stamina, reducing exercise related fatigue and muscle soreness and when taken an hour before intense physical training has been shown to have performance increasing potential.

L-carnitine helps to develop optimum testosterone levels. Studies have shown that levels of carnitine within the body were associated with free testosterone levels. Lower levels of carnitine translated into lower T levels. It was also shown that l-carnitine can help restore levels of lutenizing hormone in men with low testosterone. As we have discussed earlier, LH is fundamental in the production of testosterone.

Carnitine also offers a protective effect on the testes. This enhances the conversion of LH and FSH within the testes in the production of testosterone.

Because of its known positive effects on improving androgen sensitivity, carnitine is a supplement seriously worth trying and the benefits to testosterone are too good to ignore.

It is important to note that when supplementing with l-carnitine it is advisable to also supplement with a fat soluble antioxidant. The increase in energy production facilitated by l-carnitine will also result in an increased production of free radicals being released from the mitochondria, which naturally occurs as a result of ATP (adenosine triphosphate) production. Mitochondria are contained within cells that specialise in extracting energy from the foods we eat and converting into ATP.

Vitamin E is a fat soluble antioxidant that is known to be effective in limiting free radical production, and in helping to prevent the diseases associated with free radicals. Once of the best sources of natural vitamin E is extra virgin olive oil, which also happens to be very beneficial to testosterone.

Possible side effects include nausea, vomiting, stomach cramps, diarrhea and a fishy body odour.

Taurine.

Taurine is an amino acid that is found in many foods such as meats, fish and eggs. It is derived naturally in the body from the amino acid cysteine. Cysteine is important for making collagen, it affects skin elasticity, and has antioxidant properties.

Taurine can also be sourced in supplement form and has been found to have many positive health benefits, including a positive effect on T levels.

Taurine is known to be effective in stress management and has been found to play a part in lowering cortisol production. It can also improve sleep and improve athletic performance. It can also help to reduce insulin levels and help to facilitate improved energy production.

It can also have a positive effect on cognitive function and in elevating your state of motivation and in improving your moods.

Stress and anxiety are known to play havoc with our DHEA and testosterone production. Taurine can help to calm the nervous system by aiding the production of a neurotransmitter known as GABA, or Gamma AminoButyric Acid.

The production of GABA aids the body to manage anxiety and stress. This in turn helps to inhibit the cortisol spikes that are associated with high stress. If your taurine intake is low your nervous system will be more susceptible to reacting to stress in a negative way.

This of course will leave you being more prone to producing high levels of cortisol in reaction to the stress.

For anyone engaged in intense physical training, or hard physical work will find that their taurine levels will be depleted rather quickly. Taurine is particularly involved in the burning of fat stores during training and the recovery post workout. Taurine is known to improve the fat burning process and can be very effective in any weight loss program, but this will also mean that stores of taurine will be rapidly depleted.

Taurine consumption either during or before physical training helps to increase stamina and energy levels and help to prevent exercise related exhaustion. This will increase your performance and endurance levels during physical activity. I can confirm this to be true from personal experience.

Because taurine is mostly found in meats and animal products this does mean that vegetarians and vegans are going to be pretty prone to taurine deficiency and thus more susceptible to stress and anxiety. It is interesting to note that vegans tend to have lower T levels in general compared to carnivores, this could possibly be due to the diet being lacking in taurine.

Taurine supplementation is also known to have an effect on increasing T levels in men. During studies it has been shown that men who used between 2-5g of taurine supplement daily all showed significant increases of up to 20% to both free and total testosterone levels. These increases remained consistent over time.

It was also shown to improve endurance and athletic performance, and to reduce fatigue when directly compared to a placebo group.

And interestingly enough, taurine has been proven to raise T levels while not raising estradiol, which is an estrogenic hormone. It is also safe to use daily and does not have any adverse affect on natural production, nor does it disrupt hormone production in any way.

Taurine is not known to have any adverse side effects. It can interact with certain medications, for example meds for managing a high blood pressure.

I use 2g, 2000mg of taurine daily. I take it in the mornings 30 minutes before training. On rest days I split the dose and take 1g in the morning and 1g in the afternoon. I am 55kg and a short guy.

Bear in mind if you are a bigger guy you might need to consider using somewhere between 3-5g.

During trials and studies they determined a recommended dose of between 2-5g daily, and it was based on an 85kg man.

This is a very effective supplement with so many benefits and no side effects, which for any supplement is pretty rare. And it increases T levels by up to 20% without affecting natural testosterone production in any way. Add to that the increases in physical performance, recovery efficiency and energy levels, its ability to combat stress and anxiety and to improve well-being this is a supplement that you should seriously consider adding to your regular diet and regime.

Caffeine.

Caffeine, which is found in tea, coffee and energy drinks is known to be great when looking for a quick energy boost. It has also been recently attributed to increases in T levels by some. And there is *some* truth to this.

When you drink coffee the caffeine affects your brain and nervous system directly and the results are usually quite quick to be felt. It triggers the release of neurotransmitters, such as serotonin and dopamine. These neurotransmitters help to speed up the signals sent between the brain and the body, which in turn, induce a state of wakefulness.

Considering its stimulant properties it is the go to drink for many upon waking in the morning, myself included.

Because of this I have included caffeine here to consider whether it is a worthwhile T boosting supplement to consider.

And the answer is yes, and no. Those who drink coffee on a regular basis were found to have higher T levels when compared to men who do not drink coffee.

The increases in testosterone are only temporary and last only for a short time after the coffee had been consumed. Which is contradictory. Temporary increases that only last for a short time resulting in generally higher levels when consumed on a regular basis?

Detailed studies have confirmed that consuming up to 800mg of caffeine was linked with T levels increases of up to 14%. But this increase also required it to be combined with physical training. Also the caffeine had to be consumed directly before training. Again these increases only lasted for a short duration. An interesting note is that the T increases associated with training seem to manifest after working out, and they too, only lasted for a short time.

High doses of caffeine have been linked to heart palpitations, anxiety and restlessness. A 250ml can of Red Bull energy drink contains 80mg of caffeine. A dose of 800mg seems excessive for a temporary elevation of 14% to T levels. That is the equivalent of 10 cans of Red Bull, which does not seem like a good idea in terms of health benefits.

So it is true that caffeine can increase T levels if combined with a workout. The increases in T levels however, seemed to last for only a short time after consumption.

However what the study also discovered was that there was also a corresponding increase in cortisol levels of up to 44%. Cortisol production is known to inhibit natural testosterone production so in moderation seems the best strategy. Too much caffeine will produce more cortisol, and on a regular basis, could lead to declining T levels. And of course could suppress DHEA levels.

For me a morning coffee to kick start my day before working out is no bad thing. But in my opinion a dose as high as 800mg, in one go, before a workout doesn't seem such a good idea. Might give you a boost right now but in the long term could have a negative effect.

L Arginine.

L arginine is an amino acid that our bodies mostly create on their own. However if there is a deficiency in this essential amino acid then there can be cause for concern as it can lead to hormonal imbalances.

Research confirms that there is a positive and direct effect on T levels so it is certainly worth mentioning here.

Because it is a completely naturally occurring amino acid it means that if and when supplementation becomes necessary, or if you feel that boosting your arginine levels might be of use to you, then there are no side effects associated with its use.

In studies involving men with erectile dysfunction, supplementation was shown to help with erectile problems as well as producing increases in testosterone.

It has also been demonstrated that in men who had diets that were deficient in L arginine, taking a supplement had a very positive effect.

In athletes and those observing a well balanced diet combined with exercise however it was shown that supplementing with L arginine had little noticeable effect on their T levels.

However it has been observed, and well documented, that it has been proven to be essential to muscle growth during physical training.

It certainly has many benefits toward body function and health. The best course of action seems to be in observing our diet to ensure that we are getting enough. Supplementation seems to be a viable option in those who already have low T levels.

It can be found in beans and pulses, such as seeds and lentils, dairy products, meat, seafood and nuts. And eggs are particularly packed with L Arginine.

By getting enough of these foods in our diet we should be getting an adequate supply and have no real cause for concern.

Maca Root.

Maca root supplements are becoming increasingly popular in men who train and who are looking to increase muscle mass.

Whereas they have been shown to not have much of a direct influence over testosterone levels it is widely accepted that it can contribute towards supporting testosterone. This is due to its adaptogenic properties.

For this reason it is worth considering here.

Various studies seem to correlate to the fact that maca can be very beneficial in physical performance but the majority of studies agree that there is not any evidence of any corresponding increases in testosterone levels.

One particular study found that maca root did stimulate testosterone production but this was a test involving male rats and not human subjects.

Maca is a small, nutritiously abundant root vegetable which is packed with vitamins and minerals, amino acids, anti-oxidants and plant sterols and its health benefits are now becoming more widely known.

Research suggests that maca may be very beneficial in its ability to balance hormones within the body. Its abundant nutrient profile helps to give it adaptogenic properties, which are known to help to support natural DHEA production, and as we have already discussed, DHEA is converted by the body into testosterone and plays an important role in our T production and T levels.

It is also said to have anabolic properties, which explain its rising popularity among gym users seeking to increase muscle mass and improve their physical performance. Due to the presence of essential minerals and amino acids it is also thought to be beneficial in helping to improve post workout recovery.

Due to its adaptogenic properties it can also help the body cope better with stress and also aid in reducing inflammation of the muscles from physical training.

One of the research proven aspects of the maca root is its ability to aid in correcting hormonal imbalances. This has huge potential because it can help prevent the production of too much estrogen. Having well balanced hormone production is certainly a good thing in the long term.

It can also help to regulate the production of stress hormones, like cortisol which are known to also have a negative affect on T levels and testosterone production.

And of course hormones also play a significant role in muscle growth. This could be why this root has been thought to be so effective as a muscle bulking supplement.

We already know that muscle growth happens through a combination of the muscles being damaged through intense workouts and then repaired. It is the correct balance between muscle stress, or the intensity of the workouts and in then getting the correct amounts of nutrients to be able to repair the muscles and to stimulate the growth of new muscle tissue during this repair process. This is called hypertrophy.

Maca just happens to be abundant in these important nutrients that are fundamental in this process of growing and repairing muscle tissue. It contains a good dose of all the essential amino acids along with other vital fatty acids and crucial muscle repairing nutrients such as potassium, magnesium, zinc, phosphorous, calcium and iron and also it is rich in vitamin C, vitamin A, and also vitamins B2, B6 and niacin. It seems the perfect addition to any muscle building diet and regime.

However there are different types of maca root supplements available so it can be a little confusing which one to buy.

It is not a case of there being different varieties of maca plant or maca root but rather different colours that the powdered root comes in. This is because for some as yet unknown reason the maca plant produces root vegetables, in the same harvests and from the same ground, that are different colours. Each different colour also has slight differences in its nutrient profile.

There are three main groups of maca root supplement. There are red maca, black maca and white or yellow maca, and each of these is more suited for certain aims and goals than others. It is well known that each colour variation of maca produces varying effects.

The maca of muscle mass and the one most suited to the gym user is black maca. It is also the rarest form of maca root and thus is usually the most expensive. It is known to be the one that has its main potential in its energy benefits and its potential to improve the hypotrophic process. Therefore it is the maca that is more suited to body building and gains in lean muscle mass. It also has been found to be beneficial in increasing libido, it is also the maca that seems to most effective for boosting sperm count, boosting memory and focus, strengthening the immune system, enhancing moods, increasing stamina and metabolic rate.

Red maca is found in around 25% of the harvest and contains the most anti-oxidants of the three varieties. It is more well known for its adaptogenic properties and its ability to regulate hormones, improve mental focus and mental clarity and to be of great help in managing stress and anxiety. It has also been found to be effective in relieving depression, increasing stamina, enhancing libido, building muscles and bone strength and improving prostate health.

White, or as it is also commonly referred to yellow maca is the most common type of maca. It is usually the least expensive. It is the one that is considered to be the most neutral in effects and arguably the least beneficial. But this does not mean that it is a supplement to be avoided.

It contains plenty of mood boosting flavonoids its chief benefit seems to be in its ability to alleviate depression and anxiety and in balancing hormones. It can also be effective in enhancing your inner sense of vitality.

It is also abundant in nearly all of the essential amino acids and the fatty free acids prevalent in the other varieties and also contains a significant amount of vitamin A, vitamins B1,B2 and B3 and also vitamin C. It also has a healthy dose of iron, zinc, calcium and magnesium.

It is also effective in supporting decreasing stress levels, enhancing mood, improving skin health and improving focus and mental clarity.

As you can see they all have similar properties, but with a few differences here and there. It therefore could be confusing as to which one you should choose, it also comes in tricolour format, which is a blend of all three varieties. Best rule is to choose the one most suited to your own personal requirements.

Being a completely natural product there are very few side effects and those that can occur have been mostly reported as mild. These include, insomnia, upset stomach, excess stomach gas, feelings of being bloated, stomach cramps and moodiness.

Because of its potential adaptogenic properties and its potential to support hormone balances and the healthy maintenance of the endocrine system it is certainly well worth considering for that alone. Add all the other potential benefits listed above and it definitely deserves to be tagged as a super-food. There is no doubt that it makes a great addition to any diet.

It is also a great, completely natural multi vitamin and amino acid supplement and it is also worth using it for that reason alone.

Cordyceps Mushroom.

The cordyceps mushroom is a type of parasitic fungi that grows on the larvae of insects. This mushroom has been used in traditional Chinese medicine for centuries and are thought to have great health benefits.

The cordyceps is not a supplement that is widely known. I discovered its existence when I once bought a T booster product and noticed that one of the listed ingredients included was cordyceps. The other core ingredients listed were all ones that I knew to be very effective so I took the product to the clerk in the store and asked what this cordyceps was.

He had never heard of it either so he looked online and did a quick search and he concluded very quickly that it had T boosting potential and many health benefits.

This of course piqued my interest, so I carried out my own research to find out more. And they do have proven potential in improving our testosterone so they are certainly worth some consideration.

So what are cordyceps mushrooms? Well to begin with they are a type of adaptogenic mushroom, and we have already established that anything with adaptogenic properties can benefit us in the arena of T levels and hormonal health.

As I have already stated they are a type of parasitic fungus, and they feed on insect larvae. They can also live as parasites on insects such as moths and caterpillars and they eventually kill their hosts. They are elongated and shaped like a club. They contain many bioactive substances, which have a wide range of potential health benefits.

So the important question for our purposes here. Can cordyceps increase testosterone?

In numerous lab tests involving mice and rats there seems to be overwhelming corroborating evidence that it can increase testosterone production in the Leydig cells of mice. These Leydig cells are the machinery within the testicles that are responsible for the production of testosterone. This process works of course in much the same way in humans. But of course what applies to mice does not necessarily apply to humans!

In studies involving humans it has been demonstrated that it has the potential to treat some of the reproductive problems associated as being caused by low testosterone.

The results of all this research indicate that cordyceps can be used as a natural, and it seems to be a relatively harmless way to improve male sexual health. Cordyceps has also been found to enhance sperm production and sperm mobility.

Cordyceps have been found to have powerful anti-inflammatory properties. This is due to a compound called cordycepin, which is one of the main compounds of the cordyceps mushroom. Cordycepins have been found to be very effective in reducing inflammation in the human body.

As we already have discussed earlier, reducing inflammation is one of the things we can consider for maintaining good DHEA levels. With our DHEA levels being correlated to our testosterone production and with the decline of these two hormones seeming to go hand in hand, these anti-inflammatory effects are going to have a positive effect on testosterone levels.

Cordycepin has been found during research to have positive effects on reducing age related testicular inflammation and has shown great potential in treating inflammatory related erectile dysfunction in men.

In fact cordyceps seems to be able to benefit the entire human body. Along with what is mentioned above it can also improve energy levels and boost athletic performance, improve skin health, help lower blood sugar levels, boost the immune system, enhance digestive tract function, prevent oxidative damage, help you to sleep better, reduce anxiety, promote heart health, improve kidney function and even promote the respiratory system. And research even suggests that it can even help to prevent certain forms of cancer.

With all these suggested benefits it makes you wonder why it is not more well known?

You can source cordyceps supplements in capsules extracts and in powdered form.

The recommended dosage of cordyceps seem to vary with many different opinions available. The common denominator here seems to suggest that 2000mg daily is ideal. Some say as little as 500mg and others say from 3000-6000mg per day. Best advice here would be to start small at maybe 500mg to begin with.

Because cordyceps have been used for centuries they have been widely thought to be safe to consume and unlikely to cause any harm. However there are some things that you should be aware of when considering this supplement.

There is evidence that cordyceps can interact with certain types of medication and some health conditions.

If you are using any type of blood thinning medication such as warfarin, or any anti clotting treatments then cordyceps could increase the risk of bleeding and also carries an increased risk of bruising. It is also advisable to not use cordyceps during the weeks leading to any surgery.

Since cordyceps are known to have an effect on lowering blood sugar levels it is very probable that it will interact with any diabetes treatments and it is possible that complications could occur.

If you are already prone to allergies to other fungi, yeast or mould then exercise caution with cordyceps because there is a possibility of experiencing an allergic reaction. Although quite rare, there have been a few recorded incidents of allergic reactions that have been directly attributed to cordyceps. If this should happen to you then stop use immediately and consult a doctor or other healthcare professional.

Due to its energy boosting properties this is a supplement that is best taken in the morning. You could even add it to your pre-workout routine. Because of its ability to increase energy there is a possibility that it can cause insomnia or disrupted sleep patterns. Especially if taken later in the day.

Other side effects that have been noticed in some people are digestive issues such as constipation, diarrhoea and stomach cramps. However these have usually been linked to using higher doses of cordyceps.

For most people cordyceps is safe to use and any side effects are unlikely. It is also considered to be relatively safe to use long term. It is certainly worth considering this supplement based upon its possible benefits to your health. Your overall health after all plays a part in healthy hormone production.

As far as it being a highly effective T booster the jury is still out as most of the data available relates to testing performed on mice and rats. As far as taking it as a supplement with the intention of boosting T levels it is probably a good idea to look to other available supplements.

However that said it is still worth considering adding this amazing fungi to your diet.

Rhodiola Rosea.

Rhodiola is a relatively unknown supplement in the field of testosterone supplements. It is a completely natural plant based supplement made from a herb that is native to Siberia and parts of Asia. It is another highly effective adaptogen. Adaptogens are very effective at balancing hormones and bodily functions. I use rhodiola on a regular basis for this purpose.

It has been shown to have some real potential for being beneficial to human health. In various human studies it has been shown to be very effective in improving moods and sense of well being, improves cognitive function and that it can also reduce muscle damage and be effective in aiding muscle recovery and in reducing tiredness and fatigue.

I discovered numerous studies that confirm it improves mood and sense of well being. It is also effective in boosting energy and combating tiredness. It has been confirmed to improve cognitive function and mental focus and be beneficial to reducing muscle damage and inflammation and in aiding post exercise recovery.

It has also been attributed to having anti-inflammatory properties and also very effective in combating stress, and oxidative stress, all of which can help indirectly with testosterone production.

It has also been shown to have adaptogenic properties, which as we have already discussed, can have a positive effect on regulating and optimising hormone production, and on overall health and well being.

Rhodiola was found during human studies to be very effective in reducing high cortisol levels. And of course as we already know, high cortisol levels have a profoundly negative effect on our hormone production.

Side effects are rare and practically non existent in the majority of users. However some side effects could occur and these include insomnia, dry mouth, upset stomach, drowsiness and headaches.

Recommended dosage ranges from between 100mg to 600mg. It is considered safe for daily usage. The most commonly recommended dosage is 200mg twice a day.

In reality any supplement that can help to manage or reduce cortisol levels is going to provide T boosting benefits, and for this purpose Rhodiola has been proven to be very beneficial.

Not so much a T boosting supplement but an adaptogen supplement that is highly effective in fighting and reducing factors that can harm T levels.

Mucuna Pruriens.

This is another little known supplement that can be extremely useful for our purposes here. It is also known as velvet bean. It is a natural plant based supplement made from the seeds, or the beans, of a creeping vine type plant that is native to India, the Caribbean and the tropical regions of Africa. It is also considered to be an adaptogenic herb.

It is known to be a great natural source of L-Dopa, more commonly known as dopamine, and it can increase dopamine production in the brain. Dopamine is a neurotransmitter associated a sense of inner well being and satisfaction.

In recent times the concept of getting a dopamine fix has been associated by some as being a means of instant gratification, associated with laziness and a lack of motivation and it has been suggested that dopamine is something related to bad lifestyle choices.

There is some truth to this and it is probably not a good idea to try raising your dopamine levels by watching porn, masturbation, or any other unhealthy or immoral practises. Now forgive me, I am not trying to lecture anyone on what they should or should not be doing here, I am just saying this to provide context.

However by increasing the production of this neurotransmitter you can boost your moods and of course your inner sense of well being. Well being and moods have a direct influence over stress levels and reactions to stressful situations. Dopamine can also help enhance the production of growth hormone, which is directly related to muscle mass gains.

So dopamine can in fact be a positive thing. A sense of well being and improved moods also lead to more positivity and better motivation and can also be correlated to increased confidence and an increased sense of belief in one's self. This can only have a positive effect on hormone production?

During an extensive study into the effects of mucuna pruriens on testosterone, it was found to have very significant results. Test subjects were comprised of 150 men, half of whom were fertile, with good sperm levels and good sperm mobility. The other half were infertile. All subjects were aged between 25 and 40.

Subjects were all given 5000mg of full spectrum mucuna pruriens daily for a period of three months. At the beginning of the test all of the men had blood samples taken and their testosterone levels and Lutenizing hormone levels were recorded along with prolactin levels.

According to a medical science journal, "Elevations in prolactin inhibit the release of Lutenizing hormone and follicle stimulating hormone, which blunts (decreases) gonadal (the testicles') production of testosterone."

Prolactin is also associated with stimulating the production of milk in lactating women, something that men would want to avoid, and prolactin is also associated with the development of gynecomastia, a condition which consists of the development and having the appearance of female type breasts in men.

So levels of prolactin that are too high in men inevitably leads to decreases in the production of Lutenizing hormone and along with that, ultimately, testosterone production.

OK, now back to the test.

The test concluded after three months and the men had their levels checked. And the end result was very positive.

All the subjects were shown to have significantly increased both their levels of testosterone and their Lutenizing hormone. Prolactin levels were shown to have significantly decreased. And this happened right across the board with no exceptions. In both the fertile and infertile groups.

T levels went up by up to 43%. Lutenizing hormone was elevated by as much as 56% and prolactin levels dropped by as much as 32%.

And this is what sets mucuna pruriens aside from most other T boosting supplements currently on the market. Its ability to boost T levels while at the same time inhibiting prolactin production.

Please be aware when buying a mucuna pruriens supplement to look out for a product that states that it is a full spectrum mucuna pruriens. The test involved the full spectrum supplement. If it does not specifically state that it is full spectrum then it probably is not.

Possible side effects are relatively mild and quite rare but include headaches, nausea and a sensation of bloating in the stomach. In rare instances it has also been said to cause a pounding heartbeat, and it has also been attributed in rare cases as being associated with symptoms of psychosis such as agitation, confusion and delusions.

It is also recommended that if you have any history of cardiovascular disease, diabetes, liver disease, or mental illness, particularly depression, psychosis or schizophrenia, that you do not supplement with mucuna. Also mucuna should not be used alongside any medications used for the treatment of mental illness such as anti-depressants or anti-psychotics, any meds used for the treatment of diabetes or any forms of anaesthesia.

Although the lab test subjects were given 5000mg per day, it is recommended not to exceed a dose of between 1000mg and 2000mg per day. For smaller guys a dose of 1000mg per day should be enough. For bigger guys perhaps a dose of 2000mg per day.

A sound recommendation is to begin use for the first time in a lower dose, starting with 200mg daily, and increasing the dose gradually if there are no signs of any unwanted side effects, although these are quite rare.

The supplement will not interfere with your natural testosterone production in any way, making it a perfect supplement to include in your regime.

Tongkat Ali.

Tongkat Ali is an ingredient found in many T boosting supplements and can also be found as a stand alone supplement. It is sometimes referred to as Malaysian Ginseng. It is considered by some to have adaptogenic properties.

It is a natural herb from South East Asia and has been used in this region in traditional medicine for many generations and is reputed to have many benefits.

It is primarily thought to be an aphrodisiac and is used for the treatment of erectile dysfunction and libido problems in men. The extract from the roots of the plant has also been traditionally used to increase T levels in men. It is also said to improve mood, to combat stress, lower blood pressure, for the treatment of fever and bacterial infections, to increase physical performance, increase muscle mass and help to combat fatigue. It is also said to contain anti-oxidant properties.

The research into Tongkat Ali is still relatively new and there is not much independent data out there. Much of the research conducted so far suggests that it can help to treat male infertility, improve mood, boost energy and increase muscle mass.

In one study conducted on older men with confirmed low T levels, it was found that taking 200mg of a Tongkat Ali root extract every day for one month, improved their T levels to a normal level for 90% of the subjects.

Also studies in both animals and men demonstrate that Tongkat Ali stimulates sexual desire and seems to improve erectile dysfunction in men. This does tend to correlate with the claimed benefits from its use as a traditional medicine.

Another correlation is that it does seem to have achieved results in improving fertility. During a study involving 75 couples with infertility issues it was shown that 200mg of Tongkat Ali taken daily for three months improved sperm quality. The trial also resulted in 14% of the couples becoming pregnant.

Of course, of the other 84% of the couples, it was not revealed as to how many of them had male or female infertility issues.

So it does show that Tongkat Ali does have some potential as a T boosting supplement. Personally I decided not to use Tongkat Ali because of some reports of toxicity and a possibility of DNA damage of the stomach. This sounds quite serious.

According to research and a subsequent report by the European Food Safety Authority a high dose of Tongkat Ali, stated at 2000mg per kg of bodyweight, was probably unsafe. The panel concluded that they could not establish the safety of tongkat Ali use.

Bear in mind that this is a far cry from the 200mg daily cited in the trials, which were producing positive results. For me, at 55kg this would amount to a daily dose of 110,000mg! But proceed with caution because there could be potential issues with long term use that have yet to be discovered as no studies have examined and monitored its long term use.

Studies have shown that with a dose of between 200 and 600mg per day in humans, this did not result in many side effects. Mainly upset stomachs and cases of itching.

The issue for me was that there are no regulations for the preparation and extraction process for its commercial preparations in supplements. But with any supplements it pays to always source quality products.

There have been studies into the quality of Tongkat Ali supplements, sold in the western marketplace, that have shown contamination of heavy metals present in quite a lot of available supplements. Including lead and mercury that were deemed to exceed safe levels.

Ingesting too much mercury can result in mercury poisoning and this can involve symptoms such as negative mood changes, memory problems and motor skills problems. This possible outcome caused me to pass on trying Tongkat Ali supplements.

I was fortunate enough to find someone who has used Tongkat Ali and it is his experiences that I will relate to here.

He noticed a massive improvement in motivation and enthusiasm in the first week. He felt good inside and his overall mood improved significantly. His training also improved due to the increase in motivation. He also noticed that he could train for longer and he was able to increase the weights he used in resistance training for most exercises. He also stated that he hit a PB on the leg press machine while using Tongkat Ali.

He did notice however that the effects seemed to wear off after about a month. He did not notice the benefits any more. He said he felt the same as he used to feel before he started taking Tongkat Ali, in himself, his moods and his energy levels. This is probably him building up a tolerance to the supplement. I have experienced this with many supplements. Building up a tolerance to them in only a short time.

He did say that there was no catabolic effect and that when he stopped using Tongkat Ali he was training the same as he used to. No drop in motivation or energy levels. But he did state that the weight lifting increases stayed with him. Apart from the tolerance issue after a month he did not have any adverse side effects at all.

This supplement has possible potential risks so I would advise to avoid Tongkat Ali as there are many more viable alternatives without the risks of toxicity.

Viagra.

Now you might be surprised to find this here in terms of being a testosterone boosting supplement. For many it is considered to be a medication rather than a supplement.

It is man made and of course not a natural product. Everyone has heard of its effectiveness in treating ED in men. It contains an active ingredient called sildenafil, which works well for erections because it inhibits an enzyme responsible for relaxing the penile tissues and in regulating the blood supply in the penis.

It effectively removes the restriction of the enzyme leaving the penis less prone to relaxing (staying soft) and removes the regulation of blood flow to the penis allowing the penis to get hard more efficiently. And whether you have ED or not it seems to affect all guys the same.

But Viagra is not only beneficial to penile blood flow and increasing sexual performance. It also has testosterone boosting qualities and is now being used as an effective treatment for low T levels. And being a pharmaceutical medication, this has been extensively researched.

In one study they considered 140 men who had confirmed erection problems and who also had confirmed low testosterone levels. This was stated as being *lower* than 300ng/DL.

The men were given a dose of 50mg per day and they were monitored for a period of three weeks. They found that total testosterone went up by 40%, free testosterone by 50% and also it was observed that DHT levels increased too. This is only natural because around 10% of your testosterone is converted into DHT anyway.

However there was a tolerance issue. Some built up tolerance fairly quickly and needed to increase the dosage. This is fairly common with many prescription drugs.

In another study Viagra was taken by a group of 100 men. After 3 years they contacted the men and 43 of them were still using Viagra. Only 16 of them said that they had to increase the dosage to get the same effect. This was a tolerance test and their T levels were not recorded.

These tests, which both gave positive results were funded by the drug companies that manufacture these types of drugs and thus could be biased in favour of presenting a positive outcome.

Dr Geoffrey Hackett, an expert in sexual medicine when speaking in 2010, stated that Viagra will not work on all men because the real issue is low testosterone. By this he explained that for the men for whom Viagra doesn't work the Viagra needed to be combined with TRT in men with low T levels.

The question that arises here is that if Viagra is supposed to be an amazing T booster, as the manufacturers claim, then why is an independent sexual medicine expert suggesting otherwise?

There is a lesson to be learned here in terms of research data. Some of it is biased towards the supplement it is testing, usually this occurs because the testing is funded by the manufacturer, or some other party with a vested financial interest. When relying upon research and data as part of your supplement research it is important to try to look at independent studies carried out by third parties who are not connected to the product in any way.

Why? I will explain this in our viewing of the last supplement on the list.

Turkesterone.

Turkesterone is a supplement that has been making waves in the fitness and gym scene recently. It is a natural supplement that has been reputed to be able to increase muscle mass in the same way as anabolic steroids, but with no side effects and no damage to natural T levels and testosterone production.

There are many different sources online claiming that it is possible to gain up to 10 pounds of muscle in only 8 weeks. With claims like this and the suggestion of no adverse side effects this kind of supplement hype is naturally going to grab the attention of any guy into training who is looking to increase muscle mass.

But how accurate are these claims? After conducting a detailed research using as many sources as I could find I quickly noticed that there seems to be conflicting opinions. And the downside is that there is not much reliable research available to settle the matter.

Some state that it is great, and that they have had very positive results and they confirm its potential for increasing muscle mass. Sometimes this opinion occurs on sites selling the supplements, or fitness blogs providing affiliate links for you to click to buy the products. They are naturally going to have a vested interest in inducing you to buy turkesterone.

Others are saying that its not at all effective and that they have seen little or no results to their muscle gains. But I did notice that some of these sites were saying not to use turkesterone, but they were also suggesting alternatives that you could buy with links provided to do so. Interesting considering that they have a vested interest in convincing you *not* to buy turkesterone!

Think about it. If the claims are true, then of course most of the other supplements available could become obsolete. This is because they are nowhere near as effective as the claims being made for turkesterone. The supplement industry could then be in trouble because gym guys especially are only going to buy turkesterone and forget about all the other T boosters that are available.

However when analysing the reviews for these supplements left on third party marketplaces, the same conflicts of opinion occur. Usually with third party marketplaces that have no vested interest in the products, we can often get a clearer picture. But here too, there also seems to be a mixed bag. Some reviewers singing the supplements' praises, and others stating that it is useless and had no real effect. And this even occurs in users of the same product and brand!

So lets get into this supplement in more detail.

It is said that Turkesterone is a natural supplement that comes from various plants that grow in East Asia and Siberia. It is what is known as a naturally occurring edcysteroid. Edcysteroids help to make more proteins and can inhibit the production of cortisol.

Edcysteroids do not bind with the same part of the cells as testosterone, for example the androgen receptor. The body does not recognise it as testosterone and thus keeps producing natural testosterone.

So this considered it does not change the balance of hormones in the body like artificial hormones do. For example in the case of steroids, they mimic testosterone and the body then detects it has enough, and then shuts down natural production. This does mean that it may have less negative effects than these artificial hormones.

This also seems to indicate that it does not increase testosterone levels as it does not affect the hormones in any way.

It is reputed to improve energy and fitness levels. It is also said that it can increase muscle mass and endurance during physical exercise. It is also said that it can help to reduce body fat, reduce the risk of injuries and speed up recovery times.

It is also said to improve libido, provide better focus and mental clarity. There is no scientific evidence available to back up these claims. Most of the studies have been conducted on animals and there have been no significant human studies.

There is some evidence that turkesterone can help reduce fatigue. One study on rats found that it reduced levels of the stress hormone cortisol after exercise. Interestingly enough in one study using rats, which observed increases in musculature, it outperformed, albeit only marginally, the potent anabolic steroid Dianabol.

It is recommended that the dosage is between 400mg and 800mg daily. It is advised to begin at the smaller dose and then increase if there are no side effects. It is also recommended to cycle the supplement and to use for 8 to 12 weeks followed by a 2 week break before resuming.

A big problem with turkesterone supplements is that they contain less than the label states. Most of the turkesterone used in supplements is an extract so this means that if the label says 500mg of extract this correlates to around 50mg of turkesterone.

In an independent ingredient analysis of many popular turkesterone supplements, the ones that sell the most, it found that most of these popular products actually contained less than 1mg per capsule!

When challenged the manufacturers response was that it was necessary to add other ingredients to the turkesterone supplements to reduce the likelihood of any negative side effects. Now wait a minute. Didn't they claim that turkesterone didn't have any side effects?

It was found that also present in the supplements were tribulus terrestris, fenugreek and zinc among others.

Now this would help to explain why some guys have reported positive results and others negative results in third party marketplace reviews. Only they left conflicting reviews for exactly the same product! So this only causes further confusion.

So why do the manufacturers add other ingredients to minimise the possibility of unwanted side effects?

These side effects include increased risk of liver damage. Turkes-terone is metabolised in the liver and there is the risk of liver damage caused by toxins. Now hang on, isn't this a similar side effect to ana-bolic steroids?

It can also increase the risk of kidney damage. This is due to its diuretic effect. This means it strips water and makes you pee more of-ten. Also kidney damage also correlates to your adrenal glands, which are situated at the top of the kidneys, so can this actually contribute to harming hormonal production such as DHEA production? And ultimately T levels?

Turkesterone can also cause high blood pressure. Another side effect that can occur with steroid use.

It can also cause acne. This apparently is one of the most common side effects of turkesterone. This usually occurs with increased testos-terone levels and it is claimed that it does not affect natural hormone production or the body's hormone balance so how acne can be a possible side effect is beyond me! Acne is also a very common side effect from steroid use.

Aggression. In one study it found that subjects who took turkes-terone supplements were much more likely to be prone to aggressive thoughts and aggressive behaviour. Like roid rage, there seems to also be a turkesterone rage!

Other noted side effects included increased heart rate, anxiety, rest-lessness, insomnia, headaches, nausea, vomiting and diarrhoea.

Now that's quite a list of side effects for a product that is claimed does not have any side effects! And for a product that is claimed to be able to provide increases in muscle mass comparable to steroids, and in rats this has indeed been confirmed, then there do seem to be many similar side effects associated with turkesterone use, that are also associated with steroid use.

So it seems that this could be a supplement to avoid. This is certainly my own personal opinion from what I have seen. This is why is is very important to carry out your own research into any supplement before starting use.

And that includes the supplements that I have recommended in this guide. If you are reading this then I don't know you personally and I am not familiar with your lifestyle and any medical conditions you may have or any medications you are taking.

Also consider that you might experience side effects from the supplements that I use whereas I haven't. We are all different. Most supplements carry with them the risk of side effects despite all of their possible benefits.

Bear in mind that my recommendations are based upon the premise that you are in good health, and that you have already optimised your diet, got into the habit of being active, you have your sleep patterns down and that you are managing your stress effectively before considering supplements.

Another thing to note is that I have discovered that only a few core supplements have been that effective for me. I have them found useful

enough to adopt them into my regular regime, many of them do not or
have not benefited me enough to warrant me continuing to use them.
It is certainly of no benefit to continue using something that I don't
really need.

You may well experience different results to me. Please bear this in
mind. A supplement that has worked well for me may not work so well
for you. Also a supplement that I have found not to work particularly
well for me may work really well for you.

Another thing that does spring to mind is that if you take as many
T boosting supplements as you can, will this give you even better T
levels? Sadly the answer is no.

Many supplements have been shown to increase T levels by a certain
percentage. Does this mean that all the percentages will add up into
a combined testosterone increase? Lets say one has been shown to
increase T levels by 20%, and another by 40% and another by 50%.
Does this mean that you will boost your T levels by a total of 110% by
taking all of them?

Probably not. But then no research has ever been conducted to test
this theory. The research, the vast majority of it, has been focused on
just one element or supplement and the effects and benefits of just that
one supplement.

But it could also be true that taking a combination of supplements
which have all shown to have a positive effect could give you a bigger
boost to T levels than you would get from one supplement alone. It

is entirely possible. It would be interesting to discover whether this is true. Logically there could be a lot of truth to this.

But taking too many supplements might not be the best approach.

This could ultimately have a detrimental effect. Better to keep it to a few tried and trusted go to supplements rather than taking too many. In truth I have found many of the benefits of multi ingredient T booster supplements to be short lived. I discovered that tolerance is built up rather quickly, and they lose their effects over time.

My supplement regime consists of a few core supplements that I have found to be beneficial and ones that can be taken regularly. And most importantly supplements that I can keep getting benefits from with prolonged use.

And one last important thing with T boosting supplements. None of the studies have ever examined whether any testosterone increases are permanent, or whether they can be maintained long term with repeated supplement use. The jury is still out on this one and hopefully more research will be available in the future.

I will reveal my exact routine and give you an explanation of why I use certain supplements and everything else I have done to optimise my T levels as I get older.

Staying with the subject of supplements, lets now consider some beneficial vitamins and minerals that are important for T levels.

21

Vitamins and Minerals Essential For Testosterone

I f you have low T levels then we all know that paying attention to our diets is important. Getting the right healthy balance of carbohydrates, proteins and fats is extremely important. My diet is geared towards getting all the nutrients I need, and maintaining my T levels.

Getting the right amounts of micro-nutrients, such as vitamins and minerals in our diets is equally important. There are so many important micro-nutrients that it can be difficult to ensure that we are getting enough of all of them every day.

For this reason, especially when it comes to our hormone levels and hormone production, it might sometimes be necessary to use vitamin and mineral supplements to help optimise our testosterone levels.

As a primary concern, always seek to get as many vitamins and minerals as you can from natural food sources. Eating a varied diet including as many different foods needed to ensure all nutritional requirements are met.

One of the most important things to consider is correcting any deficiencies. Vitamin and mineral deficiencies are common in cases of low testosterone. A very simple solution if you think you might have a deficiency is to start using a multi vitamin supplement.

A good strategy here is to use for a week or two daily and get the micro-nutrients levelled out and then after this initial period then maybe use once or twice a week to help keep your levels topped up.

Some of these micro-nutrients are even known to help increase testosterone levels. And the best thing of course is that being something our body needs and can get from foods anyway, these micro-nutrient supplements will not affect our natural testosterone production at all.

Let us first consider some of these T boosting micro-nutrients.

Vitamin D.

In the last section on supplements we covered the importance of vitamin D in the maintenance of our natural DHEA production, which has a positive effect on T levels. We also considered the importance of getting ample vitamin D in the section covering T boosting lifestyle choices.

It is also an essential vitamin for overall health. It helps to maintain strong healthy bones, good cognitive functioning and can play a part in helping you sleep. All of these elements can also be conducive to healthy T levels.

It is a fat soluble vitamin. Fat soluble vitamins are vitamins that are found in high fat foods such as fatty fish. They are absorbed into the body in much the same way as fats. This means that any excess of fat soluble vitamins do not immediately leave the body and they are effectively stored in our fatty tissue for later use. This of course is one of many reasons why it is recommended to maintain healthy levels of body fat. Body fat percentage that is too low makes it more difficult for the body to store these fat soluble vitamins.

The best source of vitamin D is being exposed to sunlight. For lighter skin types all that is recommended is 10 to 15 minutes per day and for darker skin 20 to 40 minutes per day. And this must be direct sunlight. Sitting in an office window with the sun shining in will not work. The glass of the window blocks the absorption of vitamin D.

The recommended daily intake of vitamin D for adults is 600 IU, or 15mcg. It is also not recommended to exceed 4000 IU, or 100mcg per day. Remember that too much of something is often just as bad as having not enough.

I have seen one blog post, from a qualified physician, who advised using a dose between 4000 and 5000 IU daily to fix a vitamin D deficiency. This of course is not a good idea. The recommended daily amount taken for just a week is more than sufficient in most cases to restore a deficiency.

There are only a few foods that are rich in vitamin D. The best foods by far are fatty kinds of fish, and fish liver oils, such as cod liver oil, oysters, salmon, swordfish, tuna and sardines. Smaller amounts can be found in egg yolks and cheeses. It can also be found in beef liver.

Vitamin D is also a kind of steroid hormone that our bodies make. It is involved in many of our bodily functions, including hormone production.

In numerous studies it has been demonstrated that there is a correlation between vitamin D and testosterone levels. The studies have also discovered that those who have a vitamin D deficiency are more likely to also be suffering with low T levels.

It has also been found that supplementing even with smaller doses of vitamin D can increase both total and free testosterone by 25%.

Based upon that statistic alone there is a quarter of the problem solved if you have low T levels. When it comes to testosterone it is essential to keep your vitamin D intake optimised.

Being a fat soluble vitamin, this does mean that you are less likely to suffer a deficiency. However this does not mean that you cannot get a deficiency. All it takes is a poor diet of processed convenience foods and a lack of sunlight for any length of time to make it happen.

Another point to note is that most people do not have any outward visible symptoms when their levels are too low. They are often completely asymptomatic.

With prolonged deficit in vitamin D intake, there are some symptoms that can occur. The body usually sends you signals that something could be wrong or abnormal. With vitamin D deficiencies this can often occur as pains in the bones, tiredness and muscles that become weaker. Due to its benefits in cognitive function, mood changes such as depression can occur with deficiency.

Other signs can also be pale skin, disturbed sleep patterns, hair loss and if you seem to all of a sudden start becoming sick more easily.

However these symptoms can also be signs of an underlying health condition so it is always best to seek medical advice if any symptoms occur.

As always and this is true with our diet, an ounce of prevention is worth a pound of cure. Eating a well balanced healthy micro-nutrient rich diet with all the essential macro-nutrients is the best form of preventing deficiencies.

When it comes to supplementation, this can be a good strategy if you live in climate without adequate sun exposure. A good way to go is to supplement during the winter months. Anyone engaged in physical training who is constantly depleting their fat stores to fuel their training sessions it can be a good idea to supplement all year round.

A word of warning. Vitamin D has quite correctly been associated with T level increases. This could lead to some thinking that more Vitamin D means more testosterone? This is not the case. It is possible to induce vitamin D toxicity. And this tends to happen with excessive supplement use, or using the supplements in larger doses. It can lead to a build up of excess calcium in the blood. This leads to fatigue, nausea and vomiting. This can even progress to the formation of calcium stones in the kidney.

Magnesium.

Magnesium is an essential mineral involved in maintaining healthy muscles, the central nervous system and in regulating blood sugar levels. It also plays a part in our testosterone. Various studies have concluded that magnesium frees testosterone and makes it bioactive. Research also found that magnesium supplementation combined with physical exercise resulted in increases in testosterone levels by as much as 24%.

A magnesium supplement alone will not work, this research demonstrated that it must be taken in conjunction with physical exercise, healthy body fat levels and good sleeping patterns to achieve these results.

Magnesium also helps to regulate cortisol levels by relaxing the nervous system and in preventing excess cortisol production. It also helps to improve sleep quality. And as we already know quality sleep is conducive to testosterone production.

Magnesium also supports thyroid function. Thyroid imbalances are mostly caused as a result of an autoimmune response caused by inflammation. Magnesium helps to reduce this inflammation. Our thyroid hormone is known to affect our sex hormone production. An over or under active thyroid can contribute to lower T levels in men.

Magnesium has also been shown to be essential to the production of hormones such as testosterone, estrogen and DHEA.

It is also said to be beneficial for bone quality, brain functioning, joint health, reducing muscle pain and recovery, improving muscle contractions, combating fatigue, healthy skin and in improving digestion.

Magnesium is present in many foods and including these in your diet should provide enough. It has been recommended that we should be taking in around 400mg per day.

Eating foods such as beans, lentils, seeds, whole grains, nuts, leafy greens, avocados, milk and yoghurt should provide you with the recommended daily intake.

Guys who are engaged in physical training are advised to supplement because with physical training your nutrient supplies are more likely to be used up quicker. There are many magnesium supplements that are usually combined with potassium sold in fitness nutrition stores. Alternatively an average daily dose of a multivitamin usually contains around 125mg and this will usually be sufficient in helping to make up any diet deficiency.

Magnesium deficiencies are often hard to detect. This is because levels must usually drop to very low levels for any symptoms to show. With extremely low levels over a long period of time can increase your chances of high blood pressure and diabetes. It can also play a part in the weakening of the bones.

Magnesium is also present in the popular ZMA supplements along with zinc and vitamin B6. This supplement became popular with gym users after it was suggested that it can increase testosterone. However most studies agree that in healthy men with good T levels and in men who engage in physical exercise it has been shown to not have any effect in increasing testosterone.

It can help increase testosterone in men with low T levels due to the zinc content, and it has been demonstrated to increase T levels in men with a zinc deficiency.

All three ingredients are beneficial for T levels making it a useful supplement in maintaining good testosterone production.

Zinc.

Zinc is an essential mineral that is fundamental to the endocrine system and to hormone function. It has also been shown to be able to increase T levels in men in some cases, usually in men with low testosterone or a zinc deficiency. It is also thought to be of great benefit in maintaining T levels.

It can also help to boost the immune system and to improve your metabolic function. It can also help to prevent many age related diseases, and reduce inflammation and oxidative stress. It is also helpful in healing wounds quicker. It also plays a part in skin health, cell growth and protein synthesis.

Although zinc is essential to our overall well being it is not produced naturally within the body. It must be ingested by eating foods that contain zinc, or through supplementation.

The recommended daily intake of zinc is 11 mg per day for adult males.

Many foods that are high in protein usually contain zinc. The best food source of zinc bar none is oysters. Just 2 oysters will give you 100% of your daily intake. Other shellfish such as crab, prawns and mussels also contain zinc. Red meat also contains a high dosage of zinc. Just 100g of beef contains 44% of your daily intake. Good amounts of zinc can also be found in meats such as pork, wild boar, lamb and veal.

Legumes such as chickpeas and beans, nuts in particular almonds and cashews, dairy products like milk and cheese, eggs, some seeds such as hemp seeds and sesame seeds, all contain good levels of zinc

Research found that zinc deficiencies are mainly nutritional in origin. A lack of meat intake, excess alcohol consumption, excess phytates, present in beans, seeds, soy products, and whole grains, or excess oxalates, found in spinach and nuts can cause a zinc deficiency.

You will probably notice that some of these foods are rich in magnesium, but it seems that consuming too much of them can cause your zinc levels to drop along with your T levels. Its all about balancing everything. This is the true art to the well balanced diet.

Too much of something is often as bad as not enough. This is the fundamental principle of a balanced healthy diet. Not too much of anything and neither too little. Forgive me if I keep repeating this but it is *that* important. Balance.

Completely avoiding these foods through fear of getting a zinc deficiency could possibly result in a magnesium deficiency. And some of them are also good sources of zinc.

One of the obvious symptoms of zinc deficiency is low T levels, which can result in tiredness, decreases in muscle mass, loss of libido and erectile dysfunction.

Other symptoms of deficiency include skin problems such as rashes, hair loss, an increase in infections, losing your sense of taste or smell, wounds taking a long time to heal and eye problems.

B Vitamins.

The B vitamins are 8 water soluble vitamins that are fundamental to the function of various cells and for energy metabolism, also neural function and in combating oxidative stress. Being water soluble this means that your body cannot store them for any length of time so regular intake is going to be necessary.

Several of the B vitamins also play a significant role in the natural production of testosterone. Vitamin B6, the third element of the ZMA supplements, is active in the production of testosterone as it inhibits estrogen synthesis.

Vitamin B3, is known to be a growth hormone booster with benefits in cell repair and recovery, and in building muscle mass. Vitamin B2 plays a role of converting testosterone into DHT, which is a potent androgen responsible for many of our masculine features.

Vitamin B1 converts nutrients into energy and plays a part in improving muscular strength. It is also beneficial to the heart, brain and nervous system. Our nervous system and cardiovascular system also have an effect on testosterone levels so consuming this vitamin can play a role in increasing T levels.

Vitamin B5 is also known as panothenic acid. Panothenic acid helps to enable the testes to produce testosterone. Recent studies into panothenic acid have shown that it has a positive effect on T levels and in sperm production.

Vitamin B12 is proven to help prevent testosterone damage and to increase energy levels.

To sum up, all 8 of the B vitamins are essential to our metabolic function. Without them we wouldn't be able to metabolise any of the nutrients we need, so any deficiencies are going to have a negative effect on the absorption of nutrients, which in turn can impact our testosterone levels in a negative way.

Vitamin B1, or thiamine, can be consumed through food and is also available in supplement form. The recommended daily intake is 1.2mg for adult men. Thiamine is found in meats, fish and whole grains. It can also be found in beans, lentils, sunflower seeds, fortified cereals, green peas, breads, noodles, rice and in yoghurt.

Due to the low amounts required, it is quite easy to get the sufficient amounts in our diets. Deficiency is therefore quite rare. Excessive alcohol consumption can cause decreased absorption and result in a deficiency. Symptoms of a deficiency can include unexplained weight loss, muscle weakness and fatigue, lowered immunity and being more prone to infections, impaired cognitive functioning such as confusion and memory loss.

Vitamin B2, or riboflavin, is available in foods and also in sup-plement form. It is key to cell growth, fat metabolism and energy production. Most riboflavin is used up immediately and it is not stored in the body in any way. Any excess amounts exit the body in the urine when we pee. The recommended daily intake is 1.3mg for adult men.

Riboflavin is found in milk, yoghurt and cheese. It is also found in lean meats such as beef, pork and chicken breast, and also in organ meats such as liver and kidney. It can also be found in eggs, salmon, fortified cereals, some nuts, particularly almonds, and in spinach.

Again because of the small amounts required deficiency is rare. It can usually be consumed in the relevant amounts through food and supplementation is rarely required.

Possible symptoms of deficiency include hair loss, swollen throat accompanied with soreness, skin rashes, itchy eyes and cracked lips.

Vitamin B3, or niacin, is another water soluble vitamin that is not stored in the body and excess amounts are passed in urine. It can also be obtained easily through foods and in supplement form. Niacin plays a role in converting nutrients into energy, and in the creation of cholesterol and fats and it also has antioxidant properties. The recommended daily intake is 16mg for men.

It can be found in fish, poultry, red meats, legumes, bananas, nuts, seeds, and in fortified cereals. It also is a common ingredient in many multivitamin supplements.

Deficiency is quite rare because it is easily found in foods and direct supplementation is rarely required.

Signs of deficiency are headaches, tiredness and loss of energy, memory loss and impaired concentration and depression.

Vitamin B5, or panothenic acid, can be obtained from foods or through supplementation. It is primarily involved in breaking down fats, reducing cholesterol and in metabolic functioning. The recommended daily intake is 5mg for adult males.

It is available in many foods. It can be found in organ meats, chicken breast, beef, pork, fish especially tuna and salmon, eggs, milk, yoghurt, mushrooms, avocado, sweet potatoes, broccoli, spinach, nuts, sunflower seeds, lentils, chickpeas, bananas, and whole grains.

Because it is so easily obtained from a wide variety of foods this means that deficiencies are rare. It usually occurs in cases of malnutrition, such as maintaining extremely low body fat percentages.

Possible symptoms of deficiency are tiredness, irritability, restlessness, muscle spasms and cramps, nausea and vomiting, and also disturbed sleep patterns.

Vitamin B6, or pyridoxine, is responsible for the metabolism of proteins, carbohydrates and fats and it also helps to support the immune system and plays a role in preventing sickness and diseases and in cognitive functioning. The recommended daily intake is 1.7mg for men. There is also an upper limit for B6 consumption at a level where it is considered to be toxic. This is 100mg.

It can be found in milk, ricotta cheese, salmon, tuna, eggs, chicken liver, beef liver, poultry, beef, carrots, spinach and leafy greens, sweet potatoes, green peas, chickpeas, avocado, bananas, papayas, oranges and cantaloupe melons.

Vitamin B6 deficiencies usually occur when other B vitamin deficiencies are also present. Often there are no symptoms that are noticeable. Certain conditions such as auto-immune diseases can cause deficiency as can excessive alcohol consumption.

In severe deficiencies there can be some possible symptoms such as skin problems and lowered immunity and increased susceptibility to infections and sicknesses.

Vitamin B7, or biotin, is the vitamin that helps to convert food into energy. It is also a water soluble vitamin that is not stored by the body any excess amounts are passed in urine. Regular absorption through food or supplements is necessary. The recommended daily intake is very low, only 30mcg, or 0.03mg per day.

Biotin is readily available in many different foods making it an easy nutrient to obtain without the need for supplementation.

Biotin can be found in meats, such as beef, pork and in liver. It can also be found in salmon, tuna, yeast used in making bread, eggs, sunflower seeds, nuts especially peanuts, almonds, walnuts, and in many fruits and vegetables such as sweet potatoes, mushrooms, spinach, avocados, cauliflower, bananas and asparagus.

It is very readily available and only a tiny quantity is needed each day so deficiencies are very rare. Excessive alcohol intake can lead to a deficiency as is the case with most nutrients. It has also been suggested that B7 deficiency can cause hair loss, along with skin and nail problems.

Research seems to suggest that there is no evidence to support this. Biotin supplements have been promoted as being beneficial to healthy hair and skin and many people have been influenced into the belief that it can be beneficial to hair and skin. These claims are unfounded.

Vitamin B9, or folate, is another vitamin that cannot be stored in the body, any excess is passed from the body and daily intake is required. It can be obtained from food and in supplement form. The common name for these supplements is folic acid. Its main role is in the production of red blood cells. The recommended daily intake is just 400mcg, or 0.4mg per day.

It can be found in legumes such as lentils, peas and beans and in fortified grains. It can also be found in vegetables such as avocado, broccoli and Brussels sprouts, leafy greens, asparagus and beetroot. It can also be found in eggs, beef liver, nuts and seeds and in citrus fruits, papayas and bananas. It is a micro-nutrient that is abundant in a healthy balanced diet.

Vitamin B12, is a water soluble vitamin that can be obtained through foods or supplements. Vitamin B12 also contains the mineral cobalt. It is needed for the production of healthy red blood cells and to support the central nervous system. It is also associated, in its supplement form, as an energy supplement.

The recommended daily intake is only 2.4 mcg. This means that the body requires it only in trace amounts for normal levels to be fulfilled.

It is readily abundant in a healthy diet and can be found in many foods. 100g of either beef liver, cooked clams, tuna and ground beef all provide more than 100% of the recommended intake. It can also be found in eggs, milk, cheese, meats, fish and poultry.

There is rarely a need to supplement vitamin B12 as it is so easily obtained through your diet. I have found that it is sometimes included in some multi ingredient T boosting supplements, usually because of its reputed energy boosting qualities.

As you can see from the above information it is relatively easy to get enough B vitamins from your diet if you are eating a well balanced diet. For most guys who train, meat, fish and other protein sources are usually consumed on a daily basis so they are probably getting an adequate supply.

The main thing to be aware of really is that many of these nutrients are not stored in the body and any excesses are passed in urine. Therefore regular daily intake is required.

Vitamin A.

Vitamin A has been linked with androgen production in various studies. If there is little or no vitamin A in the body then levels of serum testosterone can drop. Also any deficiency means that you cannot properly metabolise dietary fats. Healthy fats play a role in the production of testosterone. So not so much of a testosterone boosting vitamin but more of a vitamin that is essential to maintaining T levels. Vitamin A can be obtained through foods and is often an ingredient in most multivitamin supplements.

Vitamin A can also support eye health and it helps to stimulate the production of white blood cells and also regulates cell growth. It is a fat soluble vitamin and the body can store any excesses in the body for later use.

The recommended daily intake is 900mcg, which is the equivalent of 3000 IU in supplement form.

It can be obtained from these foods. Leafy greens, kale, spinach and broccoli, carrots, sweet potatoes, pumpkins, tomatoes, red peppers, cantaloupe melons, mangoes, fish oils, milk and eggs. As mentioned before a multivitamin usually contains the RDI of vitamin A.

Deficiencies are quite rare but it is not quite so abundant in our diets as other micro-nutrients. For this reason using a multivitamin is usually a good idea especially for men who engage in physical training.

Mild deficiency can cause tiredness and increase susceptibility to infections and viruses. A more serious deficiency can cause night blindness, dry itchy eyes, dry skin and dry hair.

Because of it being a fat soluble vitamin there is a risk of toxicity especially when supplementing. Best advice is to stick to the multivitamin as they usually contain the correct dosage of vitamin A. Symptoms of possible toxicity are blurred vision, nausea and vomiting dry skin and extreme light sensitivity.

Vitamin K2.

Vitamin K is not often cited as a potential testosterone boosting micro-nutrient. In fact it plays a fundamental role in testosterone production. Researchers have recently discovered that every process in the body that determines the function of testosterone needs vitamin K.

Another study, which focussed on a long term observation of guys reaching puberty discovered that their levels of vitamin K correlated with their T levels.

This is quite important because many diets are deficient in vitamin K. It is only found in high levels in a few foods, which not many people enjoy eating such as leafy greens. For this reason supplementation might be required.

I do not particularly like leafy greens but I make a point of eating them at least twice a week simply because they are packed with many different micro-nutrients. I drown my leafy greens in extra virgin olive oil to make them more palatable.

The good news is that vitamin K is a fat soluble vitamin. As we have already discussed this means that it can be stored in the body's fat tissues for later use.

Another piece of good news is that in addition to being available in foods and in supplement form it is also produced naturally, the intestine can produce vitamin K from the bacteria in your stomach that is produced during the digestion process. However it is a little more complicated than that. Don't just think problem solved. There are two forms of vitamin K as I will explain.

The recommended daily intake of vitamin K1 is 120mcg. For vitamin K2 it is between 100 and 300mcg. Which are not huge amounts so that is a good thing. And because when it is utilised within the body it is broken down very quickly and passed in urine and stools so there is no risk of toxicity, as with other fat soluble vitamins.

When it comes to foods it is important to note that the food sources for each form of vitamin K are different. Vitamin K1, or phylloquinone is found in leafy greens. Vitamin K2, or menaquinone, is found in some animal and dairy products. Menaquinone is also the form of vitamin K that is produced naturally in the intestine from bacteria.

A single sprig of parsley contains more than 100% of your daily intake of K1. I mean that's just one mouthful of food and it goes well sprinkled over some fish.

Another great source is the leafy green mixed salads you can buy. All of these leaves are rich in vitamin K. 100g of kale provides 680% of your recommended intake. So considering that your body will store what you do not immediately use means that eating kale along with a steak or a piece of fish a couple of times a week should be enough to maintain an adequate level.

Other leaves such as spinach, beet greens, mustard greens and Swiss chard, which usually feature in the mixed leaf salads, all contain K1 in abundance. So including mixed leaf salads into your diet once or twice a week should give you more than enough. Remember that being a fat soluble vitamin it is best to consume these greens along with some fat to aid better storage of the excess.

Fatty fish, meats or just some olive oil drizzled over them will all work well for this purpose.

Likewise 100g of either cabbage, broccoli or brussel sprouts will all provide at least 100% of your daily intake. However they are less abundant in vitamin K so you will need to consume them a few times per week to get the required amounts.

Vitamin K1 is also present in smaller amounts in avocados, green beans and green peas. It is also present in some fruits in smaller amounts for example kiwi fruits, blueberries, blackberries, red currants, tomatoes, grapes, figs and pomegranates.

When it comes to vitamin K2 you should look predominantly to animal products. Beef, chicken or pork liver, chicken, pork chops, ground beef, bacon, duck breast and beef kidneys all contain K2. It is also found in dairy products such as hard cheeses, soft cheeses, eggs, whole milk butter and cream. The amounts are smaller in relation to the percentages of daily intake found in greens but with K2 being naturally produced from the bacteria in the stomach during digestion this should provide a sufficient amount for our purposes.

Deficiency is rare in those who follow a balanced healthy diet. Symptoms of deficiency include excessive bleeding due to the failure of the natural clotting mechanism and possibly weaker bones.

Calcium.

Calcium is well know for its benefits to bone health and good teeth but it also helps with proper blood clotting function, regulating normal heart rhythms, muscle contractions and to aid proper nerve function.

99% of calcium is stored in the bones and the other 1% in the blood and other tissues. If levels in the blood drop too low then the bones release calcium into the blood to keep levels up and to keep the body's systems functioning.

Recently it has also been linked to testosterone. In one recent study for example, researchers took 30 healthy men and divided them into 3 groups.

One group was given 35mg of calcium per day along with no exercise. Another was given 35mg of calcium combined with exercise. The third group received no calcium but performed the exercise. The results found that training increased testosterone but that increase was greater when combined with calcium.

Now that hardly classes it as a testosterone booster as such and this was a study involving only 30 men in 3 groups of 10 so these results are limited. And bear in mind the group not training but taking the calcium supplements did not see the increases that the exercise only group achieved.

Still calcium is essential to normal functioning of our body and there is no doubt that this has an effect on T levels. Calcium is found in abundance in our diet and the recommended daily intake is 1000mg.

It can be found in dairy products such as milk, cheese, yoghurt and also in canned fish like salmon and sardines which include the bones of these fish. It can also be found in almonds, edamame beans and in leafy greens.

Bear in mind that calcium is not so easily broken down in the intestine, so this means if you are in the habit of measuring the exact quantities of nutrients that you consume, your body will not absorb all of that calcium.

The calcium quantity that will be absorbed into the body is the nutrients' bioavailability. Dairy products have roughly a 30% bioavailability and greens only 5%. So bear this in mind. Also note that calcium can block the absorption of other minerals such as zinc and iron. In many multivitamin supplements these are often all included together and some inevitably get cancelled out.

A downside to the complete A-Z multivitamin supplements that have become popular.

As calcium levels in the blood are regulated deficiency is rare. It usually occurs as a direct result of severe nutritional deficiency and can be difficult to detect because other symptoms associated with other nutrients will probably also be present.

One obvious sign is deterioration of the condition of the nails and teeth, and the long term implication could be osteoporosis. Deficiency can also occur in people with a lactose intolerance as dairy products are the best food source.

Boron.

Boron is a trace element that is reputed to help to increase testosterone. It has an important role in cell metabolism and supports the growth and maintenance of bones and aids in recovery and wound healing. It also has an effect of the body's use of estrogen, testosterone and the absorption of vitamin D and magnesium.

It has been mistakenly believed by some to be an estrogen blocker, but as we know, all men contain small amounts of estrogen as part of our healthy hormonal balance. In effect, blocking estrogen excessively will also contribute to lowering testosterone. And of course increasing T levels will naturally result in a corresponding slight rise in estrogen as the balance is maintained. And this is no bad thing. After all you would then have a higher T level?

So what does the research suggest? Recent studies seem to agree that boron increases the conversion of total testosterone into free testosterone, which in turn can augment sexual function. It also increases T levels by up to 25%, while reducing levels of estradiol by as much as 50%. It also allows for more free testosterone to bind in the blood which could have benefits as we age. These benefits were seen in just a week of supplementation in doses of between 6 to 10mg per day.

In older studies the results were different. In a study into male athletes in the 1990s, it did show that exercise increased T levels, but that boron supplementation made no difference when compared to a placebo group. This could be due to T levels in men being higher in the 1990s than they are now, due to the generational decline in T levels. But this is just speculation on my part.

Boron also seems to be effective in treating ED, but only if the problem is low T levels, or higher levels of estradiol. So it seems that for certain it can be very effective for helping to sort out hormonal imbalances, and potentially, a useful supplement to help combat exposure to endocrine disruptors.

The maximum recommended daily intake of boron is 20mg for men. The recommended intake is 1-1.5mg. It is safe to use long term as a supplement of no more than 20mg. But too much boron can cause toxicity, and in extremely high doses can even be fatal. It is advisable to supplement in doses of up to 10mg to begin with, then drop the dose for maintenance purposes.

Symptoms of toxicity can include indigestion, nausea, vomiting, diarrhoea, headaches, seizures, and even skin colour changes. It seems that with trace elements such as boron, less, or not too much, is definitely more.

The body does not produce its own boron but you can also find it in some foods as well as in supplements. It can be found in prune juice, raisins, peaches, apples, broccoli, avocado and coffee.

Half an avocado contains 100% of the recommended intake. A cup of prune juice 140%. A whole peach 80%. Considering this it is easy to get the sufficient daily amount without the need for supplementation.

In my opinion, and this is partly supported by research, supplementation would be more beneficial to guys with low testosterone levels than to guys who already have good T levels.

To give you more of an idea of the fundamentals of a well balanced diet, let us consider all of the micro-nutrients in turn, and the foods that you can find them in. There are many different diets recommending many different strategies but the real truth is that regular intake of micro-nutrients along with proteins, carbohydrates, fats and dietary fibre forms the basis of a healthy balanced diet. To go further would just be to complicate things unnecessarily. Just tracking all these micros will complicate things enough already.

Vitamin C.

Vitamin C, also referred to as ascorbic acid, is essential to the human body and regular intake is necessary. This is because the body cannot produce it on its own. The body also cannot store it for very long. It is a water soluble vitamin.

It plays a role in the formation of collagen, which is used to help skin quality. It aids the absorption of iron, has antioxidant properties, and helps to fight infections. It also helps the function of neurotransmitters in the brain.

The body requires around 45mg of vitamin C per day. The recommended intake is 90mg for men. Any excess that is not used is passed from the body. It can be mainly found in fruits and vegetables. Fruits and vegetables are considered to be the best sources. It is also heat sensitive meaning that the cooking process depletes the vitamin C content so it is best consumed in raw fruits and vegetables. It is worth noting that many nutrients are depleted during the cooking process. It is something to be aware of.

Smoking depletes vitamin C so it is recommended that smokers increase their daily intake to 125mg.

It can be found in citrus fruits such as oranges, lemons, limes and grapefruit. Also in kiwi fruits, pineapples, melons, mangoes, tomatoes, strawberries, plums, cherries, guavas, blackcurrants, bananas, lychees and papayas. It can also be found in fruit juices such as orange and pineapple juice. Avoid fruit juices from concentrates because they are excessively high in added sugar.

It can also be found in some vegetables. In particular green vegetables like leafy greens, green peppers cabbage, lettuce, broccoli, Brussels sprouts, cauliflower and green chillies.

Just one green chilli contains more than 200% of the required daily intake.

It can also be found in white potatoes, red chillies, red and yellow peppers.

Vitamin E.

Vitamin E is an antioxidant that helps to protect the body from what are known as free radicals, things like cigarette smoke, air pollution and radiation. Free radicals are basically elements found in our environment that can cause cell damage. It is also helpful to our skin, vision and immune system.

Vitamin E is a fat soluble vitamin meaning that our body can store vitamin E for later use in our fat tissues. The recommended daily intake is 15mg per day for adults.

It can be ingested in foods or taken as a supplement. It is found in oils such as wheat germ oil, soy-bean oil, extra virgin olive oil, sunflower oil and also in sunflower seeds.

It can also be found in meats, particularly in organ meats such as liver. It is also present in egg yolks, most nuts and seeds, and it is also in peanut butter or almond butter. Leafy greens, pumpkins, red peppers, asparagus, avocados, mangoes and broccoli all contain vitamin E.

Vitamin E supplements are popular due to their reputed benefits to our skin but considering that the recommended intake translates to 22 IU and that vitamin E supplements usually contain between 400 and 1000 IU there have been recent studies which discovered that there was a higher risk of death in those who were ingesting more than 400 IU per day. It was suggested that the body's ability to store vitamin E played a significant role in the potential for toxicity.

Most of the supplements that are available have doses that are too high, so it is best to get your vitamin E from food sources.

Iodine.

Iodine is essential to healthy thyroid function. It helps the thyroid to produce hormones, which control your metabolic rate. It is a trace element mineral that the body cannot make for itself so must be ingested via food or supplements.

Normal thyroid function has an affect on T levels. An over or under-active thyroid can contribute with various negative side effects in the body, including an affect on hormones.

The recommended daily intake is 150mcg. It is probable that most people are already getting enough in their diet. Supplements are rarely required. Too much iodine can be harmful. The upper limit is considered to be 1100mcg.

Iodine can be found mainly in animal proteins and in sea vegetables such as seaweed and kelp. Fish, such as tuna, prawns, North Atlantic cod, and oysters all contain iodine. The is also the iodized table salts, milk, cheese, yoghurt, eggs, beef liver and chicken.

Iron.

Iron is an important mineral that is involved in the transportation of oxygen into the blood, and the transference of energy into the cells, this aids the maintenance and development of muscles. Iron deficiency is the most common deficiency in the world and it can cause extreme fatigue.

Basically without enough iron there are not enough red blood cells to transport oxygen.

Iron is stored in the body in the liver, spleen and in the muscle tissues. The recommended daily intake is 8mg for men. Guys who engage in intense physical exercise are at a higher risk of deficiency so a supplement could be useful.

This said it is probably not needed daily. Personally I have found that using an iron supplement every day affects digestion and gives your poop the consistency and appearance of sticky tar. This is an indication of perhaps a little too much iron in the body. The supplements can also cause nausea, stomach cramps and diarrhoea in some people.

Iron in foods comes in two forms. Heme and non heme.

Heme iron is found in animal flesh and seafood, and non heme iron is found in plant foods. Non heme iron can also be found in animal foods in animals that consume plants such as cows.

Heme iron is more readily absorbed by the body. Heme iron combined with vitamin C improves non heme iron uptake. Large amounts of calcium can inhibit the absorption of non heme iron. Just a few interactions to be aware of if you are the type to carefully measure the micros of your diet.

The best sources of heme iron are organ meats, such as liver, and also beef, poultry, canned tuna, oysters, mussels, clams and eggs.

For non heme iron good sources include beans, lentils, chickpeas, nuts, seeds, dried fruits, broccoli, spinach and dark chocolate (minimum of 70% cacao).

A thing to be aware of is that too much iron can have an effect on SHBG levels. With high levels of iron present in the body, the body can then have higher levels of SHBG, which can result in more testosterone being bound, and this could lead to reductions in free testosterone.

Iron overload can also produce a condition called hemochromatosis. With this condition it is important to note that 75% of cases go undetected and display no noticeable symptoms. Left unnoticed over time this can have a detrimental effect not only to depleted T levels but loss of libido, abdominal pain, joint pain and inflammation, chronic fatigue and weakness.

Long term this can lead to arthritis, liver disease or even liver failure, hypothyroidism, heart disease, pancreatic disorders, endocrine system issues such as impaired adrenal and pituitary function and testicular failure and hypogonadism. If you observe an animal based or carnivore diet then you will need to pay particular attention to this.

To help prevent the condition the most effective remedy is calcium rich foods, such as dairy products, or a calcium supplement. Calcium helps to significantly reduce iron absorption. Also plant phenols found in foods such as leafy greens, legumes and avocado can be effective. Drinking tea or coffee can also have the same effect.

If you are observing an animal based or carnivore diet then you may want to consider adding some other foods to your diet and a well balanced diet is far more nutritionally abundant than eating just meats alone.

Potassium.

Potassium is a mineral that all the tissues in the body need. It is also an electrolyte, which effectively carries fluid that supports various cell and nerve functions. Its principle role is to maintain normal levels of fluid inside our cells.

When training we lose a lot of electrolytes in our sweat. This effect increases in warmer conditions, it is important especially in hot weather to keep our electrolyte levels up. Drinking a lot of water in hot conditions without keeping electrolyte levels up can lead to water poisoning in extreme circumstances. It can easily be neglected to consider electrolytes when thinking of hydration.

Potassium is also extremely important for the nerves and muscles and it can also help to lower blood pressure. Potassium helps to relax the walls of the blood vessels and to carry out any excess salt in the urine. Tight blood vessels and high sodium levels both contribute to high blood pressure.

Potassium deficiency is much more likely to occur if lots of processed foods are consumed. We humans are designed for a high potassium diet and food processing destroys the potassium levels in foods and increases the sodium levels. Sodium and potassium intake must be balanced out.

The recommended daily intake for men is 3400mg. It seems a lot but this is because all the cells in our bodies need it and that is a lot of cells! Potassium is available in many foods and can also be taken in supplement form.

It is also said that our bodies need at least 800mg daily to avoid deficiency. A lot of our potassium is passed in our urine. It is also lost through sweat and stool and because we excrete so much we need to continually consume it to avoid a deficit occurring.

Our diet is abundant in potassium because it is found in so many different foods. So it is not difficult to get the required amounts.

Potassium is found in fruits such as bananas, water melons, cantaloupe melons, honeydew melons, oranges, kiwi fruits, tomatoes, coconut, grapefruit and also in some dried fruits such as apricots, raisins, dates and prunes. Any fruits that contain potassium can be consumed as juices too, such as orange juice, grapefruit juice, tomato juice, coconut water etc.

Some vegetables are also rich in potassium, these include leafy greens, cooked spinach, zucchini (courgettes in the UK), cucumbers, avocados, broccoli, mushrooms, potatoes, sweet potatoes, butternut squash, peas and pumpkins. Also some legumes contain potassium such as lentils, lima beans, kidney beans, soy beans and pinto beans.

Potassium is also present in some fish including salmon, tuna, trout, cod, halibut and sea bass. It is also available in dairy products like milk and yoghurt, and also plant based milks like almond milk and soy milk, and molasses, some nuts, meat and poultry, rice, pasta and bread.

So it is really easy to find sources of potassium in our diets, just steer clear of processed foods. But I am sure you know that already!

Sodium.

Sodium and salt intake is linked to poor health and there is truth to this if you consume too much but it is also an essential mineral that our bodies cannot do without.

Excesses of salt can cause high blood pressure, kidney problems and heart disease and even strokes. However you still need some sodium in your diet as it keeps your electrolytes balanced with your water intake. Sodium is the counterpart of potassium and it maintains fluid levels outside of cells. Potassium maintains fluids inside of cells.

If you engage in physical exercise, or physical vocation and you sweat a lot then you are going to deplete your electrolyte stores. To restore electrolyte levels you need potassium and salt to maintain a good balance. Having one without the other is not a good thing so completely cutting out salt intake is never a good idea. With many people who observe a healthy balanced diet eating whole foods it is easy to neglect sodium intake and levels can get too low.

The recommended daily intake is NO MORE than 2300mg. About 1500mg is fine. 1000mg is preferable. And the good news is that there some food sources that contain sodium that can also have health benefits.

Of course one way to get enough salt is to lightly salt your meals or to cook with salt. Provided you don't use too much it is fine. To keep your iodine levels up at the same time use iodized salt.

Or alternatively salted nuts are an option. Nuts contain protein, essential fats and many essential micro-nutrients. Eating salty nuts in moderation could be an option. Another good way to get sodium, and this is one of my preferred options is canned fish such as tuna or salmon a typically sized can contains 400 to 600mg of sodium. Or there are canned beans, which also contain sodium in the liquid that they come in.

Another protein packed option is cottage cheese, which also contains sodium. But best of all, in my opinion are olives. Packed with good fats, anti-inflammatory properties, and also containing many vitamins and minerals, but also naturally salty.

Proceed with caution though as four good sized olives contain about 140mg of sodium.

Your electrolyte ratio should be 3:1. For every 1000mg of sodium you consume, you should consume 3000mg of potassium. Electrolyte balance is important. The average western diet produces an imbalance as we often consume more sodium.

An imbalance will occur if you fail to observe the above recommended ratios. You preferably want to avoid having too much or not enough. Balance is the key.

Symptoms of an electrolyte imbalance include fatigue, diarrhoea, nausea, vomiting or constipation, headaches, quicker heart rate, muscle cramps, muscle spasms and muscle weakness, numbness in fingers and toes confusion and irritability.

You are much more likely to experience an electrolyte deficiency in hot weather. This risk will increase when you are doing any physical activities. If you suspect that you have an electrolyte deficiency or imbalance then the best course of action is to consume drinks containing electrolytes.

Prevention is the best course of action. Always consume electrolytes during periods of hot weather.

You should seek to include all of these essential vitamins and minerals in your diet as they all serve a purpose in the normal functioning of our bodies and as previously mentioned they form the basis of a well balanced diet with no deficiencies. Deficiencies in any element can lead to imbalances and unwanted symptoms within the body. This will no doubt have a corresponding effect on not only our hormone output, but in many bodily functions.

Lets now look at the T boosting diet and ways we can use our diet to optimise our T levels and to avoid dieting methods that can lower testosterone production.

22

Phytonutrients.

Phytonutrients are nutrients that are found in plants. They are effectively the immune system of plants and they protect the plant from any environmental hazards. And consuming them offers many benefits.

Plants are often exposed to pests, toxins and pollution and this generates harmful free radicals within their cells. As we know humans are also vulnerable and affected by free radicals.

The plants develop these phytonutrients to protect the plant from such damage.

So what do phytonutrients do for us and our human bodies? They help to protect us in much the same way as they do for their hosts, the plants.

We are exposed to radiation, pollution and many toxins. These toxins are everywhere in many everyday products that most of us use.

So we need phytonutrients to help our body fight off the potential damage from these free radicals.

And how do we get these phytonutrients? By eating lots of different fruits, vegetables, herbs and roots in our diets. Not something that meat only guys want to hear and their community often deny the benefits of eating fruits and vegetables.

But consider this. I have been consuming vegetables for years and getting plenty of these phytonutrients in my diet. I am in good health and all my markers are within normal ranges. My energy and vitality levels are high and so is both my total and free testosterone.

Consider also that endocrine disruptors are toxins and that consumption of phytonutrients will offer you some protection against the effects of these chemicals on your body.

Phytonutrients also help to support our immune system and our normal cellular activity. They can help to protect cells and make them less vulnerable to infections and diseases they have also been shown to protect against some forms of cancer.

They also help to protect the brain from age related cognitive decline and help to protect the organs. All of the longevity gurus make no secret to the fact that they consume phytonutrients daily as part of their protocols. There is a reason for this.

During the covid pandemic my wife tested positive and for three weeks we were isolated together in a small apartment. We shared the same space, ate together, sat together, shared the same bed, and exchanged bodily fluids during bedroom games. At every test I tested negative. My immune system is so powerful I very rarely get sick. This is no doubt helped by consuming phytonutrients.

To get the best results when it comes to maxxing out your T production potential it is important to treat your body as an entire organism. Any problems or imbalances and this can and does inevitably affect testosterone.

And phytonutrients have many health benefits. All these benefits and the prevention of any of these conditions will help to ensure that not only are your T levels optimised, that they will also stay optimised as you get older.

Phytonutrients help to reduce blood pressure. Blood pressure can cause many health issues and blood pressure medications can negatively affect T levels.

A diet rich in phytonutrients also helps to improve skin health and potentially help to decrease the risk of skin cancer. They can also decrease disease causing inflammation. Inflammation is also detrimental to T levels. Inflammation is also the number 1 root cause of many health conditions.

If you are optimising your testosterone and hormone production by consuming at least a moderate intake of cholesterol then phytonutrients can help regulate cholesterol, preventing excess cholesterol build up within the body and also help to reduce LDL cholesterol.

It is vital for hormonal health to consume cholesterol as all hormones are made with cholesterol a deficiency will cause hormonal problems. But too much cholesterol can be harmful to our health so it is important to balance cholesterol and phytonutrients can help balance cholesterol levels.

Phytonutrients also help to optimise digestive functioning allowing for improved uptake of nutrients. They promote the growth of intestinal bacteria and intestinal flora which play a significant role in digestion and absorption of nutrients.

It is important to consume a well balanced diet to get the best results when it comes to testosterone. A balanced diet results in a well balanced body. A well balanced body results in optimised bodily functioning.

Consumption of plant based foods and phytonutrients will help significantly in the maintenance of a well balanced body and balanced hormones.

23

Glycogen Stores.

Why Glycogen Stores Are Important.

There are many who are promoting low or no carb diets and claiming that the body will adjust and adapt to not receiving regular carb intake.

Well there is some truth to this. The body will adapt and adjust but not necessarily in a positive way. Carbohydrates are responsible for our glycogen stores within the body.

Consider that ATP, or Adenosine Triphosphate, is the sole fuel for muscle contractions. When training at or near maximum intensity the muscle store of ATP will be depleted quite quickly.

Therefore to maintain normal muscular contraction functioning and to get the best from your training, ATP must be continually topped up.

So it seems that when the depletion of muscle glycogen stores are low, muscle cells cannot produce ATP rapidly enough to maintain exercise intensity. The perfect definition of the word "fatigue."

Glycogen is excess glucose stored within the body to be used by the cells as energy. Glucose generates ATP which is the ultimate fuel source for the body.

So how do you know that you are glycogen depleted?

Decreased strength and power.

Muscles rely upon stored muscle glycogen to fuel explosive muscle contractions. When lifting weights the body is primarily working anaerobically, this means without oxygen.

Carbs are necessary for the body to kick-start this metabolic process. Even fats are oxidized through the krebs cycle, which also requires carbs.

The krebs cycle is a series of reactions occurring in mitochondria, through which almost all living cells produce energy in aerobic respiration. And this process requires carbs.

Without sufficient carb intake the body will not be able to produce enough energy to promote forceful muscle contractions.

Workouts can seem harder than usual.

Muscular glycogen is stored in muscles, and along with that comes increased muscle volume from water being drawn into the muscles.

A muscle with a good supply of glycogen often holds water giving it a feeling of fullness. If you are feeling muscular flatness or a loss of fullness this could be due to glycogen depletion.

This will also correlate to depleted muscle recovery.

There can be many reasons for post exercise recovery issues to occur. And nutritional factors are often to blame and should always be the first thing to consider if you find this happening to you.

During intense physical exertion you are asking your muscles to work at much higher rates. If you fail to replenish glycogen stores then this can diminish the amount of muscle glycogen that you will have available and eventually depletion will occur.

Often the solution is to replenish glycogen stores immediately after training or even during training to avoid this catabolic reaction.

And of course the risks increase during longer and harder workouts glycogen depletion can start happening as little as 30 minutes into any hard training session. This is why many athletes engaging in strength, power and endurance routines, will often supplement during training with carbs and BCAAs to keep their muscle glycogen levels high, which helps to trigger protein synthesis and this helps with post workout protein uptake and ultimately muscle repair.

Of course fatigue can lead to depleted testosterone production. The body cannot be functioning at an optimal level if you are suffering with fatigue. And depleted glycogen stores can contribute towards this.

And testosterone plays a role in signalling glucose uptake into the cells to be used as energy. A vicious circle. So if you are suffering with lower than normal levels of T, blood sugar levels can rise after eating a meal and stay high for a longer period of time. Low testosterone inhibits glucose uptake.

So it seems that carbs are necessary for the human body. This need increases along with your levels of physical activity. And physical exercise is a great way of managing glucose levels within the body.

If you want to optimise your T levels taking care of your glycogen stores is going to be of great benefit to you. Exercise and activity levels correlate to good T levels. Exercise requires consistent energy maintenance. This all requires glycogen. For this you will need to consume some carbs.

24

Carb Intake is Personalised.

Optimise Your Carb Intake

The trend right now, at the time of writing, is low carb diets. And the problem with this trend is that it is not suitable for everyone. For many this will cause energy crash and this can throw the body out of sync. What is not often considered is that when it comes to nutrition we are all different and have different requirements for our body to be functioning at its own individual optimum. In this section we will look at optimising carbohydrate intake.

For people with diabetes or high blood sugar levels of course low carb could be beneficial.

But what is often overlooked is that your unique genetics and your unique microflora profile are probably the biggest factors in how you convert food into energy, while at the same time keeping your blood sugar and insulin levels balanced. High insulin can have a negative effect on the endocrine system.

There is a lot of generic info out there about carbs. We know that processed carbs, refined carbs and sugary carbs are known as bad carbs and carbs derived from whole foods are generally considered to be good carbs. But it is not that simple. Not all good carbs are the same and depending on the digestive system of the individual, not all good carbs are digested and converted into energy in the same way.

Also when it comes to carb intolerances some cases are obvious and deliver obvious reactions. Other levels of intolerance can be harder to notice. Everyone's level of either tolerance, or intolerance, to carbs is different.

I am going to consider ways you can discover your own optimum carb intake levels and determine which types of carbs or foods are going to work best for you. Carbs are essential to energy so this is pretty important.

Towards the end of this section I will show you a system for measuring your carb tolerance and how to monitor your absorption of carbs.

The first thing to consider is that there are some factors not even directly related to diet that can affect digestion. Stress levels, mental state, sleep patterns and exercise levels will all have an influence over your digestive system.

When the bodily stress response is activated then digestion can be suppressed because the body can re-route its resources to secrete cortisol. In the case of chronic stress or prolonged and consistent stress, the central nervous system can shut down digestion by slowing the contractions of digestive muscles and decreasing the secretions for digestion.

This can then manifest itself with many symptoms including heartburn and indigestion, nausea, vomiting, diarrhea, constipation and abdominal pain.

Stress occurs within the mind. The brain directly affects the stomach. The stress response inhibits the digestive system while the relaxation response activates it. There is information in another section of this book about balancing cortisol and offers insight in how to fix this.

In truth the digestive tract is sensitive to emotions. Anger, anxiety, elation, sadness and many others can all trigger symptoms in the digestive system. This is why developing a calmer and more centred being and having our mental and emotional states under our control is so important. A balanced mind correlates to an equally balanced body. And like it or not, your mental state affects your digestion and often can display digestive symptoms that can be mistaken for other factors such as intolerance.

So first and foremost address your mental state and seek to fix any imbalances that may be there. Your digestive tract will definitely improve if there are any problems in this department. My book, The Full Breath, offers instruction and insight into how to manage stress effectively and to become a more calm and centred being.

Connected to stress and mental state is our sleep. Changes occur in the digestive process during sleep. The oesophagus becomes more prone to gastric acid because during sleep the number of swallows is reduced, this reduces the amount of saliva and a reduction in the contraction of the muscles of the gastro-intestinal tract. In effect sleep slows down digestion. So a full stomach at this time of the day can be detrimental.

The time you take you last meal of the day will also affect your nocturnal digestion. And how long before bedtime you should eat is best adapted to your metabolic rate. A rough guideline is to wait at least 2 hours after eating to get into bed. For those with a slower digestive tract, maybe longer will be needed. Gravity also aids digestion and digestion works more efficiently with the body in an upright position. Laying down too soon after eating can be detrimental to digestion.

Another very important factor that is fundamental to digestion is chewing food properly and fully masticating the food to the consistency of a soft gel in our mouths before swallowing. Ideally the consistency of a smoothie. This significantly improves digestion and makes digestion much, much more efficient and cannot be understated. It also significantly improves nutrient uptake, and the body will also use up less energy during the digestive process.

When food is bolted down quickly, which many have a tendency to do, and only chewed for a very short time before being swallowed, this results in the food entering the digestive tract in much bigger lumps. This means it is more difficult for the digestive tract to absorb nutrients from the food, this will take up more energy and can lead to after-meal tiredness. Tiredness after eating can also be a symptom of carb intolerances.

A lack of sleep, of course can also increase stress and disrupt our natural cortisol cycle, but it can also increase sensitivities to foods and cause changes in the intestinal microflora. This can lead to bloating, inflammation and stomach pains. And if you are not sleeping well and are, as a result, less active during the day this will probably reduce how efficiently you can digest and process carbs and fats in your diet. Even if you are masticating your food properly.

Exercise also affects digestion. It can improve nutrient uptake and digestion efficiency but the thing to remember is that the stomach and intestines are not athletic organs. This means that they will not adapt to increased exercise induced physiological stress. Over training and not taking adequate rest can have a negative effect on digestion. It can cause increased reflux, delay small intestinal transit and reduce absorption of nutrients. Again as with everything in the physical and mental state, balance is the key to optimisation of your organism.

There is no easy way out, quick fix, hack, or instant results when it comes to attaining balance. You need to work on your organism until you figure it all out for yourself your optimum is not my optimum. We are different and this is all personalised.

Now, when it comes to carb intake we all know already the difference between high GI and low GI carbs and to avoid eating processed carbs so lets skip that and get into good carbs and carb tolerance.

When it comes to carb tolerance it seems that the higher the starch content the more likely intolerances are to occur. Healthy whole foods such as sweet potatoes and brown rice do contain essential phytonutrients and fibre and they are healthy carbs, but they are also higher in starch. And the higher the starch content, means a greater ability of that carb to cause disruptions and spikes in blood sugar and insulin. So even when considering good carbs, not all good carbs are equal.

The best type of carbs for tolerance are nutrient rich, low starch, and fibre rich carbs. Things like leafy greens, spinach, broccoli, brussels sprouts, cabbage, and cauliflower for example. And of course many fruits also fit the bill here, they tend to have higher carb content, but then they contain natural sugar content. This of course is a factor that also must be taken into consideration when considering blood sugar and insulin levels.

Because blood sugar and insulin imbalances are at the root of many health problems associated with over-consumption of carbs, and because higher starch carbs are more likely to spike blood sugar and cause digestive reactions, it is a good idea to tweak your intake of these foods to suit your own body's unique needs. Some people will find that eating fewer high starch carbs will improve their blood sugar. Others will find that they will benefit from eating a few more of them. Our responses to carbs are individual.

This only emphasises the absurdity of those in the hardcore carnivore niche, who claim that carbs are unhealthy for all, and that the body doesn't need carbs and the body will adjust to not ingesting them. For the majority of people this is practically guaranteed to lead to some kind of problems. The obvious one being energy crash due to depleted glycogen stores. The avid carnivore MD, Paul Saladino, even crashed his testosterone after 5 years of carbohydrate avoidance. He has now become an advocate of carb intake!

Now its pretty straightforward to dial in your own unique carb balance with some simple at home experimentation.

Pick one high starch carb. This could be sweet potatoes, legumes or brown rice. Consume 100g of that one carb with a meal that also includes a healthy fat source, a healthy protein source and a little fibre.

Make a note of the quantities of fibre, fat and protein you consume at this meal. Wait until 30 minutes after eating to see how you feel. Now if you are feeling satiated from the meal with steady energy and no cravings then that amount of starchy carb is probably ideal for you. Provided of course this does not affect your digestion in a negative way.

If after 30 minutes you are feeling sleepy and needing a nap or you are craving sugar or even caffeine despite being full then this can be a sign that this amount of that carb is too much for you.

If this happens then repeat the following day. Same parameters only drop the amount of carbs. Take the meal at the same time of the day. Include the same amounts of fibre, fats and protein but drop the carbs down to 50g.

If you get the same sluggish feeling after 30 minutes, or the sugar or caffeine cravings then keep repeating the process each day, dropping the amount of carbs each time until you find the correct amount. If this continues to happen with higher starch carbs then try changing the foods. If that brings no joy then use carbs with a lower starch content.

Another thing to consider with this experiment is you try this out for the first time and after 30 minutes you feel great. But then you feel hungry or irritable after a couple of hours this can be a sign that either this amount, or this type, of carbs isn't ideal for you.

If this happens then repeat the meal the following day. Keep the amount of carbs the same but slightly increase the amounts of fibre and protein on the plate. If that doesn't help then repeat again the following day only this time increase the fat content on the plate.

If adding more fibre, protein or fat to the meal doesn't erase your symptoms at the 2 hour mark then repeat the meal again only this time slightly increasing the amount of carbs on the plate. This might seem illogical but this particular pattern of symptoms can indicate low cortisol and reactive hypoglycaemia, and this can be relieved with a few more carbs.

Another common scenario. Back to the meal on day one. Immediately after your first test meal you feel tired, irritable or have cravings for sugar or caffeine.

If this happens then cut the carb amount by half the following day. If that doesn't help then repeat the meal increasing the fibre intake.

This process of tracking symptoms and reactions to carb intake over time might seem a waste of time to some. But this is your energy and vitality and optimum bodily balance we are talking here and as you get older you will thank yourself over and over for making the effort to dial your diet to your own unique requirements. It has taken me best part of 20 years to discover my own optimum diet.

For the quick fix, instant results and fast gratification types this no doubt will not resonate. But the good news for these guys is that TRT is now trending and widely available. Finding your optimum balance, both physically and mentally, is not easy and requires some work from you. For those prepared to put in that work you will be still reaping the benefits and still feeling young and full of energy and vitality decades from now.

Another thing you can do if you want to, especially if you are getting any of these reactions to carbs is to monitor your blood sugar using a glucometer. These are small devices you can use at home and they are quite inexpensive.

Monitoring you blood sugar after meals is also a great way of getting further in touch with your own bodily reaction to ingesting foods. Your blood sugar levels will give you an idea of how efficiently you are digesting foods. Best approach here is to test is about 2 hours before eating and then again 2 hours after eating.

I use my device even now, after dialling my diet to a state of perfection. I test my blood sugar levels once a month just to monitor myself and my levels are pretty consistent at between 4.5-5 nmol/L.

Carbs are highly beneficial to those who can tolerate them. And most people can tolerate them to a degree. It is all about finding your own optimum requirements. Each body can only store so many carbs, its all about managing that balance for optimal energy and vitality levels, optimum bodily functioning and optimum health.

And being at your optimum means you are far more likely to have optimised testosterone levels and to keep those T levels healthy into older age.

In an age where TRT is trending and many young guys are taking it, optimum natural hormone production is priceless.

25

Testosterone Boosting Diet.

W hen it comes to maintaining higher levels of testosterone as we get older the best strategy is to be doing everything we can to optimise our T levels. All these little things when added together will give us our best chance of achieving this. And when it comes to our diets there is no one great thing or one single food that can just jump our testosterone. Again it is the combination of many little things that when combined together will collectively make all the difference.

T Boosting Foods.

Another way of aiding the maintenance of T levels is eating foods that are specifically beneficial to testosterone production on a regular basis. We have already discovered that a healthy well balanced diet is going to be very effective in this crusade, but there are a few foods that are particularly beneficial to T levels. First we will give a little attention to each of these.

Ginger.

Ginger is already pretty well known as an immune booster and a great way of improving the flavour of certain dishes and it has a number of health benefits. One of those benefits happens to be its potential to boost T levels.

Ginger has been used in Chinese and Indian cooking for centuries. It has also been used in traditional Chinese medicine and also in Indian Ayurvedic medicine for more than 2000 years. It is considered to be a super food with multiple health benefits.

In recent years it has been studied to ascertain its abilities to boost testosterone, and with promising results. For this reason many T booster stack supplements now include ginger extract among their ingredients.

Clinical studies confirm that long term ginger consumption helps maintain healthy levels of testosterone. This obviously serves our purpose here as we are looking to keep T levels up as we get older and to help combat the inevitable decline as we age.

Clinical studies have also confirmed that ginger supplementation boosts testosterone levels. As an added bonus ginger also has many health benefits and can contribute towards improved overall health.

And there seems to be little or no conflicting evidence or results. They all seem to confirm that ginger not only helps to increase testosterone production overall, but it also increases free testosterone availability, and improves sperm production and sperm quality.

And the best part is that this is not just on older men that this works, it works for men of all ages. One study involving men of between 19 and 40 years old found that with 3 months of continuous ginger consumption, all the men increased their T levels by around 20%. And these gains in T levels remain consistent with regular consumption. Being a natural food source there is no affect on natural testosterone production, and no risks whatsoever of hormonal imbalances.

So whether you decide to use a ginger extract, or to include it regularly in your diet, it is something that you can use *permanently* to help in maintaining your T levels. No need to cycle your ginger consumption as with many other supplements. However it is best to consume raw ginger instead of supplementing.

A good way to consume ginger that I use daily is to consume it as a drink. I take around 2-3 grams of fresh ginger root, remove the skin and then chop it into little pieces. Put the pieces into 500-1000ml of water, give it a good shake then put it in the fridge for an hour. You can use a glass bottle if you want to avoid drinking from plastics. After an hour the ginger has infused the water making a very tasty and very healthy drink. Shake well before each use. I usually eat the ginger pieces as well when I have drunk all the water for added intake.

You could use carbonated water if you prefer, making a healthy alternative to fizzy drinks. Adding a little lemon juice is a good idea if you do not like the taste of ginger.

Alternatively cut the root ginger into very small pieces and swallow with water, in the same manner of taking a pill, and without chewing. This is great if you do not like the taste. In this way you can still consume ginger even if you hate the taste!

It is believed that ginger is effective to T levels because of its ability to boost circulation and blood flow. Most studies have declared that ginger improves blood flow to the testicles where the testosterone is manufactured.

Apart from boosting blood flow and its benefits to testosterone it also has antioxidant properties, which can reduce oxidative stress. It can help regulate blood sugar levels and boost nitric oxide production. Nitric oxide is effective for ED, it helps the muscles in the penis to relax allowing the penis to fill with blood more efficiently resulting in better erections. Nitric oxide also boosts exercise performance and improves recovery and even helps to reduce blood pressure.

Ginger also boost the immune system, and eating fresh raw ginger also improves oral health helping to keep teeth in better condition, providing fresher breath and reducing the build-up of oral bacteria in the mouth.

Ginger is one of the best supplements for maintaining T levels long term. Start incorporating into your diet as often as you can.

Fatty Fish.

We all know that fish is an excellent source of protein. It is also packed with essential fats and many micro-nutrients and it is something that should be featuring in any well balanced diet.

Numerous studies have linked low body fat and low fat diets to low testosterone levels in men. We all know that some fats are bad but eating fatty fish and consuming fish oils is an excellent way to get enough healthy fat in our diets.

They contain omega 3 fatty acids, which have been shown, during various studies to be effective in increasing Lutenizing hormone production in men. This no doubt has an effect on T levels, and increased levels of free available testosterone. However the studies used an omega 3 supplement and were not long term studies.

But you can see the obvious benefits here. Regularly consuming fatty fish will give you a continuous supply of omega 3 fatty acids, which will help you no doubt in maintaining your T levels long term. The intake of healthy fats will also help to combat the lowering of testosterone as you get older. This will also help to prevent the build-up of plaque in your arteries, which will help you to maintain good blood flow and sexual function too.

It is important to remember to observe the correct ratios. Omega 3 is really important. Omega 6 is equally important. But balancing the two out is fundamental. A quick reminder. Never exceed a ratio of

4:1. Four parts omega 6 to one part omega 3. The ideal is 2:1. The optimum for testosterone is 3:1.

Fatty fishes that are packed in essential good fats include tuna, salmon, swordfish, mackerel, mussels, anchovies, trout, herring and sardines.

Extra Virgin Olive Oil.

Olive oil is another good fat that can contribute to a healthy diet. It is also known to be effective for T levels. Olive oil has many health benefits such as reducing bad cholesterol and in improving heart function. It is also a source of good cholesterol.

In one recent study men between 20 and 40 were given 25ml of olive oil per day for three weeks. There T levels increased by almost 20%. Considering that a low fat diet can reduce testosterone by up to 15% you can see the benefits of olive oil.

The primary concern here is to source a good quality oil. Avoid all olive oil that comes in plastic bottles. This is an obvious sign of low quality and the oil will absorb some of the endocrine disruptors found in plastics and this will no doubt affect the oils T boosting potential.

Always buy olive oil in glass bottles that are of darkened glass. Light can damage the oil. And most good quality oils will have some kind of seal on them for example IOC, NAOOA or COOC.

Another pointer is to seek out oils that have either a harvest date or a manufactured date. Oils that have only a use by date could have already been a year or two old before being bottled. This affects the quality.

Avoid cheap oils. These are likely to be oils that have used inferior olives or that have been mixed with other oils to bulk them out and make them go further. Also cheaper oils have cheaper pressing and extraction methods. Some of these processes involve the use of chemicals and agents, for example the industrial solvent hexane, to increase quantity in relation to raw materials.

There will still be trace elements of these toxins present in the end product.

Observe the ingredients. Reject anything that includes anything other than olive oil or olives!

Oysters.

Oysters have been reputed to be an aphrodisiac and beneficial for sexual health for hundreds of years.

Oysters are rich in zinc, which is known to have an effect on testosterone. In studies using zinc supplementation it was shown to increase testosterone in human subjects. Because of their high zinc content, just 2 oysters contain 100% of the recommended daily intake, oysters have some potential as a testosterone boosting food.

Zinc is essential for male sexual health and fertility. Low levels of zinc will also help contribute towards low T levels. Zinc is also necessary for maintaining levels of dopamine, a neurotransmitter involved in male sexual health. Research suggests, albeit not conclusively, that increasing dopamine production increases sexual arousal. This could be why it has been considered to be a powerful aphrodisiac by some.

There is no doubt that zinc plays a role in testosterone production and in T levels and oysters are packed with zinc, and omega 3 fatty acids, so this means that oysters should sometimes be on the menu of anyone looking to optimise their T levels.

Leafy Greens.

Not often associated directly with testosterone, leafy greens can be very beneficial to our hormone levels. This group of leafy vegetables is packed with so many essential micro-nutrients that are good for your overall health and well being, your immune system and in optimising your T levels.

Always seek to include foods from this group into your regular diet at least once or twice a week.

Leafy greens have such an abundant nutritional profile. They are high in dietary fibre, and have substantial amounts of vitamins A, C and K, and most of the B vitamins. They also contain iron, magnesium, calcium and potassium. With such an abundant nutritional profile they make a great addition to any T boosting diet. Deficiencies in micro nutrients can contribute towards declining T levels.

Chillies / Spicy Foods.

It has been confirmed that men who like it hot are more likely to have higher testosterone. It seems that men who consume hot foods regularly are more likely to be risk takers, have greater ambitions, and be more adventurous in the bedroom too. And of course these things are also associated with higher testosterone.

In one study at a French University, the resulting article interestingly was entitled "Some like it hot," it was found that eating spicy foods correlated with higher T levels.

The men, aged between 18 and 40 were given a bowl of mashed potato and then invited to season it with as much hot sauce and salt as they liked.

After they had eaten the researchers measured how hot their meal had been and took saliva samples. They discovered that the men who had smothered more hot sauce on their potato had higher testosterone. And the more sauce and heat they applied it seems the more testosterone they had.

This was of course salivary testosterone and not results gained via a blood exam. The study did not observe lifestyle habits such as exercise, alcohol consumption, etc, so this is not 100% conclusive.

In another study on mice however it was shown that consuming capsaicin, which is the active ingredient that makes chillies hot, had resulted in increased levels of total testosterone.

So it seems that plenty of chillies and hot sauces such as Piri Piri, Tobasco and Sriracha sauce consumed on a regular basis can potentially increase testosterone and help to maintain T levels if adopted into your lifestyle as a regular habit.

Chillies also help to prevent allergies, fight infections and boost the immune system. They can improve circulation and boost cardiovascular performance in exercise, prevent bad breath, reduce the risk of some types of cancers, improve your metabolic rate.

Improving metabolic rate helps to prevent storing excess fats, promoting a healthy heart, and in aiding digestion. They are also said to enhance sexual performance, this could be due to their T boosting potential and their circulation stimulating qualities.

So getting some heat and spice into your diet on a regular basis is a must for anyone looking to optimise their testosterone production. Try to include this kind of food at least twice a week.

Lean Meats.

There seems to be a conflict of opinions regarding meat as a testosterone boosting food. The vegan community swear that it makes no difference in T levels to not be eating meat. And there are many studies that confirm this. But there are also many other studies that have found that meat eaters tend to have higher T levels than men who abstain from meat.

With such a conflict apparent I read many articles and papers on this exact problem to discover which is true. And it is difficult to conclusively answer this. There are many studies that support both camps. So we must look beyond the carnivore vs vegan debate and apply some logic and nutritional factors.

But one thing that I did discover is that none of the studies into supporting the vegan position that I read specified whether the test subjects engaged in physical training or led sedentary lifestyles. Papers and journals that are published tend to be pretty detailed and include lots of scientific jargon and parameters so it would be fair to suggest that they would mention "athletes," or something similar if that were the case?

If we rely upon mere facts here it is fair to say for example that meats contain taurine and creatine, which both contribute to T levels. It is also well known that a vegan diet can be lacking in these elements. Also it is more of a challenge for vegans to get adequate protein and especially fats (think cholesterol here) in their diets when compared to carnivores. This would at least give carnivores a slight advantage?

If we look at the typical nutritional analysis for meat we find the following ingredients present in practically all unprocessed meats. Only the exact quantities are varying a little depending upon the meat.

Most meats contain protein, vitamins A, B-complex, and K. Vitamin D3. Fats, both saturated and mono-unsaturated. Omega 3 and omega 6 fatty acids. Zinc, magnesium, potassium, taurine, phosphorus and creatine. These are pretty well established nutritional facts and many of these elements *do* contribute towards T levels. Now some of these are also present in veggies too but the amino acids, creatine and essential fatty acids are not particularly abundant.

Of course where it can be a challenge for vegans to get adequate amino acids, creatine, taurine and essential fatty acids in their diets, it is not impossible. And there is always the option of using supplements. The real challenge for vegans lies in getting enough cholesterol to make enough testosterone.

Meat eaters certainly have a distinct advantage here simply because it is easier for them. It is a fact that animal and fish products have the highest protein content of all foods. They contain more amino acids, fatty acids and cholesterol.

Another question arises here being where do vegans get their omega 3 and omega 6 fatty acids? The best source by far is fish and meats?

The Vegan Societies' website advises: "Include good sources of ALA (Alpha-Linolenic Acid) in your daily diet, such as chia seeds, ground linseed, hemp seeds and walnuts, and use vegetable oil as your main cooking oil."

Now this, for me anyway, sets an alarm bell ringing in my mind. Because vegetable oils contain industrial solvents used during the manufacturing process that can harm testosterone production and testicular health when consumed on a regular basis. This is confirmed by many different sources and also by numerous studies and research.

And trace elements of these chemicals are present in the oils that are on supermarket shelves. It would cost money to remove the industrial solvents completely. The chemicals are present to save money. You come to your own conclusion here.

Vegans are also at an increased risk of vitamin D3 deficiency. Even most D3 supplements are made from animal products. Vegans are also prone to deficiencies in iodine, calcium, zinc, vitamin B12 and iron. And deficiencies in these elements can affect T levels either directly or indirectly.

I am not trying to condemn vegan-ism here. This is a guide to optimising T levels and if you are reading this and you are vegan, you need to be aware of all this. Remember that it is going to be more of a challenge for you. But certainly not impossible.

But returning yet again to the research it seems that if you add some intense physical exercise into the mix then the results seem to be rather different. And these results remain consistent in all studies that specify that "athletes," or men who engage in "intense physical activity" have been used as test subjects.

The study that really highlights this particular element fairly is a comparative study in athletes, who were engaging in training for the entire study. They were observed for three weeks while following a strict vegetarian diet. Then *the same* athletes were also observed for another three weeks while following a meat rich diet.

It was found that T levels were 35% lower when they were following the vegetarian diet. Their T levels were recorded at the beginning of the study, then recorded again at the end of each 3 week diet regime. Now the study did not show that meat consumption increased their baseline T levels but it did clearly find that with a vegetarian diet combined with exercise their levels fell to 35% below their baseline T levels.

The researchers also suggested that because the meat is rich in fat, this influenced the findings. A diet more rich in fat, which of course means more cholesterol, and it is already an established fact that (good) cholesterol, contributes towards better testosterone production. This fact is also widely agreed upon.

Other studies, comparing low fat diets to a diet containing fat rich foods like meats found that there was a decrease in T levels for those following a low fat diet. Later in this section we will get into this a little more.

One thing that cannot be disputed is that the nutritional elements found in unprocessed meats are beneficial to testosterone production. So if your dietary preferences allow for meat consumption you should be aiming to be eating lean meats at least 3 times per week. I consume either meat or fish, and often both, every single day.

Garlic.

Garlic has many health benefits, it is so much more than just a flavour enhancer. It can boost the immune system because it has anti viral properties. It can help with toothache, lower the risk of cancer and improve heart health. It can also help to reduce blood sugar, improve your mood, and is great for unblocking nasal congestion when eaten raw.

It can also help with an over active thyroid, which of course can affect T levels. It is beneficial to detoxing the liver, lowering bad cholesterol levels, it also helps with stomach disorders, and to reduce water retention. Anyone using creatine knows that water retention is possible so that could be of benefit to you.

It also boost blood flow and can aid sexual potency and athletic performance. It also has benefits in preventing or treating ED. If that wasn't enough reasons for including it in your diet it also naturally boosts testosterone levels.

It contains a chemical called dialyse-disulfide that helps produce testosterone in the testicles. And that has been proven in studies. And this is enhanced when it is combined with physical exercise and foods high in amino acids such as lean meats. No surprises here. It also aids protein synthesis, which can contribute to building muscle mass more efficiently.

To get the full benefits it is best consumed raw as cooking reduces its effectiveness. However eating it regularly in cooked form will still provide benefits.

If the taste is too strong for your palate then you can still consume it raw by cutting it into small pieces and swallowing them with water.

One to two cloves of fresh garlic per day seems to produce optimal results. It can be chopped finely and sprinkled raw onto meats or fish or added to salads to improve the flavour. In this way it goes great with leafy greens!

I consume at least one whole garlic, raw, every week. I also add it to cooked meals to improve the taste. For anyone looking to maintain T levels into older age it is an *essential* part of your diet.

Turmeric.

Turmeric is another flavour enhancer used extensively in cuisine and it comes from a plant belonging to the same plant family as ginger.

It has many health benefits including anti-inflammatory properties, boosting the immune system and in reducing the risks of heart disease. But it also has the potential to boost testosterone.

In this respect it works in many ways. It improves the synthesis of cholesterol. Turmeric has been shown to be effective in lowering bad cholesterol levels and also in augmenting good cholesterol. And testosterone is manufactured from good cholesterol so this effect will enhance your T level potential.

It also has been shown to enhance the processing of vitamin D meaning that your body can use up more available vitamin D. Vitamin D is fundamental to testosterone production and the higher your uptake of vitamin D, the higher your T levels tend to be. Please be aware of the possibility to vitamin D toxicity. Not *too* much.

Turmeric is best consumed together with black pepper. If you decide to supplement with turmeric it is essential that you buy a supplement that combines turmeric with black pepper.

Research found that combining the piperine in black pepper with the curcumin in turmeric increases turmeric absorption by as much as 2000%. And of course this in turn will increase the benefits.

As a food it can be sourced either as a dried powder, which can be added to foods or as a fresh root, similar in appearance to ginger but with an orange flesh.

Again best consumed raw, as cooking tends to deplete the effects of the curcumin. It can be finely chopped and added to salads. If you cannot get the fresh root then the powdered form can be added to foods or to hot water as an infusion.

Now when it comes to testosterone, any foods which contribute towards a healthy well balanced body are going to benefit T levels. Any deficiencies certainly are going to increase the risk of worsening the natural decline in testosterone as we age.

So the base rule is that if the food benefits you, eat it. If it doesn't benefit you in anyway at all, don't eat it. The space inside your stomach is sacred. There are so many vital macro and micro nutrients that your body requires. That's a lot of nutrients from a diverse range of foods. It seems detrimental to be wasting valuable stomach space on things you don't *need*.

If you are the kind that likes to treat yourself once in a while, and cheat meals are very beneficial, especially when to adhering to any weight loss plan, then try to choose something useful for that treat. Difficult but not impossible.

My own personal cheat treat choice is dried and crystallised ginger pieces. Ginger is an ace T boosting food, the cheat is that it is dried and lightly coated in sugar. A tiny bit of sugar now and then is OK. Just not too often.

Other foods that are reputed to be excellent choices for any T boosting diet include milk, eggs, honey, oats, bananas, cabbage, pumpkin seeds, spinach, chia seeds, Brazil nuts, pomegranate, red grapes and avocado.

I decided not to go into any further detail with this last selection of foods because there is not enough evidence directly linking them to increases in testosterone production or T levels. Apart from the eggs, but they are coming up very soon. But they are all beneficial foods containing essential nutrients our body needs and are well worth including in your diet.

DHEA Boosting Foods.

There are also some foods that are rich in DHEA. As we have already discussed, DHEA is a naturally produced hormone that is closely linked with ageing and in testosterone production. DHEA is effectively converted into testosterone and is connected to how well you age. Depleted DHEA levels will not only leave you more prone to many age related diseases, it will also have an adverse effect on your naturally declining T levels.

Therefore, as already mentioned, preservation and optimisation of DHEA production and DHEA levels is absolutely fundamental to our purposes here. So anything that you can do to aid this process is going to benefit you in the long term. And this includes eating foods that are rich in DHEA to enhance DHEA production.

Here are a few foods that are rich in DHEA and worth your consideration.

Wild Yams.

Wild yams are packed with diosgenin, which is a compound that is converted within the body into DHEA. This makes yams a top choice as a DHEA food and a great way to boost your hormone levels.

One thing to be aware of is to not confuse these with the more common sweet potatoes, also called yams in some countries. They are similar, being root vegetables but here their similarity ends, they are two wholly different vegetables.

The difference is that yams have a rough skin, akin to tree bark and yellow flesh similar to a standard potato, and they are not sweet. Sweet potatoes have a smooth skin and orange sweet tasting flesh.

They are not so easy to get hold of in some parts of the world. They are native to Africa, Asia and parts of the Americas. A good place to find them is oriental food stores if there is one in your region.

If you cannot find them then don't despair, there are other options that are abundant!

Soybeans.

With such a reputation (unproven it seems) as a testosterone killing food you might decide to steer clear of this one. Yes they contain phytoestrogens, but they are also absolutely stuffed with DHEA. Moderation is the key. Too much could be bad, too little and you could be missing out. I know it is controversial to even include soy in this guide, and in this context, but it would not be a complete and honest guide if I just ignored the facts. However soy is not essential, skip soy products if you like in favour of these other DHEA rich alternatives that many of you will find more acceptable. I hardly ever consume soy and I have survived well without it.

Eggs.

Eggs as we already know are beneficial to T levels in many ways as they are packed with many essential elements that our body requires on a regular basis. But eggs, particularly the yolk, are brimming with DHEA. I am sure that many of you will prefer eggs to soybeans! And next time you think about an egg white omelette you might just want to go all in and include that cholesterol rich, and DHEA packed, yolk too. Not to mention its also an excellent source of saturated fats.

Eggs are also packed with L arginine and are not only a great source of good cholesterol but they are also a great source of saturated fats. Many will advice against eating too many eggs but the benefits of eggs are so great. Eggs are abundant in so many essential nutrients. They are also *great* for testosterone!

Eggs are also very effective in boosting nitric oxide. Nitric oxide is known to be very helpful in achieving strong erections.

Nitric oxide also boosts exercise performance and improves recovery and even helps to reduce blood pressure.

Lean Meats.

Again we arrive at lean meats. Another factor in favour of the meat vs vegan debate mentioned earlier in this section. Best DHEA meats by far are chicken and turkey, which are also good sources of protein for anyone following an anti-inflammatory diet.

Dark Chocolate.

Anyone searching for a beneficial cheat treat need look no further than dark chocolate. Whenever choosing dark chocolate look for chocolate that contains at least 70% cacao for maximum benefits. And its stuffed with DHEA!

Legumes.

Things like beans, chickpeas or lentils are also a great source of DHEA to get into your diet. And they are a good source of protein and stuffed with many essential micro-nutrients. A great way to consume legumes is to knock up a fiery mixed bean chilli dish. T boosting chillies along with DHEA packed beans. And don't forget the abundance of micro-nutrients, the protein, the unrefined carbs and dietary fibre that will provide too. Just have a glass of filtered water handy!

Dairy Products.

I don't want to be seen as out to destroy the vegan side in that earlier debate, but dairy, which are animal products of course and not consumed by vegans, are also full of DHEA and very beneficial to a hormone boosting diet. Cows milk, cheeses and unsweetened yoghurt are good options.

Again there is a lot of talk today suggesting that these products are exposed to hormones and they are. They are made with the milk from female cows. So you would expect some estrogen to be present? But if you are concerned then you can opt for organic products as these are less likely to come from animals fed growth hormones or antibiotics unnecessarily. But bear in mind that many commercial dairy farms give substances that enhance milk production. This enables the cows to be permanently lactating and thus producing more milk.

Cruciferous Veggies.

An option for vegans to boost their DHEA intake, cruciferous veggies such as broccoli, Brussels sprouts, cauliflower and cabbage are not only jammed with many essential micro-nutrients and beneficial to any diet but they are also rich in DHEA. One downside to this type of vegetable is that they are best consumed cooked, which means that their nutritional value might be lower due to being exposed to heat.

A way around this problem is to make a veggie packed minestrone, all the nutrients leached during the cooking process will still be present in the water used to cook the vegetables. You can then either blitz with the food mixer to create a nutrient packed velouté or leave it as is for a nice chunky broth. Add some passata to flavour the water.

Nuts and Seeds.

Most nuts and seeds are also great sources of DHEA. Cashews, walnuts, almonds, Brazil nuts, chia seeds, flaxseed, pumpkin seeds. A great snack to pop into your bag when you are on the move or for a mid morning or pre-workout snack and even add them to a yoghurt or cottage cheese for breakfast.

Now to be fair there is a dark side to consuming too much DHEA. Consuming DHEA packed foods is generally safe but consuming too much could have potential side effects such as hormonal imbalances. Balance is the key to all things. Never forget this.

However most of the research tends to refer specifically to DHEA supplements, not to DHEA rich foods so this shouldn't be a problem. Consuming DHEA rich foods can be a great way to support your overall health and indeed your hormonal health. These foods can help in combating hormonal imbalances and in enhancing your physical performance and mental function and cannot be overlooked.

Now we are going to consider some specific diet strategies that can have an effect on testosterone levels.

The Carnivore Diet.

The carnivore diet is growing among guys looking to increase their testosterone and there is a good basis for this because meats and animal fats contribute greatly in providing the much needed cholesterol to make testosterone.

There are many benefits to the carnivore diet but there are a few important things to consider that are often neglected by those who promote this diet.

They tend to concentrate on the positive elements of the diet when promoting the idea and they either ignore or deny and negative, or potentially negative aspects.

With any specialised diet such as carnivore and also with the vegan diet is that there is a huge potential for nutrient deficiencies. There are vital nutrients absent from the vegan diet as we know and there are also some potential nutrient deficiencies to be aware of for those following the carnivore diet. As we have already discussed, any nutrient deficiencies can have a negative effect on our health and our testosterone production.

So for the benefit of all carnivores I am going to run through those potential deficiencies and make suggestions to compensate for these deficiencies.

First up we have vitamin A. This can be dealt with by consuming liver from beef, chicken or pork.

Also B vitamins, in particular folate and biotin, and deficiencies are linked to nerve and blood disorders. Again liver from beef and chicken are rich in these nutrients. But as B vitamins are water soluble and excesses are not stored within the body, regular daily consumption is advised. A B-vitamin complex supplement is going to be useful here too.

Vitamin C is an essential antioxidant and it appears in sufficient quantities mainly in fruits and vegetables. It can be more difficult to obtain enough if you are only eating meats. This can be compensated for by eating a variety of organ meats. Liver, heart, tongue etc.

Vitamin E is another essential antioxidant lacking in a meat only diet. Fish eggs and salmon are good sources of vitamin E that you may want to consider adding to your diet to remedy that potential deficiency. Extra virgin olive oil is rich in vitamin E and just a couple of tablespoons taken neat straight from the spoon can also solve this issue.

Vitamin K1 is typically found in plant based foods. This element is going to be difficult to incorporate into a carnivore diet without considering adding plants to your diet. A sprig of parsley provides the recommended daily intake and this can be sprinkled over the top of a steak as a seasoning. Otherwise you may want to consider using a supplement.

Boron is an important nutrient that is abundant in fruits and nuts but difficult to obtain on a strict carnivore diet. Many followers of the animal based diet include fruits, dairy and honey into their diets to overcome the nutritional shortfall of the carnivore diet. Of course if you decide that you would prefer not to switch to being animal based in this way then you may find a boron supplement useful.

Calcium is essential for our teeth and bones, muscle contractions and nerves. It is easy to get from dairy products and plant foods but lacking in meats. It can be obtained from canned fish that includes the bones such as salmon. Calcium also helps in preventing iron overload as it inhibits iron absorption. We will get into this very soon.

Potassium is another essential nutrient. Again fruits and vegetables are rich in this element. Some shellfish, octopus meat and salmon contain some potassium but not in the abundant quantities it is found in plant based foods. Potassium is an important electrolyte and it can be a good option to include an electrolyte supplement into your daily routine to ensure you are getting enough.

Magnesium is another element that is hard to obtain from meats alone. Many complete electrolyte supplements also contain magnesium so this could be an option that will cover both of those deficiencies. Many carnivores consume bone broth which can be a good source of magnesium. Other alternatives include shellfish, fish eggs, and fish such as cod and salmon.

Polyphenols and phytonutrients are considered to be the best antioxidants and are essential to human health. The participants in the longevity Olympics all include these antioxidants in their daily diet because of their proven benefits for improved health and their potential to longevity. They help to prevent cancer, infections, heart disease and more. It is only possible to get these powerful nutrients from plants and only emphasises the limitations of the carnivore diet. The only options you have are either supplements, or a more varied diet.

Fibre is completely absent from the carnivore diet. Many of those who promote this diet claim that the body does not need fibre and will adapt to not ingesting any. This is simply not true. A healthy digestive system contains bacteria which are known as microbiota or gut flora. Fibre is essential for healthy human gut flora. When we don't eat enough fibre the gut flora eats away at the mucus of the intestinal wall, which medical science believes makes us more prone to being sick and developing stomach cancers. Fibre is also beneficial because the gut flora uses fibre to produce short-chain fatty acids, which are anti-inflammatory compounds that nourish the lining of the intestine.

Meat contains no fibre. Supplementation is the only option other than reconsidering your approach to a healthy balanced diet geared for testosterone production. An animal based diet including fruits and vegetables would provide adequate dietary fibre.

A meat only diet also leaves you more prone to oxidative stress. This is because cooking meats releases substances that increase oxidative stress. These substances build up when meat is cooked at high temperatures such as barbecuing, grilling and pan frying. Cooking methods that don't brown the meats such as slow cooking can potentially inhibit these substances.

Keto diets have been associated with improved mitochondrial functioning and lower oxidative stress. So carnivores could benefit from eating fattier meats to help in inducing ketosis. Also taking antioxidant supplements and consuming olive oil can be beneficial.

Plant based foods are much richer in antioxidant compounds than animal based foods. This is why it is better to consider an all rounded, varied and balanced diet not only for testosterone, but also for optimal health.

The carnivore diet is also known to have the potential to increase cholesterol levels which can develop into health issues if left unattended. The section on balancing cholesterol will be particularly useful for carnivores. Any diet that limits or neglects essential nutrients can harm testosterone levels.

The well known American MD, Paul Saladino was an avid follower of the carnivore diet. He found that this diet lowered his testosterone levels, increased his blood cholesterol levels to exceed normal levels and induced abnormally high iron levels. By switching to an animal based approach including fruits, honey and dairy was a game changer for him as he fortunately was able to recover his testosterone. He now routinely has his blood examined and now keeps an eye on his cholesterol and iron levels. I am subscribed to Paul's channel on You-tube and would highly recommend that any carnivore check him out.

Iron overload can be catastrophic to testosterone levels and is a risk associated with high meat consumption. Many advocates of the carnivore diet ignore or deny the possibility of this occurring. However this is an established fact. The bioavailability of iron from meats is high. Regular intake of large amounts of meats may burden the body with iron.

When this occurs it is difficult for the body to get rid of excess iron easily. It stores the excess iron in the organs such as the liver, pancreas and the heart.

Too much iron can lead to the development of a condition called hemochromatosis. This condition can cause testicular failure, pituitary gland dysfunction and can even result in testicular cancer. It also causes symptoms of low testosterone in men.

It increases levels of SHBG, which cause more testosterone to become bound and this results in decreases in free testosterone which cause symptoms of low testosterone. There are an abundant number of studies which confirm this.

Of concern is that 75% of cases of hemochromatosis go undetected and display no obvious symptoms until the condition is well developed and difficult to reverse. Common symptoms of this condition include chronic fatigue, weakness, joint pain and inflammation, abdominal pain and loss of libido.

Left untreated this can lead to arthritis, liver disease or liver failure, hypothyroidism, heart disease, pancreatic disease, and endocrine system issues affecting the testicles, adrenal glands and the pituitary gland. This condition means that it will then become extremely difficult to optimise and maintain your testosterone levels. And it is difficult to correct or treat and the medication prescribed for this condition is known to lower testosterone levels.

To help prevent iron overload from occurring the best way is to consume plenty of calcium. Calcium inhibits iron uptake. So does consuming coffee, and both green and black tea. Vitamin C increases iron absorption so it is a good idea to avoid consuming vitamin C when consuming meats.

Other effective strategies include reducing iron rich foods. Avoiding raw shellfish. Eating foods that decrease iron absorption such as milk, dairy, eggs, leafy greens, oily fish, avocado and beans and legumes.

The best diet for testosterone is a diet that includes all nutrients and a varied choice of foods. When it comes to testosterone in particular, the carnivore and the vegan diets are not the best options because of their limits and potential deficiencies.

The Keto Diet.

The keto, or ketogenic diet has been gaining popularity in the fitness scene for its effectiveness in helping to achieve and maintain an aesthetically pleasing and chiselled physique. It is certainly very effective for this purpose and it can also be a very effective way to kick-start any weight loss program.

Now we all know that excess fat and being overweight tends to correspond with lower T levels so any weight loss goals are certainly going to help you with the long term goal of maintaining your testosterone production as you get older.

I do not dispute that the keto regime is very useful, but taken to excess, or to remain in ketosis for too long does have a dark side. If you follow a keto diet there are a few things to consider.

I have already touched upon the dangers that maintaining low body fat for long periods of time has on T levels in a different section. I will not repeat myself here, but avid keto practitioners often pursue keto for the purposes of getting their aesthetics down to perfection and taken too far is not always a good thing. At least in the long term anyway.

Now the fundamental principle of keto is to observe a high protein, very low carb diet. Carbohydrate consumption is kept to a maximum of 50g per day. Combined with exercise the idea or principle is that the high protein intake builds muscle and the low carb intake then forces the body to consume the fats for energy, resulting in either achieving a weight loss effect, or a leaner cut look.

So the carbs amount to 5% of your energy intake. Protein consumption is around 1.5 to 2g of protein per pound of bodyweight, this tends to be around 30% of your energy intake, and the bulk of energy consumption comes from fats. There are variations to this but this is the basic principle.

This then means there is a displacement of carbs versus proteins in the body. These proportions of macro nutrients triggers the production of ketones in the body, which gives the diet its name.

Ketones are basically a type of chemical that your liver produces when you break down fats. It's a natural process. Your body also uses ketones for energy during exercise when you don't store as many carbs, and also whenever you fast.

However you can have low ketone levels in your blood without it ever being a problem.

So how does the keto diet affect T levels? Well it seems that it can boost T levels. But remember that it is not an easy diet to stick to but some studies say that it works. I can confirm that it is not easy from experience.

One study showed that after observing keto for 11 weeks, combined with exercise, and resulting in the cutting of the fat mass of these subjects, that significant gains (118ng/DL) in total testosterone occurred.

Another study showed an increase in T levels after only a week and that the increases continued going up throughout a further 4 weeks of observation. Sounds too good to be true? The test subjects were overweight men with diagnosed low testosterone.

So for sure if you have low T levels then this could be an extremely effective method to kick start and increase your testosterone production. It can also be an effective way to kick-start fat loss.

Beware of ketone supplements that are circulating in the dieting scene. They promise to speed up the ketogenic process, without the strict diet. This is the lure of these supplements. Resist instant gratification and easy results because they are not recommended. There are many health problems associated with these miracle supplements.

In a study involving pro cyclists they were found to have a detrimental effect on their performance. And that ingesting these supplements lowered their free testosterone levels. So whatever your goals with keto, don't try cheating with supplements to speed up the process. Despite all the promises it wont work.

So how does all this affect men who already work out and do not have low T levels? Well its not good. Why?

It is not recommended to follow keto during periods of higher intensity training. High intensity training relies upon the stores of glycogen in the muscles. To keep up these stores you need sufficient carbohydrate intake. Most evidence from studies on athletes also points towards the conclusion that it also harms performance. And it can lead to a reduction in weight and muscle mass.

You should expect to feel a greater level of fatigue when pairing keto with intense physical activity. This is what happened to me while following a keto diet.

There is a LOT of misleading information out there suggesting that keto can either enhance physical performance, or that athletes can adapt to ketosis and that performance is not affected. This simply is not true.

To quote a researcher of one study. "Performance was not enhanced. The price paid for the conservation of carbohydrate during exercise (lack of glycogen stores) appears to be a limitation of the intensity of exercise that can be performed. Our (the researchers) ketogenic diet did not, as is popularly believed, enhance exercise capacity. At best, only exertion at sub-maximal (considered to be 60% of their full physical potential) intensities was preserved, at the expense of ability to undertake high intensity exercise."

Beware that calorie restriction for a long time lowers testosterone levels. Depleted energy can also affect our T levels. Low carb, high protein diets can cause T levels to drop significantly. A plus side is that the high fat intake can be good for T levels combine this with moderate protein and slightly more carbs and it can work. Combined with low carbs and high protein intake it can lower T levels. You need carbs for energy and this is the huge disadvantage of keto if you engage in strenuous physical activity.

The evidence does support the theory that keto and a deficit in carbs combined with intense physical activity do not go well together. Over a longer period of time they could prove catastrophic. Keto can be very useful and highly effective for weight loss combined with lighter exercise. Just be aware of consuming too much protein on keto. It can drop your T levels.

But for a short term boost to weight loss it can be very effective. If you are looking to increase muscle mass then a low carb diet of course is not recommended.

Low Carb High Protein Diets.

So following on from the keto diet and in a way connected is the high protein/low carb diet. This is considered to be any diet where protein intake exceeds carb intake in significant proportions. There are many different diets that follow this angle. Keto is one example of this.

Protein is quite rightly associated with increasing lean muscle mass and the supplement industry has created a plethora of protein products designed to increase your protein intake and supplement your diet. The importance of protein cannot be denied, but with some the fact that it plays a significant role in building muscle has led to them over focussing their diets towards protein intake.

Carbs promote water retention and fat is the enemy of aesthetics that is true. Amino acids are the building blocks of cells and muscles and without enough protein muscle gains are going to be difficult, and that is equally true. These two beliefs have led to many adopting diets that focus on high protein intake. It is common to see and hear people in the fitness scene recommending as much as 2 to 3g of protein for every kilo or pound of bodyweight.

Along with fats and carbs, that then amounts to a lot of food to be consumed. This is why so many guys supplement with protein powders. I do use whey protein in my diet but only very occasionally.

I have also followed the high protein approach before and found it effective in building lean mass.

However this type of diet, although effective for building lean muscle mass, is not the best and most effective diet for optimising or maintaining testosterone levels. And there is a lot of evidence from studies that confirms this.

I found one particularly helpful report on this subject. It was a report based upon analysis of 27 studies into the effects of low carb/high protein diets on hormone levels. It was registered on PROSPERO (CRD42021255957). It is a very interesting and revealing read to anyone interested in their T levels.

For our purposes here I will quickly jump to the conclusion. It was found that in the first 3 weeks of this type of diet, both resting and post exercise levels of cortisol were elevated. As we know cortisol is the nemesis of testosterone. Continuing this type of diet for longer periods of time resulted in resting cortisol levels returning to baseline, but post exercise cortisol levels remaining elevated.

Another cause for concern was that the study also concluded that high protein diets also caused a large decrease in resting total testosterone of 5.23nmol/L.

1nmol/L amounts to 28.85ng/DL so that comes in at 150.88ng/DL. For someone with 400ng/DL that's more than 25% of their total testosterone. Whatever your baseline T level, these kinds of losses are significant and are to be avoided.

This study actually states that the average decrease in men observing low carb/high protein diets was around 37%. For anyone looking to maintain their T levels as they get older it is a disaster. This could explain the rise in TRT use among fitness influencers who need to have exceptional physiques to satisfy their followers. And there are a lot of guys, especially guys who workout, who are following this exact type of diet!

Ultimately there is a conflict of interest for many guys here. Building lean muscle mass or optimising T levels? The good news is that you can do both, naturally, and I will get to that in a while.

It was suggested, for the purposes of the aforementioned study that the term high protein referred to a diet that consisted of protein intake of greater than 35% of macro intake. They went further to suggest that anyone on a high protein diet should limit their protein intake to no more than 25% of all energy intake.

Now this study refers only to average men in their late 20s. There were also differences in exercise regimes and intensities, and differences in the types of carbs those on low carb diets were consuming. And the low carb element could have contributed towards the declines in T levels.

Low Fat Diets.

So what about low fat diets? Low fat diets have been plugged as something that is beneficial to our health and of course there is some truth to this.

And we all know that trimming away any excess fat can contribute to higher T levels. We also know that having excess body fat can contribute to lower T levels. So surely low fat diets are a good bet for long term T level maintenance?

Alas no. Recent research suggests that low fat diets cause men's testosterone levels to drop by 10 to 15%. One study, which was an analysis of 6 studies consisting of more than 200 subjects studied the effects of various diets on testosterone levels.

These studies first subjected the subjects to a high fat diet (consisting of 40% fat intake) and then transferred the same subjects to a low fat diet (20% fat intake). The result was that their testosterone levels dropped by up to 15%. It was also noted that vegetarian low fat diets resulted in a 26% decrease in T levels.

These studies also discovered that high consumption of the mono-unsaturated fats present in things such as olive oil, olives, nuts and avocados play a part in boosting testosterone levels because they boost the production of the good (HDL) cholesterol that is used for testosterone production. They also help to combat inflammation, which affects DHEA levels.

There are also saturated fats to consider. You need some of this type of fat in your diet. This type of fat is considered to be bad for you. For decades many doctors have always advised patients against eating saturated fats. The reasons given for this are that it ramps up your cholesterol levels and clogs up your arteries. Now to be fair there is an element of truth to this, and this element of truth applies to bad LDL cholesterol. However studies have now proven that there is no connection between good HDL cholesterol intake and heart attacks and strokes as popular medical opinion once thought.

When it comes to saturated fats the ideal is to consume in moderation. Never completely eliminate them from your diet cholesterol is the building material of testosterone. Just be sure to avoid hydrogenated oils or trans fats. When buying red meats always go for the leaner cuts. Chicken, turkey, pork, beef, and eggs are all good providers of saturated fats.

They also found that the consumption of polyunsaturated fats, mainly found in vegetable oil, contributed to the damage of testosterone production.

COMPLETE GUIDE TO TESTOSTERONE

They are more prone to oxidization, which also contributes towards cell damage. But remember that you still need polyunsaturated fats in your diet. These include omega 3 and omega 6 fatty acids. They are essential fats that the body needs for brain functioning and cell growth. You can get enough omega 3 from fish, and enough omega 6 from meats.

If you do not get enough fat in your diet you may become more prone to skin problems and a weaker immune system as well as lower T levels. The recommended daily intake of fats for men is 90g per day.

So low diet fats can have a detrimental effect on T levels. And they can contribute to fatigue and energy levels. Increasing your fat intake can have benefits but these must be the right types of fats. And you need all three types. Finding the balance is the key. Not too little and not too much.

Weight Loss and Cutting.

Now if you are carrying any excess weight then of course weight loss is going to be of great benefit to your testosterone production. There is an abundance of studies and evidence that supports this fact.

In the case of guys who are overweight or carrying excess fat it is known to be very effective.

But of course we live in a society where rapid results are the desired outcome for many. There are many examples of marketing for various diets that promise that you will shed x,y or z kg's in no time at all, or in the first month. This of course is to lure in potential customers. And this method works because there is a need to impress people, and indeed impress yourselves, with how much progress you are making.

A number of studies have researched the effects of rapid weight loss on testosterone in both overweight men and in athletes and it seems that the results are pretty conclusive.

In one study involving a group of athletes, who had normal T levels at the beginning of the study, they were put through a program of gruelling training combined with gruelling dieting. Their T levels dropped way below their normal levels in only 3 weeks.

Usually if T levels are dropping the brain will stimulate the testicles to produce more testosterone and restore the balance by releasing lutenizing hormone in a greater quantity to compensate. But the study found that levels of LH had also plummeted after rapid weight loss, so this process did not occur.

The alarming statistic that comes out of all of this is that T levels slumped by 63%! Bear that in mind next time you are considering a cut. Severe dieting and sudden changes to your eating habits and calorific intake will induce a state of malnourishment. The same happens in any situation where a calorie deficit occurs.

The ideal is to aim for gradual weight loss. Any dietician that knows their stuff will recommend against any rapid weight loss plan. You are far more likely to put the weight back on after the calorific deficit. You will be tired and probably feeling pangs of hunger too.

It is recommended that for mild weight loss you should be aiming to lose 0.25kg per week. For typical weight loss it is 0.50kg per week, and for extreme weight loss it is 1 kg per week. It is recommended that if you engage in extreme weight loss it is advisable to involve a doctor to check you periodically because to achieve just losses of 1kg per week is probably going to put you into a calorific deficit.

And in considering your required calorific intake this could involve consuming less than the minimum recommendation for men of 1500 calories per day.

So in any weight loss or cutting cycle be aware of the effects that this could have on your T levels. The best weight loss programmes are the ones that are tailored to losing weight gradually and to be maintaining a slight reduction in calories and also combined with exercise for greater calorie burning effect.

Maintaining a healthy balance in a normal BMI range for your height is fundamental to good health. Good health is fundamental to healthy balanced hormone production. Balanced hormone production is fundamental to maintaining T levels for longer. Testosterone production, natural testosterone, is also fundamental for good health and disease prevention as we age.

Speeding Up Metabolic Rate.

Exercise is great for improving out metabolic rate. But a really effective method to consider for weight loss and fat loss is the little and often approach.

Instead of the typical 3 meals per day, you instead go for 5 or 6 smaller meals throughout the day. A benefit of this approach is that is is very effective to maintaining weight loss gains. Another benefit is that you will not need to significantly drop calorie intake, you maintain enough calories to keep energy levels up, but you just spread that out more into smaller intakes at each sitting.

The little and often approach also helps to speed up your metabolic rate too. It is a useful little dieting hack that can be very effective. A faster metabolic rate is also known to have a positive effect on the absorption of nutrients.

Intermittent Fasting.

Intermittent fasting is a dieting hack that has grown in popularity in recent years and has been making waves in the fitness and wellness scene. There are many people who swear by it and with good reason too.

The idea behind this type of fast is that you fast for a short time, usually on a once per week basis. The most common practises are to fast for 16 or 24 hours and then resume your normal food intake.

The 16:8 method is pretty straightforward. Lets say the day before you fast you eat your last meal at 18:00. Then for the next 16 hours, until midday the following day you are allowed nothing to eat. Only water or maybe tea or coffee with no milk or sugar. Now considering that most people sleep for 8 hours anyway that only leaves 8 hours of actually avoiding food. This way it is pretty easy to stick to.

As a dieting technique is is also highly effective. You observe your normal diet during your eating hours, 8 hours per day, and then fast the other 16 hours. Done for a week or two and up to a month this is another way you can employ to kick-start your weight loss regime. You are not giving anything up to begin with, just altering your mealtimes. Its not what you eat but when you eat. The trick is to not gorge yourself too much during the eating window. Research found that you're not going to lose weight or become healthier if you start packing your food periods with junk food and huge portions.

But for most people, intermittent fasting on the 16:8 schedule once a week also helps to flush out the digestive tract and has numerous other health benefits too. There are also many different ways and combinations of doing them.

Longer periods without food, 48 hours or more, are not necessarily better for you and there could be potential problems too. One being that your body will go into survival mode and stop producing testosterone as it will redirect its energies into survival.

But research proves that intermittent fasting done properly can be very effective. It has been linked to a longer life, a sharper mind as well as a leaner body. It is also known to be effective in helping to prevent diseases such as diabetes, heart disease, many different cancers, bowel diseases and neuro-degenerative diseases such as senile dementia.

Various research studies have also linked intermittent fasting to improved memory, improved blood pressure and resting heart rates.

So what effect, if any, does this have on testosterone?

Does intermittent fasting increase testosterone? Well yes it can. Based on various studies it seems that intermittent fasting does affect T levels in an indirect way certainly.

We all know that reducing body fat and increasing lean muscle mass is associated with higher testosterone. Intermittent fasting is effective at reducing inflammation and we all know that inflammation can harm testosterone production by causing a spike in cortisol production. Oxidative stress can also harm T levels and intermittent fasting has been shown to reduce the levels of oxidative stress.

Not only can intermittent fasting help to inhibit and prevent many factors that can harm testosterone production it can also improve your hormonal functioning, which can help in increasing testosterone.

Intermittent fasting helps in the function of Lutenizing hormone, LH, which stimulates the Leydig cells in the testicles to produce testosterone. Intermittent fasting helps to optimise LH, which is helpful in maintaining or increasing T levels.

Intermittent fasting also helps improve the production of HGH, or Human Growth Hormone. HGH and testosterone are very closely related in relation to their effect on the male body. And HGH is also very fundamental in the process of increasing muscle mass.

HGH also functions as gonadotropin, which stimulates the release of testosterone from the Leydig cells in the testicles. So when HGH levels increase within the body, the more testosterone your body is likely to produce.

Studies have found clear evidence to suggest that short intermittent fasts of up to 24 hours, no more, can help increase HGH production by as much as 2000%, and this will result in a corresponding elevation in testosterone production. So when observing a cut, be sure to consider this method. With all that HGH flowing, it will help you to keep your muscle mass during your cutting cycle.

But beware. There is evidence that suggests that prolonged fasting can reduce Lutenizing hormone stores, which can lead to decreasing T levels.

In one study comparing two groups, one of whom observed a pattern of regular fasting and the other who did not, and with both groups consuming the same number of calories and the same ratio of macros, found that the regular fasting, which was the only difference between the two groups, actually led to a decrease in both T levels and HGH production.

Another study, which centred on the act of skipping breakfast every day produced similar results.

Now all types of prolonged fasting usually involve a calorific deficit. A calorific deficit amounts to putting the body into survival mode. The entire organism adapts to a perceived threat, which in this case is partial starvation, and the chemical and cellular processes within the body become altered as the body adapts to the deficit.

Put simply a body that engages in regular prolonged fasting is not going to be efficiently producing testosterone and building muscle mass is extremely unlikely to happen. It is not possible to enter into and maintain this state for any length of time naturally. Anyone putting out suggestions or content that says otherwise is misleading you. This is a solid fact backed by scientific evidence, extensive and detailed studies and the laws of nature.

It is proven that to enter this state for long periods of time, and especially in cases where the body fat percentage is at less than 8%, is going to produce some significant side effects.

These include infertility or lower sperm production, little or no libido, depression, sleep problems and low energy and fatigue. And of course severely depleted T levels resulting from depleted Lutenizing hormone activity. There are no escaping these facts.

So in considering these facts it cannot be possible to maintain a regime of intense physical activity during this state.

The Optimum T Boosting Diet.

So in considering all these elements and the pros and cons of each dietary method it gives us a better idea of exactly how to optimise our diets with a view to not only increasing or maintaining muscle mass and athletic performance, but to optimising our testosterone production as well at the same time.

So what is the ideal T boosting diet? Unfortunately the answer to that question is that it is different for us all. We have different weights, heights, body types and metabolic rates to consider, and all of these will require different calorific intake.

When putting together this guide I wanted to explain all of these elements in detail in order to give you a set of basic rules to follow when planning your own diet. Of course there are so many different elements to consider so even these basic rules can be pretty complicated. So lets sum up a few of these rules and I will explain how this T boosting diet works.

You need to include all of these elements into your diet. A variety of different foods, your macros and all of your micros. This is the meaning behind the term well balanced diet. You must aim to be including enough of all types of macro and micro nutrient into your diets. Of course you can use supplements to make up for any potential deficiencies of any essential vitamins and minerals. However always try to absorb as many as you possibly can from food.

What I have devised, based upon two decades of trying different diets, seeing what works and what doesn't work, is that it all boils down to a few simple equations that apply to everyone. All you have to do is input your own personal stats and then consider your own personal requirements. There is a little room for movement in a few areas and these can be decided by your own personal preferences and goals. We are all different so with this system you can fine tune your diet to your own body.

Firstly we calculate our calorific intake. I researched and tried out many different diets, opinions and recommendations. This formula takes into account that you are interested in optimising your T levels and doing everything you can to achieve this. So these calculations take into account calorific requirement based not only upon body weight, but also allowances for intense physical exercise, and the maintenance of lean muscle mass. For bulking, or cutting, should this be your aim, you make the necessary adjustments which I will explain.

Using myself as an example here I will input my own personal requirements for context.

So you take your body weight, which for me is 55kg. Convert that into pounds. That now comes in at roughly 122lbs.

For maintenance. Multiply your bodyweight in pounds by 18. For me this gives me 2196. This is my *minimum* calorific intake for my bodyweight and the fact that I train regularly.

Now multiply your bodyweight by 20. This gives me 2420. This is my *upper limit* for calorific intake to maintain my current weight more or less and maintain lean mass. As long as I fall in between these two markers I will be effectively maintaining my current body weight.

Now lets say I wanted to bulk. Now I will multiply my bodyweight by 22. This would give me a calorific target of 2684 to aim for. I would observe this for a month to see how it goes.

Now if I had increased my mass I will then weigh more. So you then go back to the original parameters and input your new information. So you can now maintain those gains.

Lets say I gained 5lbs. I am now 127lbs and now when I multiply by 18 I have a baseline calorific intake of 2286 and multiply by 20 for an upper calorific intake of 2540, to maintain my gains.

If I wanted to continue my bulking regime I would input my new body weight and multiply again by 22. This would give me a new target of 2794 kcal per day.

Now if I want to gradually lose weight. Gradually is proven to be the most effective way, both in terms of permanent weight loss and T levels. I would multiply my body weight by 17 and by 16 respectively. Any more than this and I would be running the risk of severe and sudden calorific deficit and risk crashing my T levels.

This would give me a calorific target of between 1952 and 2074 kcal to observe during the weight loss period. This I could keep going for a longer period of time because I am not putting myself into a significant calorific deficit. This will also prevent me crashing my T levels in any way.

Lets say I lost 5lbs. My weight would now be 117lbs. Now to maintain that weight loss I would then return to the original parameters and multiply by 18 and my calorific intake would then be at around 2106 kcal.

If I wanted to drop more weight then I would return to the original weight loss parameters and multiply my new body weight by 16 and 17 respectively. This would then give me a new calorific target of between 1872 and 1989 kcal.

Dropping your calorific intake in this way will prevent energy crash and feeling hungry. You are then far more likely to keep the weight off in the long term. You will also find that you will maintain energy levels sufficiently to continue with physical training.

Follow this system by just entering in your own body weight in pounds and you will get your own personal calorific requirements.

A rule of thumb here is that if you are a guy that struggles to gain weight and mass, no matter what you do, but finds it relatively easy to reveal your abs, then you probably have a fast metabolism. If you are a guy who puts on weight and mass easily but struggles with conditioning and getting your abs to show then you probably have a slow metabolism.

Only you know your own body. Adjustments will therefore be needed to accommodate your own personal metabolic rate. There is no magic remedy here and you will only discover what is going to work best for you by tweaking here and there and then observing the results. It is just a guideline to begin with.

Now on to macros. Taking into account what all the studies have shown about various dieting methods and their corresponding effects on T levels, here are the optimum macro ratio ranges for optimisation of testosterone production. You can adjust slightly to suit your own physique goals.

The ideal macro ratios for testosterone are somewhere in between 35/35/30, 35% carbs, 35% fat and 30% protein, and 40/40/20, 40% carbs, 40% fat and 20% protein. 35/35/30 being best for building muscle mass and 40/40/20 being best for testosterone.

To work out the amounts of each macro to consume we then take our calorific intake and apply the percentages. To get the percentage we multiply our calorific total by 0.40 for 40%, 0.35 for 35% etc. Then that result is then converted into an amount in grams for each macro.

I will use my own stats to demonstrate how this works.

My baseline calorific intake is 2196 kcal.

So for a macro ratio of 40/40/20, I would multiply 2196 by 0.40, 0.40 and 0.20 respectively. From these calculations I arrive at a calorific macro ratio of 878 kcal of carbs, 878 kcal in fats, and 439 kcal in protein.

There are 4 calories per gram of carbs. Roughly. So I then divide my carb calorie total (878) by 4, giving me 219g carbs.

There are roughly 9kcal per gram of fat. I then divide my fat calorie total (878) by 9, which is 97g fats.

There are also roughly 4kcal per gram of protein. I divide my total protein calorie total (439) by 4, giving me 109g of protein.

Now I will take my upper calorific intake and do the same calculations. For a macro ratio of 40/40/20 this comes in at 968 kcal in carbs, 968 in fats and 484 in protein. Using the same calculations mentioned above this gives me an intake of 242g carbs, 107g fats and 121g of protein.

So to meet my calorific targets for maintaining my current body weight at a macro ratio of 40/40/20, I would be looking to consume between:

219 - 242g carbs.
97 - 107g fats.
109 - 121g protein.

For a macro ratio of 35/35/30, we would perform the same calculations. Again I will use my own stats to demonstrate.

First I take my lower calorific intake, 2196 kcal, and multiply that by 0.35, 0.35 and 0.30 respectively.

This gives me 768 kcal carbs, 768 kcal fats and 658 kcal protein. Then I convert these calorific totals into grams of each macro using the above formula.

This gives me 192g carbs, 85g fats and 164g protein.

For my upper calorific intake , 2420 kcal, this gives me 847 kcal carbs, 847 kcal fats and 726 kcal protein. This converts to 211g carbs, 94g fats and 181g protein.

So to meet my calorific targets for maintaining my current body weight at a macro ratio of 35/35/30, I would be looking to consume between:

192 - 211g carbs.
85 - 94g fats.

164 - 181g protein.

These numbers I use as my dietary guideline. I do not count these amounts exactly I just aim to consume an amount of each macro that falls between these guidelines.

My own personal guidelines fall in between the two macro ratios. 40/40/20 and 35/35/30. I aim to consume between 35 and 40% of my total calorific intake in carbs. Between 35 and 40% in fats and between 20 and 30% in protein. My total calorific intake is determined as somewhere in between my upper and lower calorific limits. As long as I fall in between these two I am happy that I am getting enough calories.

When it comes to the amounts of macros in grams I take the upper and lower amounts and I aim to consume somewhere in between these two amounts each day. For me these amounts are:

192 - 242g carbs.
85 - 107g fats.
109 - 181g protein.

Having basic guidelines that are in between two amounts gives me plenty of room to move and I do not have to spend time working out the exact nutritional values of every meal.

To get your own optimum diet just enter your own stats and go from there. Once you have established your own personal guidelines then have these in mind when you are out buying your food. To begin with it can be a good idea to keep a journal to help you to keep track of all this. It would also be a good idea to prepare shopping lists to make sure you got everything.

Keeping a journal will also help you to keep track of all the micro nutrients you will also need to include in your diet. Your journal will also help you to identify any potential nutritional deficiencies that might apply to you. If you identify a potential deficiency you can either tweak your diet a little to include foods containing that vitamin or mineral or look to supplementation to solve the issue.

A complete healthy well balanced diet is fundamental to testosterone production. It can also be a little complicated considering all the different and varied foods you will need to eat to make a balanced diet.

A good rule is not too much of anything and not too little. And the most important rule of all, if your body does not benefit from it, don't eat it! A healthy balanced diet involves a lot of different foods and nutrients. Why waste valuable stomach space eating foods that are not benefiting you in some way?

26

Testosterone Trends.

T Boosting Myths. True or False?

In this section I am going to cover some commonly held popular beliefs that are circulating about testosterone. I have researched these myths thoroughly and here are my findings. You might find a few surprises here.

To begin with this theme I am going to start with something that I feel is of great importance to our objectives here. That is the accuracy of the information available and why it always pays to get hold of solid information before practising anything on yourself.

In hindsight if only I had thought of this earlier in my life I could have saved myself so much time chasing false leads that ended up going nowhere. The biggest offender for me was my quest to find that magic natural supplement, diet, or training routine that would push me past a plateau and give me muscle gains after I had reached my full genetic potential.

This concept applies to our T levels too. I do not want you to waste any of your valuable time chasing false leads or acting on false or misleading information. And the truth is that there is plenty of false and misleading information currently out there.

Some of that misleading info is coming from mainstream sources, think coke and bigger testicles here! *Disclaimer: I am not implying that any of these publications set out with the intentions of deceiving the public.* And some of that bad info even comes from some content creators who are *qualified physicians*. Now this is something that I have observed myself and have seen on social media platforms. But this is also backed by research. The researchers made some interesting findings.

The study, was dated 19 November 2022, and was up to date at the time of writing. It was conducted by J M Dublin et al, and involved a total of 11 researchers who all have extensive knowledge in the field of men's health. Their report was published on the website of the National Center for Biotechnology Information, NCBI, and is available to read through the National Library of Medicine, PubMed Central.

The title of the study is, "The broad reach and inaccuracy of men's health information on social media: analysis of Tik Tok, TT, and Instagram, IG. It is an enlightening read and very interesting. I would highly recommend you read it. It is a very long and descriptive report so I will just provide a only a brief summary here along with their findings.

The researchers sought to fact check information given in men's health related content. They searched the following search terms. Testosterone, erectile dysfunction, male infertility, semen retention (and nofap) The subject terms were Sexual Dysfunction and Gonadal disorders.

They discovered literally billions of instances of related content. Considering the volume of posts and the reach this has worldwide, they mention that the accuracy of this content is unreliable. They also mention that multiple studies had demonstrated a large quantity of low quality information related to various men's health topics across a wide range of other social media platforms including You Tube, Facebook, and Twitter.

Given the broad range of men's health topics they narrowed the search to the most popular topics that have generated the greatest interest. Among these topics is testosterone. For simplicities sake we shall focus on their testosterone related findings as it is the subject of this guide.

Testosterone has generated more than 700 million views on TT alone. On IG there were nearly a million posts. That amounts to a lot of content, if you are interested in T levels chances are you may have already absorbed some of this content.

When it came to the creators themselves only 2% of those had any medical qualifications. 98% of the content comes from regular content creators. 99.8% of the testosterone related content received likes, indicating that men viewing this content approved of the advise and therefore were highly likely to act upon it.

Of the account types posting this info, around 65% of the posts come from business or creator accounts. Put simply 65% of the posts have been submitted by people who stand to financially gain from the content by various means, for example by selling products, affiliate marketing, various services, courses, coaching and also paid subscription services and paid communities.

Of the sum total of all content, they provided a table indicating the mean (average) accuracy of the content and a misinformation index of 1-5. 5 being most accurate.

For testosterone related content the overall marker was only 2.3 Non physicians, those with no official medical qualifications, rated 2.3, and physicians rated 3.0. Overall accuracy was deemed to be low. So from that we can surmise that there is a huge amount of misinformation out there!

In conclusion they found a high level of content with a high level of engagement but with a low level of overall accuracy. And the physicians, although their info was deemed to be only slightly more accurate, should have scored a 5 in my opinion. So we must even be aware of information provided by mainstream and professional sources?

So on the theme of testosterone I had a look around and observed a lot of testosterone related content. I will go through some of the popular ideas concerning testosterone that are doing the rounds, which

I have not covered in the other sections, and the truth behind them. Many of these ideas have been put forward by content creators who are earning a good living from content creation and who have a significant number of subscribers. So considering they are generating income from the advice they give. How accurate is the advice they are giving?

Semen Retention, Nofap and Pron.

I have seen a huge amount of content suggesting that semen retention and nofap will significantly increase T levels in men. There is also a lot of content suggesting that watching adult movies decreases T levels. So how accurate are these claims?

Pron Decreases T Levels?

Lets break this up and look at each of these individually. It is said that nofap and semen retention will raise T levels. These two are closely related so we will look at those together in a while. Pron is said to have the opposite effect. Lets look into this first. There is a lot of content that suggests that watching erotic content is detrimental to T levels. It has even been suggested that guys who engage in this are somehow weak and inferior. All opinions aside, does watching pron decrease T levels?

A study in the Archives of Sexual Behaviour studied 8 men while they were watching erotic films. They observed their blood levels of testosterone before, during and after they viewed an erotic film. Their T levels climbed during the film and their levels were highest 90 minutes after the film finished. Their T levels had increased by up to 35%.

Mascherek 2021, observed that the testosterone levels of men increased temporarily after watching erotic stimuli, or feeling sexual desire. Another study observed the T levels of men who attended a sex club. Their T levels all increased but the ones who participated in sexual activity saw bigger increases in T levels compared to the men who just observed. The men who just watched did however see increases. These were all only temporary increases, both for the observers and participants.

Many years of research has found that men's testosterone levels increase when they are presented with visual erotic stimuli such as viewing sexually explicit images and watching erotic films. Most of these studies involved men with normal T levels and no underlying health problems.

The research agrees that these gains in T levels are only temporary and tend to subside within a few hours of this experience. But to be fair, for men with established training routines, exercise seems to have a similar effect.

Another thing that they all seem to agree upon is that T levels rise significantly more if those visual stimuli are combined with physical contact and sexual activity. They also all mostly agree that T levels did increase when only visual stimuli were present, even if the men did not masturbate or take part in any sexual activity.

In one 2011 study in men who visited a swingers club, observed that men who only watched and did not participate in any sexual acts experienced an 11% increase in T levels. But T levels in the men who did participate in sexual activity experienced an increase to T levels of up to 72%.

In a different study by the Archives of Sexual Behaviour they asked men to fantasize about sexual situations, without any visual stimulus, and then write down their thoughts. This resulted in no significant changes to T levels, indicating that it was the visual stimuli that was responsible for the increases to T levels and just thinking about sex does not have the same effect.

But it seems that more than 80% of the studies into the connection of visually erotic stimuli and testosterone have recorded a positive effect on T levels. So on the surface it seems that this idea has been debunked. It has been proven that watching pron does in fact *increase* T levels and does not decrease them as many have claimed. And if that is combined with masturbation or any sexual activity then the boost to T levels is amplified.

But to be fair, the creators who promote the idea that watching pron and masturbating lower T levels, are viewing this as a habit that is carried out on a regular basis. So to get a fairer overall view we need to address the affect on T levels in those who take this to an extreme.

The evidence from studies suggests that there is no evidence to back up the claims that watching pron and masturbation lower T levels. But there is also a lot of evidence that suggests that heavy pron users often experience erectile dysfunction. Much of this evidence is supplied by the guys themselves, that this has actually happened to, on many forums and platforms. This evidence of course is absent from the studies.

The popular consensus is that the ED is caused by low testosterone. After all ED and loss of sexual desire are known to be symptoms of low T levels.

But many of these men are also reporting that they then proceed to get tested, but the results are coming back stating T levels within the normal ranges for their age group. This is mostly men in their 20s. So the ED doesn't seem to be caused by low T levels. Many of these heavy pron users are masturbating frequently, in some cases daily, and in other cases more than one time a day. So this seems to suggest that even frequent masturbation doesn't lower T levels.

But there is evidence that suggests that testosterone receptors may decline for 3 to 4 days following ejaculation. Ejaculating every day will obviously cause that decline to be maintained, maybe even amplified. But this does not offer a full explanation because total T levels are unaffected. Or are they?

I am going to go out on a limb here and make a suggestion. This is purely theory on my account and there is currently no data available to confirm or deny this theory.

Testosterone receptors, or androgen receptors are the receptors that testosterone and DHT bind to.

As we know already physical training increases T levels in men who begin to exercise. Then with continued exercise, helps to maintain those increases, without (total T) levels really being affected much once regular training is established. Resistance training is also known to stimulate the release of testosterone and an increase in androgen receptor synthesis and function. In effect this is stimulating the amount of bioavailable free testosterone.

The body that engages in physical activity is utilising its supply of free T, thus stimulating the body to make more free T available to keep those levels up.

Training activates androgen receptors. Excessive masturbation causes them to decline. The decline could be linked to less T and DHT being bound to these receptors, theoretically resulting in decreased testosterone synthesis and function? This could result in *less* free testosterone being available, with total T being unaffected? Free testosterone is the bioavailable T that is available in the here and now for things like sex drive and libido. ED can occur in guys with normal total T levels but who have low free testosterone available? Is the same thing occurring in guys who practise excessive masturbation? Normal total T levels but at the same time experiencing ED?

Another theory that has been suggested by others is that it is the brain's reward circuitry is being re-wired in some way as a possible cause for pron-related erectile dysfunction. But one fact seems to be emerging and there is a lot of evidence. Pron related ED is a fact. It exists and guys who overdo pron and masturbation are suffering from it.

More investigation into excessive masturbation is needed to confirm or disprove these theories. But there is a possibility that this could be causing the problem. And if it is the cause of the problem, the ED, then it confirms the content creators' claims that watching pron and masturbating too much is going to have a detrimental effect certainly, but just not to overall total T levels.

So watching pron and masturbating excessively has no affect on total T levels. That one is debunked. But what has not been debunked for certain is that excessive pron use has a detrimental effect on male sexual health and possibly even their mental health too.

But as an occasional vice, evidence seems to agree that it can in fact cause a temporary boost to T levels.

So my personal verdict on this is that the creators are completely correct to be guiding men away from pron and the excessive masturbation that tends to go with that. The good intention is obviously there and its great advice. But they are wrong to assume that it does not seem to directly cause a drop in T levels. But they are also correct that it is bad on a regular basis.

So therefore it is good advice overall. Back to the study mentioned at the beginning of the section, would that study have considered this to be accurate? With some inaccurate information present it seems highly likely they would not.

Does Nofap / Semen Retention Increase T levels?

There have been as many claims that because watching pron and masturbating were suggested as being detrimental to T levels, then doing the complete opposite would have the opposite effect. This has given rise to the wide belief that abstaining from masturbation and ejaculation will significantly increase T levels.

Nofap is basically a 90 day challenge that means that a guy is to observe a 90 day period without ejaculating. The term "fap," is a slang term for masturbation. But it seems that the nofap challenge refers to all kinds of sexual activity. So it is in effect the same type of practise as semen retention.

Now it is my personal opinion that the nofap challenge is a great way to get men away from the excessive viewing of pron and the excessive masturbation that goes hand in hand with pron. Or should that be dick in hand! Whether it raises T levels or not, nothing can suggest that to promote the challenge is bad advice because if it helps someone break an addiction is has to be a good thing?

So does total sexual abstinence raise T levels in any way? Does evidence back up these claims?

Fortunately there have been many studies so there is a lot of evidence to consider. Whether you consider yourself to be observing nofap, or being on semen retention it seems to follow the same principle. You are abstaining for all types of sexual activity for a determined length of time.

Some of these men practise what is known as "edging." This is where sexual stimulation takes place, either through sex with a partner or masturbation, but no ejaculation occurs.

Before we consider its direct effect on T levels it is important to say that it has so many benefits to those who practise. If something gives so many benefits then it cannot be bad to promote it? Well its not as clear cut as that because there are a few downsides to abstinence.

First of all it depends on the individual. Some men can naturally go days without spilling their seed. Others must release it regularly. We are all different.

Here are some of the purported benefits of semen retention.

It improves sperm quality. Even for just a short time of a week or two, semen retention is known to improve the quality and mobility of sperm.

It is a great energy booster. This is down to the fact that sperm contains many micro-nutrients. Sperm contains vitamin B12, vitamin C, calcium, zinc, phosphorus, magnesium and sodium. And of course these elements are also attributed to a healthy immune system. Depleting these vitamins could also contribute towards exhaustion. And of course possible deficiencies. And maybe even pron related ED?

It can help with self control. Of course abstinence is going to take a level of discipline for many. And sexual impulses can be pretty strong to resist. We are hard-wired by nature to possess the urge to procreate. Self control is one of the most difficult things to achieve. *It takes a detailed self analysis and self observation for many years to gain any level of mastery.* A good way to begin with trying to gain more self control is to practise semen retention. It is a great exercise in self control for complete beginners into this realm.

It can help to improve confidence. Especially when used as a strategy to break a pron addiction. You will improve your mental health and sense of wellness and even focus when you are not continually depleting your sperm supply. Or thinking about your next fix? You will have more energy to channel into other activities which will also give you satisfaction, of a different kind, and this in turn could have a positive effect on your confidence.

It also can improve your libido. We already know that excessive wasting of sperm can contribute towards ED. Semen retention is going to improve your sexual experiences. Scarcity increases enjoyment and satisfaction when you are engaged in sexual activity. Doing something too much, well practically anything in fact, can make it feel pretty mundane.

It can improve sleep quality. This is believed to be down to the improvements to mental health and overall wellness.

That is a lot of good things that could happen if you retain your seed. But there are also some not so good things. For some men holding in their semen and not ejaculating can cause discomfort in the testicles. This is a condition commonly know as "blue balls," or its medical term Epididymal Hypertension. Of course if this is something that you experience then semen retention is not going to be a good idea.

A misunderstanding that can often occur in a man who suffers with blue balls is that others will often attribute him with a lack of discipline or willpower. This of course is not the case. It is a real condition and cannot ever be considered as a reason for scorn.

And other guys can suffer with mood swings and anxiety. These of course are things to be overcome on the path of life in order to find inner balance and harmony. This of course not so much a condition but more of a temporary state to be overcome. If this is you, and you want to practise semen retention, then start with abstinence for a week and go from there.

A huge benefit of sex is that it reduces the amounts of the stress hormone cortisol. Cortisol affects testosterone production. Weekly sex has been shown to improve the immune response to illness compared to those who have sex less frequently. Sex has been proven to raise levels of a germ fighting substance called immunoglobin A. But people who had sex more than 2 times per week were shown to have lower levels of this germ fighting substance. But then too much of anything is a bad thing. A healthy balance in all things is key.

And another thing to consider is that if you don't use it, you could lose it. And this applies to sex too. We all know that if you don't use your muscles, they will waste away and degenerate quicker. If you don't challenge your brain enough it also can decline over time. And if you don't engage in sex on a regular basis it can do you some harm. Taken to an extreme, sperm production can even shut down completely.

Research has shown that men who have sex once a week are much less likely to experience ED compared to men who have sex less frequently. The body balances itself. If you engage in regular sexual activity then your body will adapt to this habit and keep functioning in a way to keep you in a state of readiness for sex. This is a law of nature.

Just like training keeps your body in a state of readiness for physical exertion. It only ever becomes a bad thing when taken to excess.

Now the research suggests that there is little evidence to back up the claims that are made about the benefits of nofap or semen retention. However the research does support the fact that regular sex is a healthy practise. The science supports the conclusion that semen retention is something that can only have short term benefits.

We cannot really dispute the improvements in mental state and focus. If you are not engaging in an addiction or thinking about your next fix then that will certainly have a corresponding effect on mental focus and indeed productivity. The removal of distractions can have a great effect.

According to research in 2010, men who had sex less than once a month were 45% more likely to die of cardiovascular diseases. 45% more likely to die compared to men who had sex twice a week.

Having sex on a regular basis was shown to improve sleep quality according to a 2019 study. The men who had regular sex also reported being able to fall asleep more easily.

Another study associated regular sex with a reduced risk of prostate cancer in men.

And here is the worst part of all for the case for semen retention. *It does not give any significant long term boost to testosterone levels.* Any increases in testosterone were shown to be only temporary. And most researchers and the scientific and medical communities are all in agreement on this.

There are studies that indicate that semen retention can increase T levels and it seems that these are the studies that this myth is based upon. What many of the nofap enthusiasts don't tell you is that the increases in T levels are only very temporary.

An often quoted study from 2002 found that after only a week of not ejaculating men increased their T levels by 45%. But that increase did not materialise until day 7 of abstinence. And, that the spike in T levels dissipated the following day and their total testosterone levels returned to baseline.

Another study found that T levels went up in the first three weeks and then declined and returned to base levels. But this seems to be an isolated result. Most studies have found increases in T levels from between day 4 and day 7 of abstinence. In all studies T levels returned to baseline levels and that continued and prolonged semen retention had no effect to T levels.

A 2018 study found that after one day of abstinence sperm mobility improved. But it was shown that to abstain for longer than that actually causes sperm mobility to decline. And some semen retention advocates have suggested that it can improve fertility. Evidence actually suggests that it can harm fertility. Back to the theory if you don't use it you will lose it seems to ring true here.

But on a much more serious note. Many advocates of semen retention have suggested that semen retention can give you spiritual benefits and help you to achieve some kind of enlightenment.

This is simply not true. It is in fact absurd. Enlightenment is something that occurs after a proficient level of self mastery has been gained. Mastery of anything takes a long time. This is achieved after the conquest of the self and the transcendence of the ego. This is a very long process and it is only achievable by dedication and hard inner work practised over many years.

This is my primary field of knowledge and I teach on this subject. There is no quick hack or short-cut that can replace the many years of hard work that are going to be necessary. There are so many different elements that must be conquered along the path and many pitfalls to be overcome.

It is said that any level of mastery of anything takes 10,000 hours of practise. Minimum. And this also applies to any level of mastery over the self. In a society where it is ingrained into many peoples' minds to seek quick results or to seek instant gratification, this inevitably leads to enthusiasm for any ideas or myths that can provide short-cuts or quick hacks. These short cuts are claimed to replace many years of practise. Beware of those who claim otherwise in the field of spirituality. There is no short-cut. They are offering false hopes and misleading you.

So in conclusion we can say that on the surface, semen retention is no bad thing, in moderation. As a means of breaking a pron addiction or as a cure for pron related ED it is literally a godsend.

As for increasing T levels it can, but only on a very short term basis, and any T gains are only temporary. Long term semen retention will not significantly raise your T levels as it has been claimed.

When it comes to overall health it seems that sex practised at least weekly, or twice weekly, seems to be the most beneficial practise to engage in.

I have practised semen retention for more than a year in the past. I was overseas and volunteering and during this period sexual liaisons were not practical. We were housed in same sex dormitories. There simply wasn't the opportunity for sex. There was one woman that I was particularly sexually attracted to. To abstain, while temptation is available and before your eyes does require a tiny amount of discipline. When the project was finished we spent a memorable week together and no doubt the abstination made it so much better.

To abstain while avoiding any sexual temptation is not really a test of discipline in my opinion. To test the individual and their willpower, you are going to need to place yourself in front of either the temptation or situations where you might be tempted.

I have sex religiously twice a week. I have a healthy sexual appetite as does my wife. I believe that a body that is well prepared for sexual activity is also beneficial to maintaining good T levels as you get older. And science and the medical community tends to support that theory.

So in conclusion the claimed benefits of nofap are not backed by all the research and studies. The evidence supports the idea that regular sex is more beneficial.

However to improve the lives of men involved in heavy pron use it is good solid advice.

Mental Affirmations.

This one has come up a few times. Influencers claiming that they have used mental affirmations to double and even triple their T levels. Can something as simple as merely affirming to yourself that your T levels are going to increase going to have any real effect? And interestingly enough these influencers are already engaging in physical training and pro testosterone practises. Making doubling or tripling of T levels highly unlikely. So are they on to something here?

Now I am a big fan of mental affirmations. But I call it visualising. It's the same concept. It is a matter of self belief. If you *can* see it, you *can* be it. If you *can* see it, you *can* materialise it. And it works. Of that there is no doubt. I have personally used this method literally hundreds of times to meet and beat challenges, pass tests and exams and to realise many life goals.

But this is effectively mentally affirming and manifesting a mental state of self belief. Can this be done to change a *physical* state like raising T levels?

Well yes, I believe so. It could. It is entirely possible. But I am a big sceptic about it doubling or tripling T levels though. But nothing is completely impossible if you believe in yourself.

There is a little more to it. Those affirmations must be accompanied with *action* of some kind. If you were to mentally affirm to yourself that you will transform your body and then you put that into action by not training and leading a sedentary lifestyle, and only relying on having self belief that the affirmations are going to create a miracle with no effort then it is highly unlikely that you will see any transformation. You are going to be disappointed.

Standing in front of a mirror every morning telling yourself that "I am going to get the body of Arnold Schwarzenegger," and then proceeding to spend all day reclining on a sofa eating popcorn and swilling beer will not materialise that body. The mental affirmations are not enough on their own. No matter how much you believe in yourself.

There must also be realistic actions applied on your part. In the above example this would amount to careful dieting and some hard consistent training at the very least?

So any mental affirmations *combined with actions* can be pretty powerful. But that's just my personal opinion based upon my own experiences. What does the science and the evidence say?

First and foremost there is a dark side to affirmations. If you are really down in life and have hit rock bottom it is going to be extremely difficult to rise up over this and have total self belief. And it is the self belief element that gets the results. It is the self belief element that produces the required actions. You can affirm and visualise all you like but if that comes with any self doubts that you cannot shake then that is going to have a detrimental effect.

There are some things that are beyond your control. Affirmations will not cure a disease. They will not bring back a dead loved one and they will not rekindle a lost love. They will also not rid you of any physical limitations or disabilities that you have. The psychiatric term for all this is toxic positivity. This is basically a term to describe over-evaluating yourself and your capabilities and using self denial to try to convince yourself that these things are not real. To solve any problem or to overcome anything you must first admit to yourself that a problem exists.

You can of course begin by making affirmations to help you over-come the self doubts and disadvantages before applying them any further. But for many people standing in front of a mirror every day saying, "I am confident," or "I have more testosterone than yesterday," can seem pretty inauthentic. Denial is not an effective coping strategy.

It is very complex and is beyond the scope of this guide to explain this in detail. Just to make you aware that there is both a good side and a dark side to the use of mental affirmations.

Medical science provides a lot of evidence to suggest that affirmations are very effective at improving your mental state. Neuroscientists affirm that affirmations, formed with absolute self belief, when developed and practised properly, can help to re-wire your brain.

There are even some studies that suggest that it could possibly raise T levels. In one study conducted by the University of Cambridge in 2018, they showed that a man only needs to believe he has bested another man in some kind of competition to get raised T levels.

Not exactly confirmation though that affirmations along the lines of, "I have more T," or "my testosterone is increasing day by day," can give you higher T levels. But evidence that a level of self belief, in this case that you have beaten someone in competition, can raise testosterone. This study showed that you only have to convince yourself that you have won for this increase in T to take place.

In reality if you affirm to yourself that you are going to raise your testosterone, and then combine that with working out and making lifestyle changes necessary there is no reason whatsoever that it will not work. And add to that a big dose of self belief that you can and will make this happen then there is every reason to suggest this *will* work.

But if you are using just mental affirmations alone, and there have been many who have claimed that this is what they have actually done, then it is highly unlikely.

The real secret to making affirmations work is the self belief. And this self belief must be 100% genuine and must be ingrained into your mind. With no doubts lurking in the background.

There is currently no evidence to suggest that mental affirmations alone, aimed at your T levels, are going to make any difference.

Does Having a Cellphone in Your Pocket Affect T Levels?

This is a common theme that is often discussed on many social media platforms. Can keeping a cellphone in your trouser pocket affect your T levels, and your sperm count?

The internet is awash with advice that the electromagnetic radiation, EMR, that is emitted from these devices can cause endocrine problems and damage the testicles. And this is not only limited to cellphones, it also includes using laptops and tablets when placing them on our laps.

Now here all the evidence available seems to indicate that there is truth to this. There have been many studies particularly focused on the effects of keeping phones in trouser pockets.

The devices emit a considerable amount of EMR, this has been widely established. The tissues in the penis and testes, because of its fluid content has been shown to have a high capacity for absorbing electrical energy. Now if you take all these studies together, they all seem to agree that EMR definitely has a detrimental effect on the quantity and the quality of sperm in men. They both suffer a decline and it is thought that this decline also has a negative effect on male fertility.

These devices also generate a lot of heat. When the device is on your thighs and close to your genitals this increases the temperature of your privates.

Some studies show that this can also have a negative effect on hormone production. Andrew Huberman the neuroscientist, Stanford

University lecturer, and content creator goes into this in some detail and his verdict is that the cell in your pocket will be detrimental to not only hormones, but also to sperm and fertility.

This content he put into a pod-cast, which is very interesting and gives great insight. I highly recommend checking that one out. He recommends keeping your cell phone away from your body where possible. He particularly recommends not keeping that device in your front trouser pocket and instead a jacket pocket, or even better in a rucksack or other bag.

This is a good way to approach this. If you are at home it is relatively easy to keep your phone away from you. When you go out this can be more of a challenge, so Andrew's advice will really pay off in that respect.

After listening to his pod-cast on the subject I invested in a man bag, just to carry my phone in. Most of the time I use a rucksack, but on formal engagements in restaurants for example it is not really practical to arrive carrying a rucksack. A man bag solves the problem and I carry that in my hand mostly to keep it away from my body.

The evidence for this one is unanimous, its excellent advice.

But remember that things like obesity, stress, air pollution and smoking can all have the same effect too.

Does Smoking Increase Testosterone?

Here is another theory that has been doing the rounds recently. There have been a lot of suggestions from many content creators that smoking, and in particular smoking cigars, raises testosterone levels in men.

Smoking has been associated with bad health. But on investigating the studies into the generational decline in T levels in men, it is interesting to note that the recent trend in the reduction of smoking was not considered to be responsible for falling T levels.

The answer is not straightforward. It is a commonly known fact that smoking is bad for your health and has been attributed to many respiratory diseases including lung cancer, COPD and emphysema. It is also known to cause clogging of the arteries affecting blood-flow and the cardiovascular system.

A study published in the International Journal of Andrology involving more than 3000 men found that there is *some* truth to this suggestion.

The subjects involved had an average smoking history of 42.8 years and smoked an average of 11 cigarettes a day compared to those who didn't smoke. Now with an average smoking history of 42.8 years that seems to indicate that many of these men were older men and not engaged in any fitness or nutrition regimes. This correlates to sedentary lifestyle and possibly some other unhealthy practises.

The smokers were found to have 15% higher total testosterone and 13% higher free testosterone levels compared to the men who had never smoked. Another observation was that increasing the number of cigarettes per day correlates to bigger increases of testosterone. Both total T and free T.

This is the go to study that is usually referred to by anyone who claims that smoking increases T levels.

But the increases to testosterone levels are only short term. It seems that levels are raised after smoking and then decline again. Repeated smoking elevates T levels repeatedly. This explains why the more cigarettes per day smoked resulted in bigger T increases.

And there is of course a downside. All the health problems associated with smoking correlate to declining T levels in the long term, and to declining fitness and activity levels. And this includes bedroom activities.

Smoking will eventually decrease testosterone production. Another study found that heavy smokers, heavy smoking was considered to be more than 36 packets per year, or approximately 720 cigarettes per year, resulted in faster rates of age related T level decline when compared to non smokers.

Now most of the content that suggests that smoking increases testosterone is related to cigar smoking, and in particular big Cuban havanas. So how does that tie in with the evidence considered so far?

Well a big havana has the equivalent nicotine content of around 10 cigarettes. And the studies mostly attribute the nicotine affecting T levels as opposed to the actual act of smoking. So based upon that, 1 cigar will provide a short boost to T levels that is much greater than just a single cigarette. This is probably what the cigar and T levels myth is based upon. So it is highly possible, given the evidence, that you would get a much bigger (short lived) T boost from a cigar compared to a cigarette.

But the average cigar smoker probably smokes 5 cigars per day on average. That correlates in nicotine amounts to 50 cigarettes or 2.5 packets of cigarettes. Considering that it has been found that 36 packets per year has been shown to cause a significantly greater, and faster, age related T level decline that amounts to 912.5 packets of cigarettes per year, or the equivalent of 18,250 cigarettes!

That is a huge annual consumption of nicotine. Nicotine has a vasoconstrictive effect, meaning that it constricts or tightens the blood vessels and reduces the amount of blood that can pass through. Since an erection depends on good strong blood flow, a huge dose of vaso-constrictive nicotine is going to eventually cause sexual dysfunction.

As far as age related T level decline is concerned that amounts to a catastrophe. 18,250 cigarettes per year, or its nicotine equivalent, is a huge amount considering the harm it can do.

But cigar smokers will hit back and say that cigar smokers do not inhale the smoke. The studies that say smoking increases T levels relate to smokers of cigarettes who do inhale the smoke! The cigar smoke is held in the mouth and the nicotine and flavour is absorbed, along with all the other toxic chemicals present through the saliva and mucous membranes and then into the blood. If you are smoking that cigar indoors then you will be breathing in the smoke in the room obviously.

And there is no filter on a cigar. At least a cigarette filter catches *some* of those toxic chemicals!

And this whole myth is based upon that one, above mentioned go to study, that is often cited by those who suggest that smoking increases T levels.

But there are many studies that say the opposite. Several studies indicate that smoking reduces T levels by as much as 10 to 15%. and these studies suggested that this was caused by the toxic chemicals present in cigarettes, and of course also cigars, which affect the hormones in such a way as to reduce the amount of bioavailable testosterone, free T, in the body.

And it does interfere with your hormonal balance.

In a study published by the Journal of Sexual Medicine demonstrated the effects on hormone levels by showing that smokers had significantly *lower* T levels than non smokers. And they also proved, in a way, that hormonal balance is affected and that bioavailable free T was reduced.

They proved that smoking was related to increased levels of SHBG. If you remember this Sex Hormone Binding Globulin binds to testosterone making it unavailable for use in the body and too much of this can result in reducing levels of bioavailable testosterone. This results in a hormonal imbalance.

The majority of studies debunk the theory that smoking increases testosterone levels. Apart from that one isolated study that is often referred to. The consensus in the scientific and medical communities is that smoking has a detrimental effect on testosterone levels and causes lower T levels. It also causes a reduction in sperm production and is a contributory factor in causing erectile dysfunction.

The final verdict is that smoking causes increases in T levels is based upon only one study. The advice is misleading. Smoking has a negative effect on T levels long term and anyone promoting this theory is giving out terrible advice.

And this also applies to vaping. Testosterone levels can take a dive for the same reasons as smoking. This is because vapes also contain nicotine, which inhibits total testosterone growth.

Cold Exposure and Testosterone.

Many people now believe that taking cold showers can cause increases in T levels.

Cold showers and cold water exposure is known to have many health benefits. It can also be used as an exercise to develop situational willpower. Cold showers taken on a regular basis are known to boost the immune system and leave you much less likely to catch colds and flu in colder weather. It can also help prevent some circulating viruses.

One study found that the people (of both sexes) who started taking cold showers for between just 30 and 90 seconds over a 90 day period led to less instances of sickness compared to those who took warm showers.

Cold water also improves your circulation. Exposure to the cold causes your body to work harder to maintain its temperature. The blood starts pumping around the body faster increasing the circulation of blood flow. And while your body is struggling to stay warm it is using up energy and stimulating the metabolism to burn more calories.

The cold can also help with muscle soreness, which will no doubt aid post workout muscle recovery. When you are exposed to the cold, your blood vessels tighten up. Then your blood moves to the core and vital organs, the blood becomes more oxygenated. Then when your body warms back up to its natural core temperature the blood vessels then expand and they take all that oxygenated blood back to your muscles helping to reduce inflammation.

I take cold showers every day. In summer they are refreshing. In winter this is more challenging, but nevertheless I feel that cold showers work and are beneficial. The reasons I take cold showers are listed above.

But how does cold water exposure affect testosterone? Are the claims that cold showers boost T levels true?

Well we already know that the testes are where most of our T is produced. The testicles are situated outside of the body to help maintain the optimum temperature for sperm production. For this reason, and the widely held belief that heat affects this process has given rise to the opinion that it can also have a positive affect on T levels.

Studies on mice also showed that exposing the testes to higher temperatures caused them to shrink and it lowered sperm production as a result. This may have contributed to the belief that cold would have the opposite effect. But there has not been any correlating proof that exposure to the cold, or cold water can increase T levels.

In some human studies it has been found that cold showers can raise T levels but only temporarily. It is widely agreed upon that there is no long term elevation to T levels. But it is still a very beneficial practise.

Although there are many advantages to cold water exposure and cold temperature exposure raising testosterone production is not one of them.

So that one is debunked. But however it is still good advice. The benefits are too many to pass.

Saunas and Heat kill T Levels.

I have heard this one many times. Often the people who say that cold showers increase testosterone often state that warm or hot showers have the opposite effect. And of course this theory would also relate to the use of saunas.

Saunas and hot baths have been used for centuries and are said to have many benefits. It is thought that because the testicles are situated outside of the body and seem to function best at a temperature slightly lower than body temperature that any exposure to heat will lower T levels.

Saunas are known to provide extreme stress reduction. Stress is known to harm T levels because of the spikes in cortisol associated with stress. Saunas however can help to keep your hormones balanced, because of the stress reduction. Also with the reduction of cortisol levels in the body, it can effectively help to balance insulin, estrogen, DHEA and testosterone.

Saunas are also known to help with the healing process, for this reason many body-builders use saunas to aid muscular recovery after a workout. Saunas are also effective in boosting fat burning and the metabolic rate for better absorption of nutrients.

Saunas can also help to fight the outwardly visible signs of ageing. And improve the appearance of your skin. They are known to contribute towards the production of collagen in the skin. Saunas are also known to improve circulation, improve cardiovascular health and to be effective in removing accumulated toxins from the body.

Some say that you should wipe off the sweat with a towel while in a sauna, otherwise your body will reabsorb the toxins from the sweat back into the skin. This is true, the skin can re-absorb the toxins if they are left on the skin for too long. The downside to this is that the wiping itself will probably help the toxins to be rubbed back into the skin.

For best results a cold shower to remove the sweat prevents the toxins being reabsorbed. For best results you should spend 15 to 20 minutes in the sauna followed by a cold shower. Just stand under the water for a couple of minutes to allow the body to be rinsed off. Avoid any rubbing, or attempting to clean off the sweat with your hands as this will help the toxins be absorbed again through the skin.

However in relation to T levels, it has been shown that regular use of saunas, hot baths and warm showers has no significant effect or changes to testosterone or LH and FSH production. Some studies have even indicated that it can increase T levels. But no studies have yet found that it can reduce T levels.

Any claims that hot baths, hot showers and saunas reduce testosterone levels are not true. They can be very beneficial to health.

Dopamine Fix lowers T levels.

This theory is pretty common in the online masculinity niche. The theory is that getting a daily dopamine fix will lower T levels and is promoted as something that is bad. How true is this? Should we therefore be suppressing dopamine? This is commonly referred to as a dopamine detox. The theory that fasting from activities or pleasures that produce dopamine will reduce the drive for quick rewards.

Dopamine is known as the "feel good" hormone. It gives you a sense of pleasure or satisfaction. For example this could be the satisfaction of a great workout, hitting a goal, overcoming an obstacle or difficulty in life or passing an exam. But it could also be getting a drug hit, alcohol hit, a pron fix, even a hit from steroids. So on the surface it does seem to have both positive and negative aspects.

Having too much or too little dopamine has been linked to several mental health illnesses. Too little dopamine can lead to depression. Too much to schizophrenia or psychosis. Having too much dopamine is also linked to being more aggressive and having trouble controlling your impulses. A lack of self control can never be good.

Dopamine imbalances have also been linked to addictions. Other symptoms of high dopamine levels include, anxiety, restlessness, high energy, disturbed sleep patterns and insomnia, irritability and increased stress and increased negative reaction to stress.

So there are both good and bad sides to dopamine. As everything in nature is balanced in some way then maybe that is a good approach for dopamine too?

Dopamine is also essential and to have none would cause a mental imbalance. It is also something that we produce naturally. Dopamine is produced by converting a protein called tyrosine into dopamine. Tyrosine is found in many foods including meats, dairy products, nuts and seeds. Dopamine levels can be increased by eating these foods, or by taking exercise, meditating and getting enough sleep. So dopamine is not something bad obviously so why might a dopamine detox ever be necessary? What is this all about?

As we have already discussed, too much dopamine can be bad and lead to certain impulse behaviours and addictions. This could be alcohol, drugs, social media use, caffeine, sugar or pron. What happens is that the impulsive activities can offer sharp dopamine increases and it is this sense of satisfaction in a thing or impulse that then leads to an addiction. In effect it is the satisfaction that you have become addicted to.

Of course in the case of the drugs, alcohol and the sugar these can all cause T levels to decline. Avoid these.

This inevitably leads to a sense of discomfort or withdrawal if you do not have access to these rewards. The object of addiction is the thing that brings the sense of satisfaction. The idea of the detox is effectively to try to rewire the reward pathways in the brain by regulating these impulses.

So by restricting these activities you can then become self aware of the underlying reasons and ingredients for these impulses. With an awareness of what exactly it is that gives you the impulses, you can then become more likely to break out of those patterns.

The question you must ask yourself is; "Do I desire *not* to do this thing *more* than I desire to do it?" If you desire not to do that thing, then follow this desire. This desire will ultimately lead to you conquering the addiction. If you find yourself constantly relapsing then maybe the desire to do that thing is still stronger within you? Then you need to ask yourself why?

An effective strategy is to replace one dopamine fix with another. Sounds really counter-productive but it actually works. Lets say its alcohol you are addicted to. So instead of drinking alcohol find something else to replace that. Something rewarding that will give you a sense of satisfaction.

You feel like drinking but instead you are going to go for a walk, hit the gym, ride your bike, in fact anything that will take your mind off the desire to drink. Physical tasks or interests will work best. Ignore that little voice in your head urging you to go and buy drink. And when you do resist that desire, this will provide a satisfying feeling. Savour that feeling because that feeling is your new dopamine fix and it is going to help you destroy that addiction.

So rather than cutting out dopamine altogether, which would be harmful and almost impossible, it is more a case of breaking one cycle and establishing a new one to replace the old one. Dopamine can be a good thing if it generates a feel good factor or sense of satisfaction at having achieved something good. It is when the feel good factor comes from something not productive or beneficial that the problems can arise.

The awareness into these impulses and exactly what causes them can then be identified and then channelled into some other activity to replace the impulsive behaviour. The exact strategy would have to be determined by the individual and whatever impulses might be having a negative effect on their lives.

But what about testosterone? Well, dopamine and testosterone do have an influence over each other. Dopamine can influence testosterone and testosterone can influence dopamine. So they are kind of counter-dependent on each other.

Testosterone is thought to regulate the release of dopamine. Dopamine is also important for libido. Having too much or too little dopamine is going to have a negative effect on testosterone. There isn't a lot of scientific evidence in this area but it is pretty logical to clearly see how there is a lot of truth in the theory that while it may not directly cause a decrease in T levels, it certainly has a negative effect on testosterone.

So you can see that there is a lot of truth to some of these myths and a lack of truth in others. If unsure about anything the best way of solving these doubts is to engage in some fact checking just to be sure. You don't want to be wasting valuable time and even money chasing false leads.

Now I will take you through the personal routine I have adopted to keep My T levels optimised.

27

My Personal Testosterone T Maintainance Routine.

My Typical Routine.

Being a guy who has always been active and having spent more than 2 decades engaging in physical training I had already been doing many of the the things that the medical world recommends doing with regards to healthy living. And of course these things also happen to apply to testosterone levels.

I have mostly observed a well balanced diet and always maintained good activity levels, regular sleep patterns wherever possible, and keeping alcohol use to an absolute minimum. Which for me is practically no alcohol except social engagements where I might have one drink. This has been a lifelong habit for me that I adopted at a very young age.

I have also learned to exercise some considerable control over my mental state and my reaction to stress and the way I make use of stress.

I have been exposed to endocrine disruptors for at least 2 decades. I had no awareness of them and did absolutely nothing to avoid them. However I do not seem to have been greatly affected by them. This is because I happened to be using a supplement during the last 20 years or more that balances everything within the body. Including my hormones. This was more pure luck than intention. But I have discovered a way for other guys to also no longer be affected by hormone disruptors. Adaptogenic herbs.

I have no doubt that it has been these lifestyle choices, more than anything else, especially my diet and training, that have laid good solid foundations to maintaining my T levels to a good standard.

My awareness of testosterone began when I had been training for around 3 years. I had reached my full genetic capabilities in terms of building muscle mass and had reached a plateau. This inevitably happens. So I started to search for any supplements, diets and training routines and methods that might help to break through that plateau and make more gains. During this quest for knowledge I became aware of the importance of testosterone. I also experimented with many supplements and gained a lot of knowledge and insight into these supplements.

These supplements have no doubt made a difference to maintaining my T levels for all this time.

My Supplement Routine.

I have tried many of the multi ingredient supplement stacks that are generally marketed as testosterone boosters. To be honest I think that it would be more accurate to call them testosterone maintenance supplements rather than testosterone boosters. Many of the ingredients included in these supplements are very beneficial to *maintaining* good T levels.

Sure many of the ingredients present in these supplements have been shown in studies to increase T levels by a percentage. But many of these studies into the individual ingredients that are present in these supplements are only short term studies. And of course missing from the data is correlation to confirm that the gains in T levels are permanent, or whether they are just temporary.

I believe that these gains are only temporary and, like with many nutrients, repeated intake is required to keep those benefits manifesting. Another issue with many of the T boosting supplements and many of their core ingredients, is that tolerance is quickly built up. This then presents the problem that regular use is not viable in the case of these T boosters.

Another thing with the data relating to many of these supplements is that many of the test subjects were not guys who already work out and have all the other things down with regards to lifestyle.

The data does seem to indicate that in guys who have not been following these recommended lifestyle choices, and in guys that might already have low T, they do seem to give an increase in T levels. But in guys who train regularly, follow a strict, effective diet etc, they are unlikely to have the same T boosting effect. Another thing to note is that the results achieved in studies have involved many older guys in many cases.

My personal opinion is that these supplements are unlikely to be of any use to you anyway if you are under 40 and already have good testosterone production. A well balanced and healthy diet combined with training is going to be far more effective at maintaining T levels. If you are under 40 and your T levels are good then opt for other supplements, such as adaptogens and nutrient elements.

My personal experience with these T boosting supplements, both as supplement stacks and used as individual stand alone ingredients, is that they do not really make much difference in terms of muscle gains. And this is what the marketing suggests that they can do. On that note I found them disappointing.

As far as improved athletic performance I did notice that they can make you feel more energised. By this I mean increased vitality, and maybe even a little more motivated. But these sensations are only really apparent in the first week of use. After that you don't really feel any different. You get used to their effects quite quickly and you become tolerant to them.

Another thing to note is that there is no catabolic crash when you stop using them. There is no real noticeable depletion of performance or decreases in energy and vitality. This is a plus side to these supplements. This is important when using supplements.

These supplements have their uses and some benefits. I am not suggesting that they are crap. I use these supplements even now and based upon my own personal experience I use them only once a week.

The effects are short lived and daily use seems to lead to tolerance. But they are useful so I will take a T booster once a week as I feel that gives me the most benefit. Used in this way I do not ever build up a tolerance to them. A little boost to kick-start the week. For this I have found this type of supplement very effective.

As well as using the T booster once a week I also use the supplements listed below. The list is relatively short and I do not use all of these supplements every day. I will explain why I chose these supplements over all the others that are available, and the logic behind my preferred frequencies of usage.

Those supplements are:

Ginseng.
Rhodiola Rosea.
L-carnitine.
Taurine.

Vitamin D.

Zinc.

Magnesium.

Creatine.

Milk Thistle.

Whey Protein.

A Multivitamin, containing Vitamin A,C,E and all B vitamins.

You will notice right away that many supplements that are more commonly associated with testosterone are absent from this list. This is because these are covered in the once a week dose of T booster. In the case of micro-nutrients, I am getting plenty of these in my diet.

Wherever possible buy supplements in gel cap form and look for natural vegan caps. Even with these caps I remove the supplement from the gel cap and just consume the powder. Why ingest something I don't need?

There are many beneficial supplements for our purposes here. I went over many of them in the supplements section. However I try to keep my supplement intake to a minimum because of the other ingredients that are present in these supplements. I have narrowed these down to a few core go to supplements that I have listed above, that I have found beneficial to my lifestyle and objectives.

I use the adaptogenic herbs ginseng and rhodiola rosea on a daily basis. Being adaptogens they help to keep the bodily functions well balanced. This applies to hormones too. Adaptogens will help to maintain hormonal balance. They will also help to combat any imbalances. They also help to combat things that harm testosterone production, such as endocrine disruptors. This is important for the long term.

Adaptogenic herbs will adapt to the person using them. They have been found in some cases to even boost testosterone. What happens when you use these supplements is that they will help the body iron out any imbalances that are present within your body. Repeated use will help to maintain that balance.

For example if your T is low they will elevate it. If your estrogen is too high they will also balance that out too. Having been exposed to my fair share of these endocrine disruptors this I feel has helped to prevent them disrupting my hormones in a negative way. I can offer no other logical explanation as to why I seem to have been largely unaffected by these disruptors.

I have been consuming tap water, using soaps and other products loaded with endocrine disruptors and have eaten literally thousands of meals using foods that came packaged in plastics. Yet I have remained unaffected and my T levels are good. This I put down to my use of adaptogenic herbs, which are proven to help balance your bodily functions, including hormones.

I have used ginseng for more than two decades. I did not originally set out to take it for testosterone purposes. I discovered it was good for improving blood flow and boosting cardiovascular performance. I was doing a lot of cross country mountain biking back then so I started to include them in my diet and have done ever since.

I use ginseng for 3 months, every day, and then take a break for 1 month. I am using a dose of 500mg per day. Cycling supplements is always a good idea. I use ginseng daily to help keep my endocrine system balanced and for improved blood flow. I feel that they are an essential part of my testosterone maintenance routine.

The rhodiola rosea is also an adaptogen, it helps balance out the bodily systems in much the same way that ginseng does. The other motive for using rhodiola is its anti-inflammatory, anti-stress and anti-oxidant properties. It also helps the body fight fatigue, not by providing an energy boost but in improving the way that your body uses the energies that it already has. It also helps to actively fight factors that are known to affect testosterone production.

Both of these adaptogens are also fundamental in the maintenance of natural DHEA levels, which have a corresponding effect on T levels. Your ability to preserve your DHEA levels also determines how well you will age and how susceptible to diseases and sickness you will be as you get older. I use rhodiola because I feel that it also has a fundamental role to play in maintaining good T levels.

Be aware that all adaptogens will do the same. Other adaptogens include ashwagandha, maca root and mucuna pruriens.

I also use rhodiola daily in a dose of 500mg. I also cycle this supplement on a 3 months on and 1 month off basis. I time these cycles so that when I am observing a break from ginseng I will be using rhodiola, and when observing a break from rhodiola I will be using ginseng. I do this because I feel it is important to always be doing everything I can to maintain inner bodily balance. Adaptogens are perfect and very effective for this purpose.

I use l-carnitine because of it is useful for the maintenance of good energy levels and its effectiveness in boosting the activity of androgen receptors.

The next most important supplement is Taurine. It has many benefits, which I have covered in the supplements section. My reasons for using taurine are firstly it has been shown to boost T levels and those gains remain consistent with repeated use. It is recommended to use taurine in higher doses for this purpose. For guys who work out and are efficient at burning fat their taurine levels will get depleted pretty quickly.

I have found that exercise related fatigue is significantly reduced when using taurine. It makes a noticeable difference.

Yes you can get taurine from eating plenty of meat but I supplement because a high dose of taurine has been shown to be far more effective. I am using 2000mg, or 2g per day. I do also eat meat on a regular basis too. On training days I take the whole 2g around 30 minutes before training. On rest days I split that and take 1g in the morning and 1g in the afternoon. I also cycle this and every 3 months I take a week off. This I do when I take my week off from training every 3 months.

I also use a vitamin D supplement. Vitamin D has been proven to be helpful in maintaining both testosterone and DHEA levels. I do get regular sunshine, and I also include foods such as salmon in my diet which are rich in vitamin D. The reason I supplement with vitamin D is to ensure my vitamin D levels are always topped up. Slightly higher vitamin D levels have been shown to have an improved effect to T levels.

I vary my use of a vitamin D supplement. I cut down using the supplement in the summer because I always get enough sun. It also is unnecessary to supplement so much when taking enough sun and eating foods rich in vitamin D. Here I will use it every other day at a dose of 400 IU. At other times of the year, depending on the amount of sun, I increase my use.

For spring and autumn I will use 400 IU every day. In winter and during times of bad weather I up my intake to 800 IU per day.

I also use a zinc supplement daily. There are three types. Zinc picolinate, zinc gluconate, and zinc citrate. I use zinc picolinate because it has a better absorption rate. I use 30mg per day. For testosterone it is recommended to use between 30 and 50mg per day. The recommended daily intake is 11mg but it is recommended that guys who engage in physical training should take more.

The reason I use 30 mg is because I am a guy who trains so I will require more zinc. I am a smaller guy so the lower dose in that range is probably best for me. I am also getting zinc from my diet. The supplement is to ensure that my zinc intake is slightly elevated to take into account my active lifestyle.

I also take a magnesium supplement daily. This provides 210mg, which is roughly 50% of recommended daily intake. I am getting plenty of magnesium in my diet but I feel a top up is required because of my lifestyle. For testosterone it is recommended to get at least 400mg. Supplementing ensures that I always hit this target.

Another regular supplement that I use is creatine. Not for its testosterone boosting capabilities, which are disputed anyway, but more for its benefits in maintaining muscle mass. It increases the water volume in your body, and glycogen binds to water when it is stored and glycogen stores fuel workouts so it is good for muscles and energy.

I use creatine continuously but only on training days. I am using 5g per day, 4 times per week. My rest days are 3 days per week. I do not use creatine on these days. This way I am keeping my creatine levels adequately topped up and I do not need to cycle it. I find that this works well for me. Once every three months when I take a break from training for a week then I do cease using creatine for that week. Bear in mind that being an older guy my training centres around maintenance of my physique. I am not too concerned about bulking any more. I am happy with my current form and physique.

I also use a supplement called milk thistle twice a week. This is a great liver detox supplement and I use this because we are after all subject to a lot of toxins these days. They are literally everywhere, even in the air we breathe. I did not include this supplement in the T boosting supplements section because it has no effect on T levels at all. I am using it solely for detox purposes.

I do not use milk thistle every day, and I find that twice a week is sufficient for me, because I am actively seeking to reduce my toxin intake anyway. Some toxins cannot be avoided. A couple of doses per week are useful in aiding the liver to flush out any accumulated toxins.

The benefits of detoxing are, improved energy, improved digestion, improved skin and complexion, improved mental state and reduced inflammation.

If you feel that you need a detox, then use daily in a dose of 150mg 3 times per day for at least 2 weeks. that's all it takes for it to do its work. Then for maintenance just use either 150mg per day, or as I do twice a week in a dose of 500mg at a time.

I also use whey protein supplements. I only use this occasionally, whenever I feel my protein intake has been a little low that day. Most of the time I do not need it as I have sufficient protein intake from food. I just keep some handy for whenever I do need to use it. As I have pointed out in the dieting section, excessive protein intake can harm T levels, so I do not use this kind of product daily. When I do drink a protein shake I always put 4 raw eggs in as well. If you need a boost why not throw in some cholesterol for good measure?

I also use a multivitamin every other day containing A,C, E and all the B vitamins. This is just to keep levels of those vitamins stores up and to make sure I am getting enough B vitamins. I made this choice because I felt that these basic vitamins are all beneficial to T levels. I always try to include as many vitamins and minerals in my diet as I can and I eat a varied selection of foods to do this. But there is only so much stomach space and so much food that I can eat, so I top up every other day with a supplement covering the ones that I feel need attention.

My Diet.

When it comes to my diet I have explained this in detail in the T boosting diet section and the micro-nutrient section. These elements that I explained there form the principles and aims of my diet. What I have found to be the most effective T boosting diet is all in those sections and that is pretty much the regime that I am following. Also many of the foods referenced in the essential vitamins and minerals section are included in my diet. My aim is to include foods to cover all the micros and macros that I need. I eat whole foods, plenty of fruits and vegetables, meats fish, legumes and pulses. I include a lot of ginger and garlic for T levels and chillies, black pepper and turmeric for nutritional purposes.

When it comes to my diet I have one basic rule that I never break. If my body doesn't *need* it, I don't eat it. And this counts for sugars, processed foods and trans fats for example. If it provides me with no nutritional benefits then why waste valuable stomach space consuming it?

It might taste good but what purpose does it serve?

On waking I usually have a cup of coffee, a banana and 2 slices of boiled egg on toast. T levels are higher in the morning. Testosterone production takes place while you are asleep, so my thinking here is that I have used up some cholesterol overnight, so I top that up immediately in the mornings. I have two slices of wholemeal bread each with 2 boiled eggs, 4 eggs minimum. Every day. I also make sure to include fats and cholesterol in my evening meal.

My Training.

My training is varied. I am a pretty active guy and always have been. I do resistance training 4 times per week. I do this in the mornings about an hour after breakfast. My reasoning behind this is that firstly I am refreshed after a good nights sleep. Secondly T levels are higher in the mornings, this is well known, so I take advantage of this.

I train each muscle group only once per week except abs these get more attention. This allows for a full recovery of each muscle group and avoids over training or poor inadequate recovery. Both can have a negative effect on T levels.

My training split I covered in a previous section so I won't repeat that again here. This is my own preferred split and has worked really well for me for some years.

I also perform regular stretching exercises a few times per week and do specific neck exercises, wrist exercises and grip training. I also do cardio on a regular basis. My preferred method of cardio is to do bag work this is also an excellent way to de-stress and let out any built up anger or frustrations. I also do a lot of walking, I particularly enjoy hiking. I walk all the time except when travelling long distances. I also do various body conditioning exercises.

Sleep.

My sleep routine I have already described in the section about T boosting lifestyle choices. It is not necessary to repeat that here. Just remember that sleep is very important to testosterone levels as most of the testosterone we produce is secreted at night.

Stress.

I also observe a regular stress management routine. This involves daily meditation and contemplation exercises and also breathing exercises. Stress management is important for T levels. It goes beyond the scope of this guide to explain each of these in detail as each would take a whole book in itself to fully explain in detail. These guides will all be written at some point and will be coming sometime in the future.

I also practise self awareness on a constant basis. I practise effective time management to make best use of my time. I enjoy having a busy schedule and I thrive on this kind of environment. Also time management is effective at reducing stress. It is always better to have too much time than not enough!

Semen Retention....Erm No!

I practise sex on a regular basis. Not too much, and not too little. Twice a week seems optimal for T levels. I also want my body prepped and ready for these encounters. Sex is a very healthy way of achieving this. Regular erections contribute to good T levels. I do not believe in abstinence over long periods of time as this can have a detrimental effect on T levels. If you want it to work then use it on a regular basis. This works for all body parts. Muscles function best with regular use, so does the brain, and the endocrine system and libido works the same way. If you don't use it you will lose it!

My Approach to Endocrine Disruptors.

Another part of my regular T maintenance routine is my approach to endocrine disruptors. I filter all my drinking water and store my drinking water in glass bottles. When I go out for any reason I always carry filtered water to drink so that I do not need to buy water in plastic bottles. I drink mainly water. I also drink one cup of coffee per day in the mornings. I *never* drink sodas.

I brush my teeth with bicarbonate of soda. I buy this packaged in a cardboard container. Toothpastes contain micro plastics and endocrine disruptors. I freshen my breath by eating cloves or root ginger. I only buy colognes that are alcohol based, this means that the preservative element is alcohol and not a paraben or two. I always check the ingredients to be sure. These products are worn on the skin and remain there for some time.

With soaps and shower gels I always buy ones with natural ingredients. These are usually rinsed off after only a short time and do not remain on the skin for too long so I am not so concerned about these. Natural products are usually more expensive but are worth the extra money.

My Skin Care Secret.

My skincare routine. I did promise to reveal my secret skincare product to you at the end of this guide!

I make my own product. This is really important because a skin care product is used to hydrate the skin and it is therefore absorbed into the skin. And most products, even ones with natural ingredients contain preservatives and this is usually parabens, which means endocrine disruptors. If you are ingesting or absorbing these hormone disruptors it gives you the greatest risk of being affected by them. Therefore I focus my anti disruptor routine focusing on things that I ingest. This includes my skincare routine.

There are many products that are marketed especially for guys seeking to avoid endocrine disruptors and even many of these contain preservatives which often mean endocrine disruptors. The guys marketing these products usually fail to mention this.

So what I do is I prepare one product only for my whole face. I am not one for multiple skincare products but I do like to take care of my skin. I am often complimented on the quality of my skin so what I am doing obviously works.

And it saves a lot of money. A whole years supply of my home-made skincare product comes in at around 40-50 dollars per year.

It is a very simple idea. This keeps the oil content in the skin in a well balanced state. The ingredients are:

Pure, by this I mean 100% pure extra virgin olive oil.
Essential oil of Frankincense. Look for one that states it is 100% pure.

Totally natural and totally endocrine disruptor free. And it leaves skin looking good and well nourished too!

Take a 10ml little glass bottle. Put in 8 or 9 ml or pure extra virgin olive oil. Add around 15 drops of the frankincense oil. Put the lid on the bottle and shake well. Its that simple and it is a very effective skincare product.

Take a very small amount and apply to the whole face. It even works for beards too. The frankincense gives off a nice masculine smell and I often get asked what I am wearing it smells that good. And just one product means less time in front of the mirror too.

You are probably thinking if its that great and it works so well then why did I not produce it and sell it?

Because to commercially produce it I would have had to add a preservative of some kind. Use alcohol or ethanol as the preservative and the lovely smell is destroyed. And that leaves only parabens and other toxic chemicals. The reason it works so well is because frank-incense happens to be great for the skin. It has been used for skin regeneration since the ancient Egyptian period. And the other reason it works so well is because it contains no toxins of any kind!

Rubbing toxins into your skin will not revitalise your skin nor prevent ageing as many skincare brands claim. And most of them that make these claims are deceiving you by using models that have had plastic surgery or skin procedures performed on their faces anyway!

Give it a try. It gives the facial skin a healthy glow and restores the natural oils to the skin. And you are also not rubbing toxins into your face. I highly recommend it.

There is no one single thing that you can do to optimise and pre-serve your T levels. There is no one great thing that will be guaranteed to solve your problems. Here it is a case of combining many things together and it is these combined efforts that will ultimately bring you results.

We must be doing everything that we can possibly be doing. The decline in T levels as we age is not something that can be ignored, or completely avoided.

One thing to consider is that the age at which your T levels will begin to decline *can* be delayed to a degree. It is widely believed that this decline begins between the ages of 30 and 40 in most men. The younger age that you start to implement all this will influence the age that the decline will begin.

For a guy who leads a sedentary lifestyle, does not observe a good diet, is prone to bad reactions from stress and fails to observe good sleep patterns that decline will begin much earlier.

For the guy who is doing everything that he can to preserve his T levels pro-actively, there is every possibility that his decline will begin at an older age, in his 40s. Compared with guys who neglect to do everything they can to slow this process down, probably nearer to age 30.

Try to implement as many of these things into your lifestyle and regime as you can. There are many and it can be quite difficult to implement everything and to keep all of this going for many years. But have faith in yourself. The more things you do the better results you will achieve.

28

Still Have Low T?

I'm Doing Everything Right.

Why Do I Still Have Low T?

Many guys seem to be doing everything correctly they are training, following a good diet, managing their stress and getting adequate sunlight and sleep and still have low testosterone. What can you do if this happens?

The first thing is to implement everything in this book. This protocol is aimed at optimal bodily functioning and this will bring the the best results for your testosterone. A body in sync will produce hormones that are in sync.

Look at things that are not so obvious. A medical condition could be responsible for your low T. This protocol cannot cure pre-existing sickness and diseases but a focus on condition management could make a difference. If this is your case then optimise your entire diet and strategy around the medical condition and not your testosterone levels.

High insulin can negatively affect testosterone. So can high blood pressure. Or low blood oxygen levels. Any nutrient deficiency can also throw your body out of sync. Here you must be looking at a complete optimisation approach to your entire body. If it is out of sync in any way at all, this could have a negative effect on hormone production. And this can often be something that is not so obvious. You seem to be doing everything correctly, but you still have low T.

Why monitoring yourself is a great idea.

Because observation of your vital signs will give you an instant heads up if anything is wrong. An ounce of prevention is worth a pound of cure. Your vital signs are also a good indicator of your body being out of sync in any way.

A fitness tracker that monitors blood pressure, heart rate, sp02 and vo2 max will be very useful. I check myself daily using one of these.

These can be good indicators that everything is ok and you will immediately notice any changes and be better able to prevent any conditions developing. The sooner you notice the better.

Blood pressure, heart rate, sp02 and vo2 max are all indicators of good health and normal levels that fall within normal ranges are all beneficial to testosterone.

High blood pressure can negatively effect T production. An elevated heart rate can be an indicator of increased stress or cortisol imbalance. Low sp02 can mean less efficient blood flow which can affect T production. Vo2 max is an indicator of good cardiovascular health. If all these are in order then you will be far more likely to be producing optimum testosterone.

If any of these are not in order then they can all individually or collectively have a negative effect on T production.

Also a blood glucometer can be highly useful. This can help you in optimising your diet. High blood sugar levels and high insulin can also be bad for testosterone levels and they play havoc with adrenal function and can mess up the balance of your endocrine system.. Keeping a regular check on this can also help you maintain good health and good T levels. I check my blood sugar at least once a month.

Monitoring your health markers is important when considering long term maintenance of health and hormones. These bio-markers can give you an early warning if your body has gone out of sync in any way and if it has you can act on that before it causes any real problems.

Treat your entire bodily organism. Not just your hormones but everything. A balanced body and a balanced mind will give you balanced hormones and optimised testosterone.

29

Ideal Physique For T.

Something not often considered when it comes to testosterone production is what is the ideal physique for having optimum testosterone levels. Many perceive this as being the enhanced type of extremely muscular physique, and this image of masculinity is a common theme at the time of writing.

However I have noticed that in many older guys with well maintained healthy T levels, we all seem to have a few things in common.

David Pascoe, the well known longevity guy who is 61, eats a varied balanced diet and has a consistent and completely natural T level range of between 808 and 1262.

10 years older than me and his T levels are better than mine. My range is between 774 and 1004.

I have a friend at 47 years who was recently tested at 915. Another guy I know at 53 years tested at 894. None of us have that stereotypical super muscular physique associated with high testosterone and there are many many more like us out there.

We all eat balanced, complete and varied diets. We eat a bit of everything. We could call this the testosterone diet, it consists of a bit of everything. Restrictive diets are best avoided long term.

Us older guys with healthy T levels all also treat our body as an entire organism, and we are all lean, slim, athletic and wiry men who are not obsessed with packing on mass or on extreme aestheticism.

David Pascoe runs marathons and has a varied training routine. My friend at 53 years does no weight training at all, but is another long distance guy, he is a road cyclist. My 47 year old friend trains as I do. Resistance training focused on stamina and endurance rather than the gaining of mass. We all do cardio too. Varied training and activity. Balance. The development and maintenance of a functional musculature.

So it seems that focusing on bodily functioning and body performance seems to correlate to having higher testosterone as you get older, as opposed to focusing on mass.

But of course more research is needed here. It would be interesting how what I have noticed pans out. But the physical evidence points to this being true. Many guys who focus on building mass and aesthetics do seem to more commonly suffer a decline in testosterone after the age of 40. And many of these guys have never taken steroids, nor done anything that would obviously cause low T. You only have to look in the comments of many testosterone related videos and blogs to see how common this is becoming.

Often it is not how but who. Want to find out how to do something? Find someone who has already done it. Not someone with a protocol or methods that just happens to be on TRT. For these guys the TRT *is* their real protocol, and yet they are happy to earn revenue advising you how to increase your testosterone naturally. Their advice didn't seem to work for them.

Cardio might decrease your mass but it is very important for blood flow. And for maintaining a good vo2 max. Blood flow is important for erections and testosterone production. Vitality, good energy levels, stamina and endurance are all important in a man. Ask any woman and she will confirm this. And she will also tell you that these things are much more important than big muscles.

So what is the logical basis for me suggesting that the stereotypical archetype guy with huge muscles and lots of mass is not the optimum ideal physique for testosterone?

A thing to consider is that many gym guys tend to observe mass gain cycles followed by cutting cycles then repeating the process. This is done to increase muscle mass and then to chisel and hone the appearance of their musculature. This is quite normal and there must be millions of guys doing just that.

But in reality if you are using steroids to gain mass you will end up destroying your balls. For these guys there is little hope, the vast majority of them will end up trashing their natural hormone production and they will end up on TRT.

However even for natural guys who have never taken steroids or other PEDs this could have a detrimental effect. Why?

Because when guys are following a mass gain diet they are observing a calorific surplus on a daily basis. This calorific surplus of course is needed in order to increase size and mass. This type of dietary strategy often involves eating more meals and bigger meals.

Eating bigger meals and/or eating more frequently consumes much more energy, digestion uses up more energy than any other process in the human body, and this results in an increased level to the depletion of testosterone levels each day. On a bulk you are constantly digesting food and this constantly uses up energy. Constantly using up energy will deplete testosterone. This is unlikely to be noticed on a day by day basis, because testosterone is being replenished over night. However the body has a specific capacity for producing testosterone. And consuming even more cholesterol will make absolutely no difference. The more your testosterone is depleted throughout the day the more effect this will have on your testosterone level first thing the following morning. On a day by day basis you are unlikely to notice much difference. But it is slowly chipping away at your testosterone levels.

Over time, particularly in guys who observe this kind of regime for some years, this will contribute towards a gradual depletion of total testosterone levels. Over a decade or two of training and following this regime, this will make a *huge* difference.

Another thing to consider is the time that it takes to consume more meals and bigger portions. If you are pushed for time, which many are, then this can lead to eating quickly and not masticating the food properly. Why would this matter?

Because properly masticated food means increased nutrient uptake, up to 5 times more, and the body uses less energy to digest that food and convert it into useable energy.

Ideally the food should be masticated to the point that it has the soft gooey consistency of hummus or a smoothie for optimum digestion.

When the food is swallowed with bigger lumps still present in the food, many of these lumps, which are not properly broken down at the time of swallowing, pass through the intestine without all the nutrients being absorbed properly. It is much more difficult for the walls of the intestine to absorb nutrients from these lumps as they pass through the digestive tract. It also takes considerably more energy for the digestive tract to attempt to break down these lumps. The more energy you use, the more this depletes testosterone.

The more the food is broken down before being swallowed the more nutrients can be taken from it and the less waste there will be.

This all results in the body using much less energy during the process of digestion. With fully masticated food most of the work of breaking down the food has already been done before the food was swallowed. This results in levels of testosterone not being depleted as much during the day. The less energy your body uses during the digestive process the less this depletes testosterone.

The higher your T levels are at the end of each day helps determine the level they will be on the following morning after nocturnal testosterone secretion. It all makes logical sense according the the laws of nature and yet nobody else in the testosterone niche has figured this out. But its all pretty obvious if you think about it. Most people now chew food quickly for a few seconds at most and then swallow it, without fully masticating the food.

When guys are observing a cut this process then travels in the opposite direction. A caloric deficit is observed for a time to be able to cut the physique. In studies observing natural body-builders during a cutting cycle in preparation for a contest, their testosterone levels were found to have been depleted by as much as 75%! Again the meals consumed during the cutting cycle are often not masticated properly and this can lead to a loss of nutrient uptake and a greater caloric deficit than was intended.

This typical continuous cutting and bulking regimen that the majority of regular gym guys seem to be observing in modern times, is effectively switching between caloric deficit and calorific surplus on a long term permanent basis. Both of these methods of dieting have a negative effect on testosterone. Combining the two together and being on either one or the other all, or most of the time can be catastrophic to testosterone production. You are continually putting the body into a state of stress. Deficiency or overload. Carried out on a long term basis this will have a seriously detrimental effect.

I remember many years ago being advised by a big guy in the gym that I needed to be eating between 3000-4000 kcal per day if I wanted to increase my size and mass. He recommended that being 5 or 6 meals a day.

At the time I was consuming just over 2000 kcal per day. I tried this diet out. It resulted in me feeling stuffed, bloated and full all the time and depleted of energy because my body was continually using high amounts of energy in this constant state of digestion. My gym sessions suffered. And no doubt this had a negative effect on my T levels. Thankfully I saw the negative effect this was having and did not continue.

And this is the reality of this kind of dietary strategy. Over time it will deplete your testosterone levels. This is probably why many gym guys who are doing everything right and are natural and never used steroids end up with low T, typically after a decade or two of training.

Then consider the energy it takes to build and repair the muscles and increase size added to this process. It is all using huge amounts of energy and utilising testosterone and all the time slowly chipping away at testosterone levels. Could be an insignificant amount in terms of ng/DL each day, but it mounts up over time.

This constant nutritional deficit followed by nutritional over-load probably has an influence over many gym guys deciding to use steroids. Steroids will no doubt enable a guy to push through this. When you have developed your physique naturally to its full genetic potential then further gains in size or mass become extremely difficult.

And attempting to push your body past that genetic potential is going to take its toll.

Solution? Blended foods. Before you dismiss this idea as the ramblings of a crazy guy, consider the brutal logic behind this. Blended food is already broken down and is ready for swallowing and digestion. It also takes less energy to be digested meaning more meals can be consumed for less energy. It also allows for increased nutrient uptake, around 5 times more, meaning the body and the muscles will receive more fuel.

And this will also save you time. And enable you to consume more meals for less energy. And this will correlate to less depletion of testosterone!

However I advise against bulking up too much. The optimum physique for testosterone is a lean, hard athletic physique.

I always fully masticate my food before swallowing it. At every single meal. I only swallow my food when it is broken down into tiny pieces and is the consistency of a soft paste. Eating an average sized plate of food takes me at least an hour to consume because of this. I often add fruit and vegetable smoothies to my diet as well because this is a great way of increasing nutrient uptake and is a real time saver. And sometimes I add meat or eggs to these to make a complete easy to digest meal.

And despite what you would think, this does not affect the consistency of your poop in any way. The only noticeable difference you will see is a reduction in the amount of waste that comes out if you do not normally masticate your food enough.

But also consider that building size and cutting consistently also places the body under continuous stress. This whole process uses up not only energy but also human growth hormone, which the body needs for cell regeneration.

When the body is placed under continual stress, it is highly likely that the growth hormone is redirected away from cell regeneration. This could explain why guys who pack on mass tend to look a lot older for their age. Guys who inject synthetic growth hormones tend to age even quicker.

Cell regeneration of course also includes replenishment of testosterone levels on a daily basis. So it seems that the ultimate physique for optimum testosterone levels is a slim athletic physique maintained by a consistent, complete and well balanced diet. It takes less energy for the body to maintain this physique, this means less depletion of testosterone levels each day and increased stamina, energy and vitality into older age. This can be further enhanced and optimised by fully masticating your food.

Cutting is known to be bad for testosterone levels. And so is a continuous bulking regime. Combining the two together can have disastrous results in the long term. Have a good long hard think if you happen to be observing this kind of regime. Or if you are thinking about doing it.

Maintaining good levels of stamina and endurance will help you to keep higher T levels as you age. This is the ideal physique for testosterone. This is the tried, tested and proven protocol that cracks the code of optimised testosterone levels.

30

This is the Ultimate Protocol That Cracks The Code.

The main consideration when it comes to your testosterone levels is to remember that your hormone cycle operates on a daily basis. Your testosterone maintenance routine should also be done on a daily basis.

What you do today will have an effect on how much testosterone you produce during the night, and what your testosterone levels will be the following morning.

It is not advisable to skip a day in this protocol. It is much easier and much quicker to deplete testosterone levels compared to the time it takes to restore and recover your testosterone levels after they have been squandered.

It will probably take you between three days to a week, depending on your age and fitness levels, to recover from just one evening of alcoholic drinks followed by the consumption of fast food. Try to keep these evenings to a minimum.

Hormonal imbalances can take months or even years to recover from in some cases. It is important to maintain healthy balanced hormones. The best way to achieve this is to cultivate a healthy balanced body. Do not focus on testosterone only. Focus on your whole bodily organism. This brings the best results.

Anything that you do that is detrimental to testosterone production certainly all adds up over time. And by doing as many things to promote testosterone production as you can will also all add up over time. And this is the real truth about testosterone. There is no one thing that will increase your testosterone.

To do this it is a combination of many things all combined together on a daily basis to ensure optimum testosterone secretion tonight. And every night.

Remember that when it comes to increasing testosterone you are in reality promoting testosterone synthesis during the next night while you are sleeping.

Remember that your testosterone levels are at their highest when you wake up and are steadily depleted throughout the day. Every time to use energy in any way or do anything you are utilising and depleting testosterone. Even training and eating deplete testosterone.

Training and eating also promote testosterone when they are done right and balanced out. Not too little and not too much. Do not over-train. Take rest days and allow for adequate rest and recovery. Eat a complete whole food diet and try to avoid deficiencies in any macro or micro nutrients.

The more things that you do to promote or increase testosterone, the more you are doing to prevent the depletion of testosterone in the long term. You also stand the best chance of increasing your testosterone levels over time. There is no one single section in this guide that you must prioritise. The priority is the entire guide.

You do not need to take absolutely every supplement listed in this guide. Your diet and nutritional intake are just as important if not more important to relying upon supplements to increase your testosterone.

Supplementation is just another method you can utilise to make further improvements to your regime. The more of the things related to in this guide that you implement into your regime the better results you will achieve.

This is the ultimate testosterone protocol. Optimisation of physical body. Optimisation of lifestyle. Optimisation of diet and nutrition.

This will all bring you optimisation of hormonal output. And it works.

31

Final Words.

I want to thank you for buying my book and spending your valuable time absorbing my content. I hope that I did not disappoint you.

I hope that you enjoyed this guide and that you have found it useful. Please leave a review for this book if you found it beneficial. Please also feel free to let me know if there is any way that I could have improved the guide. All constructive criticism is gratefully received and will only serve to make me a better writer.

By applying as many of these things as you can into your life you will be able to optimise your T levels effectively and to keep them maintained at a good level as you age.

It is entirely possible that you will also be able to considerably slow down the age related testosterone decline. By following the advice laid out in this guide you will minimise the chances of ever needing TRT.

I wish you all the best and hope that your testosterone levels thrive for decades to come! I am sure they will because now you know everything that you can possibly be doing. All that you need to do is put all this into action.

If you found this guide useful then please check out my other books aimed at men as they might interest you.

Also by James Francis:
Bull in the Bedroom

Do you want to enhance your sexual performance?

This guide will give you all the information you will ever need.

Explained in very simple terms which are easy to follow.

Every man dreams of being a lover who has the sexual stamina to satisfy the desires of his partner. He wants to be sure and confident that he can have intercourse for as long as he needs to without suffering premature ejaculation. And what if he begins to experience erectile dysfunction? He does not want to begin to rely on erectile dysfunction medication to be able to rise to the occasion?

You are about to learn the secrets of male potency and male enhancement. You will become a rampant bull in the bedroom! You will be in full control of your ejaculations and you will have no performance limits when it comes to sex.

In this book, I'm going to show you all the methods and techniques you need to know to maximise your sexual potential and to turn you into a legendary lover that anyone would be happy to be with.

Your understanding of male performance will be changed forever. You will learn to be the master of your own body and its functions and you will be in total control over your sexual performance.

Whether you are young or old these methods will work for you if you set aside the time to practise these techniques.

What you will get from this guide.

All you need to rid yourself of erectile dysfunction.
Cure yourself of premature ejaculation and gain total control in the bedroom.

Increase your sexual stamina and endurance.

Gain male sexual potency and enhancement.

Help in getting the right mindset. Increase your confidence and believe in yourself.

Become the rampant bull that your partner will constantly desire.

Learn a simple exercise program designed and proven to increase sexual performance.

Learn about supplements and foods that will help prevent erectile dysfunction.

Learn the supplements and foods to avoid to give you the best chance of keeping it up for longer into old age.

Learn about adopting lifestyle changes to help you prevent erectile dysfunction.

Learn to increase your blood flow and circulation, resulting in harder more powerful erections.

If you want to say goodbye to erectile dysfunction and never again have to suffer the embarrassment of premature ejaculation........

The book can be found here:

https://www.amazon.com/BULL-BEDROOM-SEXUAL-POT
ENCY-ENHANCEMENT/dp/B0B5RH39K6

The Art to Attracting Women.

The Ultimate Guide to Getting More Dates.

Welcome to the ultimate guide to attracting women.

This guide is aimed at the average guy with just average looks and resources available to him.

This book will give you an insight into how to make yourself a much more attractive prospect in the world of dating and relationships.

This guide cuts right through all the bullshit of other guides that are misleading and will only lead to frustration.

Most guides to attracting women will tell you that you need to be an alpha male in order to succeed with women.

They give little chance to most guys and especially to average guys like us.

I am going to show you why this concept is false and how it is possible for any guy to make himself a better prospect in the eyes of a woman.

There are so many pick up gurus with so many pick up bibles. They all tend to say the same things. And now there are so many guys following their advise that women can see right through it.

I will show you the things you can do to achieve this but remember this. If you have a normal 9 to 5 office job, you can be masculine and attract women. You are an average Joe working a construction job, you can be masculine and attract women. In fact whatever job you have you can become more masculine and attract women. It is even possible to attract women with no job if you set your mind to it.

Anybody can learn to be more masculine. And women are hard-wired to be attracted to masculine men.

I provide you with all the information you need to make that happen for yourself.

I give you insight into the things that you REALLY need to know to attract women and get more dates.

I will talk about the thing that puts women off more than anything. And there are so many guys doing this.

I will teach you how to develop your masculinity the correct way to make you a more attractive prospect to women.

I will help you to develop your mental strength so you can become more confident. You will also be able to cope with anything that life throws at you. And, you will deal with rejection without giving a shit. And EVERY guy gets rejected many times. Something that not many will admit to.

I will offer tips on developing your own unique style in your appearance and your conversational skills.

I will show you how to maintain the natural balance between masculinity and femininity. The secret to any successful relationship. And this is a big part of the attraction phase.

I will show you how to become a high value man without needing an abundance of wealth. High value men are very sought after by women.

And how to select a high value woman and what to look out for.

Also what to beware of to avoid being taken for a ride.

I will give you some great tips on how to approach women confidently. From complete beginner.

Some good advice in using technology in the field of dating.

And of course how to handle the make or break first date. You will increase your chances of things going further with her.

If you are looking to realistically improve your chances of becoming more successful with women then this is the guide for you.

You can find a copy here:

https://www.amazon.com/Art-Attracting-Women-Ultimate-attra cting-ebook/dp/B0BCBX63GW

The Art to Masculinity.

Welcome to the ultimate guide to becoming the real traditional masculine man.

This is the blueprint to becoming Mr Cool, Calm and Collected. The man who can be relied upon in a crisis or extreme danger. Achieve anything you want to!

You have been told that you need to be more confident. More high value. To have impeccable behaviour, character and a high moral standard. Here you find out exactly how!

We need to be mentally tough to meet the demands of the modern world. We need to exercise a very high level of emotional self control. I will show you exactly how.

Many modern guides to masculinity are asking you to renounce your manliness. Not this one.

This is real positive masculinity. For real tough masculine men.

I will dispel the alpha male myth and give you the true path.

Get mental strength.

Improve your mindset. Make goals. Set targets. Execute.

Increase confidence.

Become extremely self efficient.

Master the art of total mental self control.

Become totally calm and centred. Banish anger forever.

Become a real masculine man. The true path.

You can find the book here:

https://www.amazon.com/Art-Masculinity-blueprint-becoming-Collected/dp/B0BTKQSBG5

Made in the USA
Middletown, DE
22 August 2024

59587138R00258